P9-DNE-655

TREATING THE JUVENILE OFFENDER

Treating the Juvenile Offender

Edited by

Robert D. Hoge
Nancy G. Guerra
Paul Boxer

THE GUILFORD PRESS
New York   London

© 2008 The Guilford Press
A Division of Guilford Publications, Inc.
72 Spring Street, New York, NY 10012
www.guilford.com

All rights reserved

No part of this book may be reproduced, translated, stored in a retrieval
system, or transmitted, in any form or by any means, electronic, mechanical,
photocopying, microfilming, recording, or otherwise, without written
permission from the Publisher.

Printed in the United States of America

This book is printed on acid-free paper.

Last digit is print number: 9   8   7   6   5   4   3   2   1

Library of Congress Cataloging-in-Publication Data

Treating the juvenile offender / edited by Robert D. Hoge, Nancy G. Guerra,
Paul Boxer.
     p. cm.
   Includes bibliographical references and index.
   ISBN-10: 1-59385-639-3   ISBN-13: 978-1-59385-639-7 (cloth : alk. paper)
   1. Juvenile delinquency—Treatment—United States. 2. Juvenile
delinquency—United States—Prevention. 3. Problem youth—United States—
Psychology. I. Hoge, Robert D., 1939– II. Guerra, Nancy. III. Boxer, Paul.
   HV9104.T74 2008
   364.360973—dc22

                                                             2007042331

About the Editors

Robert D. Hoge, PhD, is Professor Emeritus of Psychology and Distinguished Research Professor at Carleton University in Ottawa, where he is involved in teaching and research in child and adolescent psychology, forensic psychology, and psychological assessment. He has served as a consultant to numerous government and private agencies, including the National Parole Board of Canada, Justice Canada, Ontario Ministry of Community and Social Services, Alaska Division of Juvenile Justice, Florida Department of Juvenile Justice, and the governments of Singapore and Bermuda. Dr. Hoge has published extensively in Canadian and international journals. His books include *Assessing Adolescents in Educational, Counseling, and Other Settings* (1999) and *The Juvenile Offender: Theory, Research, and Applications* (2001), and he is coauthor (with D. A. Andrews) of the Youth Level of Service/Case Management Inventory, a widely used risk–need assessment tool. Dr. Hoge is a Fellow of the Canadian Psychological Association and a registered psychologist in the Province of Ontario, with a specialty in forensic psychology.

Nancy G. Guerra, EdD, is Professor of Psychology at the University of California, Riverside. Her work focuses on the causes of childhood aggression and violence and on the development and evaluation of youth violence prevention and treatment programs. She has been involved in several national and international evaluation projects, including work for the World Bank and other international agencies in Jamaica, Trinidad, El Salvador, Colombia, and Chile. For the past 7

years Dr. Guerra has been the principal investigator for the Southern
California Academic Center of Excellence on Youth Violence Prevention funded by the Centers for Disease Control and Prevention.
She has published numerous articles, chapters, special issues, policy
papers, and books in this area. Most recently, Dr. Guerra served as
coeditor of *Preventing Youth Violence in a Multicultural Society* (2005).

Paul Boxer, PhD, is Assistant Professor in the Department of Psychology at Rutgers, The State University of New Jersey, and Adjunct
Research Scientist in the Research Center for Group Dynamics at the
University of Michigan. Dr. Boxer's research focuses on developmental psychopathology, particularly on the development of aggressive
behavior in high-risk youth populations such as juvenile delinquents,
psychiatric inpatients, and youth exposed to violence in communities
and families. His studies emphasize the effects of ecological risk factors on social development. Dr. Boxer's expertise also includes the
design, implementation, and evaluation of violence prevention programming along with the assessment of risk for violent behavior. As
principal or co-principal investigator, he has received funding for his
research from the National Institute of Mental Health, the National
Institute of Child Health and Human Development, and the Centers
for Disease Control and Prevention. Dr. Boxer was a summer fellow at
the first training institute held by the Southern California Academic
Center of Excellence on Youth Violence Prevention and consults with
agencies and schools to implement and evaluate programs that target
youth social and emotional development.

Contributors

Emily Asencio, PhD, Department of Psychology, University of California, Riverside, Riverside, California

Paul Boxer, PhD, Department of Psychology, Rutgers, The State University of New Jersey, Newark, New Jersey

Clodagh Ann Dowling, DPsychSc, School of Psychology, University College Dublin, Dublin, Ireland

Carolyn Eggleston, PhD, Center for the Study of Correctional Education, California State University, San Bernardino, San Bernardino, California

Paul J. Frick, PhD, Department of Psychology, University of New Orleans, New Orleans, Louisiana

Nancy G. Guerra, EdD, Department of Psychology, University of California, Riverside, Riverside, California

Rudy Haapanen, PhD, Office of Research, Juvenile Research Branch, California Department of Corrections and Rehabilitation, Sacramento, California

Robert D. Hoge, PhD, Department of Psychology, Carleton University, Ottawa, Ontario, Canada

Tia E. Kim, PhD, Department of Psychology, University of California, Riverside, Riverside, California

Caren Leaf, MSW, Lookout Mountain, Wheatridge, Colorado

Shoon Lio, MA, Robert Presley Center for Crime and Justice Studies, University of California, Riverside, Riverside, California

Larry Miranda, MA, Office of Correctional Safety, California Department of Corrections and Rehabilitation, Sacramento, California

Kathryn L. Modecki, PhD, Department of Psychology, University of New Hampshire, Durham, New Hampshire

Todd Negola, PsyD, Federal Correctional Institution of Loretto, Loretto, Pennsylvania

Gary O' Reilly, PhD, School of Psychology, University College Dublin, Dublin, Ireland

Robert Nash Parker, PhD, Department of Sociology and Robert Presley Center for Crime and Justice Studies, University of California, Riverside, Riverside, California

Lynda Robertson, PhD, Department of Psychology, Ottawa–Carleton Board of Education, Ottawa, Ontario, Canada

Amy Seidlitz, BA, Division of Juvenile Justice, California Department of Corrections and Rehabilitation, Sacramento, California

Elizabeth Siggins, MA, Senate Rules Committee, California State Senate, Sacramento, California

Patrick H. Tolan, PhD, Institute for Juvenile Research, University of Illinois at Chicago, Chicago, Illinois

Louis Tuthill, MA, Robert Presley Center for Crime and Justice Studies, University of California, Riverside, Riverside, California

Bonita M. Veysey, PhD, School of Criminal Justice, Rutgers, The State University of New Jersey, Newark, New Jersey

Kirk R. Williams, PhD, Department of Sociology and Robert Presley Center for Crime and Justice Studies, University of California, Riverside, Riverside, California

Contents

ix

Introduction

Nancy G. Guerra
Robert D. Hoge
Paul Boxer

Although controversies exist over the extent to which youth engage in criminal activities and whether youth crime is increasing or decreasing, there are few debates about the costs associated with juvenile crime. These costs arise from the damage to victims, the processing of youth through the juvenile justice and correctional systems, and the impact of the activity on youths' future development and contributions to society. Given the costs associated with youth crime, it is not surprising that citizens and politicians alike are regularly preoccupied with the issue.

This preoccupation often takes the form of public fear of youth crime, particularly the danger of being victimized. It frequently results in unduly harsh but politically appealing calls for increased sanctions, longer sentences, and the prosecution of young teenagers as adults (Maguire & Pastore, 1996; Zimring, 1998). Such preoccupation is also reflected in the media, where reports about more dramatic forms of crime receive attention beyond their significance for the majority of youth crime. What has been somewhat absent in recent years in the United States in particular is a focus on how we can prevent and mitigate youth crime through effective treatment.

To this end, a primary goal of this book is to direct (or redirect) our attention, as citizens and as professionals, policymakers, and researchers concerned with the problem of youthful offending, to treatment approaches and best practices that can help youth to reduce their criminal behavior. A focus on treatment is consistent with the rehabilitation goals of the juvenile justice system. However, these goals have often been pitted against public outcries for harsher sentences and a punishment orientation.

Indeed, the history of the juvenile justice system in the United States is a history of tension between mandates for punishment versus rehabilitation. An emphasis on punishing offenders suggests a primary focus on establishing legal responsibility and consequences in accordance with the seriousness of the crime. The assumption underlying this approach is that criminal acts represent moral transgressions that can be controlled only by threats of punishment. Young people are seen as making conscious and willful choices to engage in criminal behavior and deemed accountable regardless of developmental history or extenuating circumstances. This perspective leads to an emphasis on formal police and judicial-system processing and the application of punitive sanctions as a means of controlling crime. The sanctions in this case will generally depend on probation or some form of incarceration. In recent years, there also has been a downward shift in the upper age limits for even being considered a juvenile, with children as young as 12 or 13 years old being remanded to the adult justice system.

In contrast, a rehabilitation and treatment approach emphasizes the responsibility of society to provide adequate care and opportunities for children and youth, particularly those who grow up under adverse social and community conditions. The assumption underlying this approach is that criminal acts of youth stem from immature judgment, inadequate skills, poor care, and limited opportunities, wherein society, rather than the individual, carries the burden of responsibility. Of primary importance is the need for a response based on identifying and remediating the factors that contribute to offending behavior. This response enhances the behavioral, social, and emotional competencies of the young person and addresses deficits in his or her environment.

Although it is difficult to identify examples of an exclusive child welfare and rehabilitation orientation in the United States, systems in other jurisdictions at least approach this ideal. An example is Scotland, where most juvenile offenders are dealt with outside the formal justice system. Their needs are met within a larger social support system that provides services to all children and families in need of care. Another example is the Canadian province of Quebec, where the juvenile offender system also tries to deal, as much as possible, with youthful offenders outside the formal legal system.

In practice, rather than represent extremes of the punishment versus rehabilitation continuum, most systems in the United States embody a compromise between these two positions. They have a formal legal system for processing youth and a range of available graduated sanctions, including probation and incarceration, but they may also include services designed for addressing rehabilitation needs. However, these systems differ considerably in the flexibility with which youth are processed through the formal system, the severity of punitive sanctions, and the extent to which educational, psychological, and social services are available for young people. They also vary in the age limits set for being considered a juvenile. Further, the relative emphasis on punishment versus rehabilitation can fluctuate greatly from place to place and across time.

Historical shifts occur in public concern for youth, fear of crime, beliefs about treatment, and attitudes about the seriousness of specific crimes. In general, as public awareness and fear of youth crime increase, policies shift toward harsher penalties and a lack of confidence in treatment and rehabilitation. Whether punitive sanctions and related programs produce significant reductions in recidivism is of little importance to a public focused on retribution and safety. How, then, can we champion the value and importance of helping youth become productive citizens, particularly when they have committed serious offenses that threaten public safety? How can we hold youth accountable for their actions while simultaneously helping them learn from their mistakes? How do we blend legal and treatment goals in order to meet the needs of society to maintain order and provide for the welfare of children and youth?

Throughout this volume, we emphasize the dual roles of a system designed to control and care for juvenile offenders, and the importance of both accountability and rehabilitation. Accountability does not require harsh punishment; rather, it can take the form of supervision, restitution, and restricted activities (in some cases) that are not counterproductive to treatment and rehabilitation goals. We can also improve our response to juvenile offending by carefully evaluating programs and practices to determine whether they are effective and helpful or even potentially harmful. For example, some recent research suggests that grouping delinquent youth together in educational, mental health, juvenile justice, and community settings (consistent with most current policies) might actually exacerbate offending behavior, particularly when programs group new, first-time offenders with more

serious and incarcerated offenders, such as occurs in the "Scared
Straight" programs (Sherman & Strang, 2004). Still, focused and carefully targeted rehabilitation efforts have been found to be effective
(Lipsey & Wilson, 1993; Krisberg & Howell, 1998). Further, the extant
evidence base is mixed with respect to the issue of whether aggregating antisocial youth produces uniformly iatrogenic effects on outcomes
(Boxer, Guerra, Huesmann, & Morales, 2005; Weiss et al., 2005).

As we shall see, there is a growing evidence base across multiple
disciplines demonstrating the relative merits of different strategies and
programs for juvenile offenders. In many cases, this evidence base
includes assessment of those for whom the program is most likely to
work (e.g., younger vs. older youth, or more serious vs. less serious
offenders) as well as optimal conditions for implementation (Guerra,
Boxer, & Cook, 2006). Some treatment strategies are focused on specific
offender populations such as sexual offenders or offenders with demonstrated mental health problems. What is clear is that we can succeed
in addressing the rehabilitation and treatment needs of delinquent
youth in general and of special groups within the broader offender
population.

Five key themes relevant to the treatment of juvenile offenders are
reflected throughout the chapters in this book:

1. Most youth do not engage in serious offending; rather it is a
   small group of chronic offenders who should be the primary
   focus of treatment programs.
2. Serious offending behavior is learned over time and reflects a
   confluence of individual and contextual risk factors that are
   affected by life events.
3. Assessment of risk factors must address sources of dynamic
   risk that can be changed while simultaneously building on
   strengths (i.e., risk-focused, strengths-based).
4. Treatment using evidence-based programs and principles is
   effective.
5. There are subgroups of offenders with unique risk profiles who
   require focused interventions.

Overview of Chapters

In Part I, "Understanding Youthful Offending," we examine patterns
and trends in juvenile crime in the United States, contemporary models of offending, and how assessments can facilitate our understanding
of individual risk and need for specific interventions. In Chapter 1,

Williams, Tuthill, and Lio discuss official and self-report data on the prevalence of youth crime in the United States by age, gender, ethnicity, socioeconomic status, and location. As they point out, the majority of youth do not engage in any form of criminal activity beyond relatively minor transgressions involving, for example, traffic law violations, underage drinking, or petty vandalism.

As they discuss, it has been suggested that these less serious and time-limited infractions reflect adolescent experimentation driven by factors such as opportunities for independence, group norms, and immaturity of judgment. This view is consistent with Moffitt's (1993) description of adolescent-limited offending linked to the developmental period of adolescence rather than childhood-onset and often life-persistent, escalating patterns of offending. The fact is that most youth are, by and large, responsible and law-abiding citizens, even in high-crime areas marked by urban disadvantage (Guerra, 1997). Indeed, a very small number of young people commits serious crimes or engages in persistent criminal activity—a finding that was first reported in the 1970s (e.g., Wolfgang, Figlio, & Sellin, 1972). In general, this group has an early onset, a high individual offending frequency, and a relatively long criminal career. It is these "chronic" offenders who should receive most of our attention.

As Guerra, Williams, Tolan, and Modecki discuss in Chapter 2, treatment programs designed to prevent or deter juvenile offenders from future criminal behavior hinge on a careful delineation of the causal mechanisms most linked to delinquency. As they point out, a large number of individual and contextual risk factors for adolescent antisocial and criminal behavior has been identified. These risk factors include static (unchangeable) factors such as parental criminality as well as dynamic (changeable) characteristics of individuals, peers, families, schools, and communities. A central idea of integrated risk models is that criminal behavior results from the additive and interactive effects of a variety of individual and contextual risk factors over time and within a given ecology, so that interventions should modify the most influential dynamic risk factors.

However, as Guerra et al. also discuss, more recent elaborations of risk-factor models of offending behavior have integrated both developmental and life-course perspectives, providing a more complex picture of treatment needs linked to the course of offending behavior (Farrington, 2005). Of particular importance is an emphasis on distinguishing risk factors that influence the onset of offending from those that contribute to escalation or desistance. Certain life experiences or "turning points," such as job stability and marital attachment, can indeed redirect delinquent trajectories toward more positive outcomes

(Sampson & Laub, 2005). Therefore, treatment programs also must consider the enhancement of strengths that help youth successfully navigate these transitions.

In Chapter 3, Hoge discusses the complexity of evaluating a youth's risk for re-offending and his or her treatment needs, emphasizing the importance of standardized assessment instruments for these purposes. The chapter begins with a review of relevant terminology and conceptual issues, including criteria that apply to the evaluation of forensic assessment tools. Examples of standardized instruments useful in assessing youth in juvenile justice and correctional settings are reviewed under the following categories: personality tests, behavioral ratings and checklists, attitudinal measures, and academic aptitude tests. Comprehensive risk–need measures are also reviewed, and their importance in juvenile justice settings is emphasized. Finally, practical guidelines for conducting assessments in these settings are discussed.

In Part II, "Treatment Programs and Policies for the General Offender Population," we review findings from controlled studies of specific interventions, discuss the need for a balance between evidence-based programs and evidence-based principles, address barriers and challenges to effective implementation of treatment programs in the community and juvenile facilities, as well as explore challenges specifically related to policies and practices within the juvenile justice system. Our emphasis is on programs, principles, and practices most relevant for the general offender population (in Part III we turn to a discussion of treatment with special populations).

Given that risk for offending is linked to a complex sequencing of individual and contextual risk factors and strengths that unfold over time, a challenge for intervention and treatment programs is to address these multiple sources of influence in an integrated and comprehensive manner. In Chapter 4, Guerra, Kim, and Boxer review evidence-based programs, pointing out that interventions focused on only one or a limited set of causal influences on youth offending are less likely to have broad impact on behavior (i.e., delinquency) than those targeting a comprehensive array of risk factors while simultaneously building strengths (often called "protective factors"). For example, multisystemic therapy (MST; Henggeler & Borduin, 1990) has been one of the most efficacious delinquency prevention programs because it attempts to strengthen a number of interconnected systems (families, peers, schools, neighborhoods). In this intervention, the family is the primary mechanism for mitigating risk across these contexts. Families also provide continuity over time for youth, although a challenge to MST and similar programs is that youth must have families that are willing and able to participate.

Other strategies that emphasize the links between cognition and behavior can provide individuals with a core set of skills and beliefs that can reduce the likelihood of offending across time and situations as individuals "construct" their lives within specific contexts. As Guerra et al. point out in Chapter 4, reviews and meta-analyses of intervention outcomes with delinquents suggest the efficacy of cognitive-behavioral programs. Lipsey's (1992) exceptionally comprehensive meta-analytic review of about 400 intervention studies shows that skills-oriented, cognitive-behavioral treatments yielded consistently significant and robust effects on a variety of outcomes. Similarly, Tolan and Guerra's (1994) review of "what works" for youth violence prevention highlighted the effectiveness of cognitive-behavioral programs.

A timely question addressed in Chapter 4 is whether it is necessary to use only evidence-based programs following strict guidelines or whether juvenile treatment strategies should also reflect evidence-based principles. In other words, should replication be limited to formal treatment packages? Recent thinking and empirical work in clinical child and adolescent psychology indicate that successful treatment also can result from a recognition of, and attention to, the theoretical foundations of best-practice principles (Boxer & Frick, in press; Silverman, 2006). By implication, for example, although MST is a well-validated treatment package for the reduction of antisocial behavior, other coherent multimodal treatment plans based on behavioral and family system principles also can be effective (Borum & Verhaagen, 2006; Boxer & Frick, in press).

Even when evidence-based programs and practices have been established, there are a number of practical barriers and challenges to effective program implementation. In Chapter 5, Guerra and Leaf discuss these barriers and challenges, highlighting the experiences at Lookout Mountain, a facility for seriously delinquent boys in Colorado. As they note, in some cases barriers may be programmatic—for instance, if an evidence-based program is chosen that does not seem to fit the ethnic or socioeconomic characteristics of the population served. In other instances, the primary barrier may be funding availability, linked, in part, to public support for prevention and rehabilitation of offenders. States moving toward a greater emphasis on preparing young people to lead healthy lives through developmentally appropriate prevention and treatment programs must often struggle with the price tag of these changes as well as resistance within agencies and systems accustomed to certain procedures and practices. Guerra and Leaf discuss how to create a culture of rehabilitation by using the example of how a simple change in language—recasting the Lookout Mountain facility as a CommUnity (stressing unity), rather than a juvenile correctional institution—created a sweeping change in organizational culture.

As Siggins and Seidlitz discuss in Chapter 6, barriers and challenges to effective programming for juveniles also occur at the level of the juvenile justice system. As they point out, there is no such thing as one juvenile justice system in the United States—policies and practices vary across states and also vary across thousands of local jurisdictions. A central question addressed is whether reform or effective juvenile treatment programming requires a certain set of external policies, including jurisdictional and statutory practices such as age of jurisdiction, distinction between state and local control, and the placement of juvenile corrections within the specific agencies within a state structure. Similarly, the internal policies that represent the procedures and processes by which the system operates can provide challenges to rehabilitation and treatment. Siggins and Seidlitz discuss various state and local systems, with particular emphasis on the challenges and opportunities of a current effort in California to reform the state correctional system into an evidence-based model emphasizing treatment and rehabilitation.

In Part III, "Treatment Programs and Policies for Specific Offender Groups," we turn to the distinct pathways and unique needs of special offender populations, including violent offenders; gang members; sexual offenders; youth with mental health, substance abuse, educational, and learning problems; and female offenders. Despite empirical support for the broad developmental–ecological view in accounting for antisocial behavior, some have argued that a cumulative-risk model cannot account adequately for extreme subgroups of youth engaging in specific types of delinquency or for youth whose delinquency is most prominently driven by a related set of problems (e.g., mental health or substance abuse). A focus on specific groups of offenders is consistent with a developmental pathways model (Frick, 2006) that rests on the observation that for some subgroups of persistently and severely delinquent youth, the risk factors for this behavior are more specific than what typically is captured in the general developmental–ecological view.

For example, Frick and colleagues (Frick & Morris, 2004) recently have identified a pathway within the childhood-onset group of persistent offenders (Moffitt, 1993). Some children in this high-risk category manifest even more elevated risk for serious and persistent offending by virtue of their generally callous and unemotional (CU) interpersonal style (e.g., lacking guilt and remorse, disregarding others' feelings, tendency to ignore conventional obligations). Antisocial youth with high scores on measures of CU traits tend to engage in more severe violent and nonviolent delinquent behaviors and show earlier and more persistent patterns of offending (Frick et al., 2003). As Boxer and Frick discuss in Chapter 7, the specific treatment of violent youth offenders must account for these CU tendencies as well as other individually located factors (e.g., social–cognitive biases; Slaby & Guerra, 1988) that enhance risk for violent behavior.

Another critical issue in the treatment of juvenile offenders is the influence of gangs in the perpetration and escalation of offending behavior both in the community and in juvenile institutions. As Parker, Negola, Haapanen, Miranda, and Asencio review in Chapter 8, the link between gangs and juvenile crime is striking, whereas the effectiveness of intervention programs designed to reduce gang membership and/or gang violence is limited. Indeed, one of the biggest challenges reported by correctional staff is the management of gang-involved youth and violence within institutions. At the community level, results from programs such as The 8% Solution, Spergel's comprehensive model, and the Gang Resistance, Education, and Training Program (G.R.E.A.T.) have been modest at best. Suppression programs such as Operation Night Light and Community Resources Against Street Hoodlums (CRASH) (Los Angeles) are often touted as alternatives to treatment, but results from these programs are also weak. As Parker et al. point out, there is a lack of well-designed evaluations of gang prevention, intervention, and control programs both at the community level and within institutions, limiting our ability to institute evidence-based programs or practices.

Just as serious and persistent violent offenders may follow a distinct pathway, O' Reilly and Dowling also suggest, in Chapter 9, that sexual offenders differ from other offenders in key psychological characteristics and can be further grouped into distinct and different typologies. In reviewing best practices for working with offenders who sexually abuse others, a particular emphasis is given to the assessment, intervention, and moving-on (AIM) framework. In Chapter 10, Veysey discusses the prevalence of mental health and substance use disorders and how they impact treatment for justice-involved youth. As she points out, screening for specific mental health and substance use problems is essential for assignment to treatments, management, and supervision. Veysey underscores the particular role of traumatic experiences in the life histories of juvenile offenders. In so doing, she proposes a treatment model aimed first at reducing the array of psychological and psychiatric symptoms often present in those offenders who have experienced abuse and other traumatic events.

Educational disabilities and school problems also increase risk for serious offending and present challenges for treatment. As Eggleston points out in Chapter 11, comprehensive treatment must address not only the psychological and behavioral needs of offenders, but also the remedial and learning needs that can limit offenders' concurrent and future employment prospects. The need to prepare offenders for future employment is an important part of treatment planning and is consistent with developmental life-course models of crime that emphasize the importance of turning points in redirecting criminal trajectories (Sampson & Laub, 2005). Indeed, as Lipsey (1992) demonstrated in his meta-analysis of treatments offered as part of the justice system, the specific effects of employment training and opportunities produced the largest impact on reducing future delinquency (i.e., these interventions predicted desistance). Successful adjustment to a noncriminal lifestyle requires psychological and practical skills that open doors for success.

In Chapter 12, Hoge and Robertson discuss the unique risk patterns and needs of female offenders. As they point out, males comprise the majority of youthful offenders and generally have been the focus of research on etiology and treatment. There is, however, a growing recognition that significant numbers of females are at risk for criminal activity, and a belief that conclusions based on research for males may not necessarily generalize to females. Hoge and Robertson review the limited empirical research on best practices for girls in both community and institutional settings.

As the organization and content of this book suggests, we set out to advance a comprehensive and integrated model for understanding how best to address the rehabilitation and treatment needs of juvenile offenders, in general, and for special groups within the broader offender population. The chapters draw from basic social, criminological, and developmental science as well as applied practice and evaluation research on juvenile offenders. They present an optimistic but realistic assessment of treatment programs and practices that should form the cornerstone of comprehensive and integrated rehabilitation programming.

References

Borum, R., & Verhaagen, D. (2006). *Assessing and managing violence risk in juveniles.* New York: Guilford Press.

Boxer, P., & Frick, P. J. (in press). Treating conduct problems, aggression, and antisocial behavior in children and adolescents: An integrated view. In R.

Steele, M. Roberts, & T. D. Elkin (Eds.), *Handbook of evidence-based therapies for children and adolescents.* Thousand Oaks, CA: Sage.

Boxer, P., Guerra, N. G., Huesmann, L. R., & Morales, J. (2005). Proximal effects of a small-group selected prevention program on aggression in elementary school children: An investigation of the peer contagion hypothesis. *Journal of Abnormal Child Psychology, 33,*325–338.

Farrington, D. P. (Ed.). (2005). *Integrated developmental and life-course theories of offending.* New Brunswick, NJ: Transaction Publishers.

Frick, P. J. (2006). Developmental pathways to conduct disorder. *Child and Adolescent Psychiatric Clinics of North America, 15,* 311–331.

Frick, P. J., Cornell, A. H., Bodin, S. D., Dane, H. A., Barry, C. T., & Loney, B. R. (2003). Callous-unemotional traits and developmental pathways to severe conduct problems. *Developmental Psychology, 39,* 246–260.

Frick, P. J., & Morris, A. S. (2004). Temperament and developmental pathways to conduct problems. *Journal of Clinical Child and Adolescent Psychology, 33,* 54–68.

Guerra, N. G. (1997). Intervening to prevent childhood aggression in the inner city. In J. McCord (Ed.), *Violence and childhood in the inner city* (pp. 256–312). New York: Cambridge University Press.

Guerra, N. G., Boxer, P., & Cook, C. (2006). What works (and what does not) in preventing youth violence. *New Directions in Evaluation Research, 110,* 59–72.

Henggeler, S. W., & Borduin, C. M. (1990). *Family therapy and beyond: A multisystemic approach to treating the behavior problems of children and adolescents.* Pacific Grove, CA: Brooks/Cole.

Krisberg, B., & Howell, J. C. (1998). The impact of the juvenile justice system and prospects for graduated sanctions in a comprehensive strategy. In R. Loeber & D. P. Farrington (Eds.), *Serious and violent juvenile offenders: Risk factors and successful interventions* (pp. 346–366). Thousand Oaks, CA: Sage.

Lipsey, M. W. (1992). Juvenile delinquency treatment: A meta-analytic inquiry into the variability of treatment effects. In F. Mosteller (Ed.), *Meta-analysis for explanations* (pp. 83–128). New York: Sage.

Lipsey, M. W., & Wilson, D. B. (1993). The efficacy of psychological, educational, and behavioral treatment: Confirmation from meta-analysis. *American Psychologist, 48,* 1181–1209.

Maguire, K., & Pastore, A. L. (1996). *Bureau of Justice sourcebook of criminal justice statistics, 1995.* Albany, NY: Hindelang Criminal Justice Research Center, State University of New York at Albany.

Moffitt, T. E. (1993). Adolescent-limited and life-course persistent antisocial behavior: A developmental taxonomy. *Psychological Review, 100,* 674–701.

Sampson, R. J., & Laub, J. H. (2005). A life-course view of the development of crime. *Annals of the American Academy of Political and Social Science, 602,* 12–45.

Sherman, L. W., & Strang, H. (2004). Verdicts or interventions: Interpreting results from randomized controlled experiments in criminology. *American Behavioral Scientist, 47,* 576–607.

Silverman, W. (2006). Shifting our thinking and training from evidence-based treatments to evidence-based explanations of treatment. *Society of Clinical Child and Adolescent Psychology Newsletter, 21,* 1.

Slaby, R. G., & Guerra, N. G. (1988). Cognitive mediators of aggression in adolescent offenders: 1. Assessment. *Developmental Psychology, 24,* 580–588.

Tolan, P. H., & Guerra, N. G. (1994). *What works in preventing youth violence.* Boulder, CO: Center for the Study and Prevention of Violence.

Weiss, B., Caron, A., Ball, S., Tapp, J., Johnson, M., & Weisz, J. R. (2005). Iatrogenic effects of group treatment for antisocial youth. *Journal of Consulting and Clinical Psychology, 73,* 1035–1044.

Wolfgang, M. E., Figlio, R. M., & Sellin, T. (1972). *Delinquency in a birth cohort.* Chicago: University of Chicago Press.

Zimring, F. E. (1998). *American youth violence.* New York: Oxford University Press.

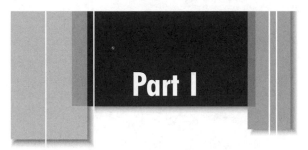

Part I

UNDERSTANDING YOUTHFUL OFFENDING

Chapter 1

A Portrait of Juvenile Offending in the United States

Kirk R. Williams
Louis Tuthill
Shoon Lio

High-profile incidents of youth crime often shape public perceptions of juvenile offending (Newman, Fox, Harding, Mehta, & Roth, 2004; Snyder & Sickmund, 2006). For example, after Americans watched on television the mass shootings that occurred in middle and high schools in the late 1990s, youth crime was seen as rising and getting worse (Bennett, DiLulio, & Walters, 1996; Glassner, 2003; Zimring, 1998). The public perception was that youth offenders are qualitatively different from previous generations in the viciousness of their crimes. The media presented an image of young, cold-blooded, super-predators pumping bullets into toddlers, parents, retirees, and one another (Glassner, 2003).

Although part of the reality of crime, such incidents are not representative of the full array of juvenile offending. Rather, they represent a distorted image, just as the image seen in a carnival mirror reflects something that is real but twisted out of shape (Reiman, 2004). A less distorted portrait of juvenile offending and the characteristics of juvenile offenders, therefore, is important for the public as well as for elected officials, youth service workers, and juvenile justice professionals who develop crime control policy and engage in crime control practice. The purpose of this chapter is to present a defensible portrait of juvenile offending in the United States, and in doing so, to address the extent of criminal offending among youth in this country, including whether a subgroup of youth is more heavily involved and therefore requires more focused interventions The portrait is produced by empirically addressing four fundamental questions.

The first question bears on trends in juvenile offending: Has it increased, decreased, or remained relatively constant in recent years? The second question pertains to the prevalence of juvenile offending: How common or widespread is it in this country, and are all youth equally likely to offend; or is the prevalence of offending differentially distributed across basic social characteristics of youth, such as their gender, ethnicity, or age? The third question is more methodological in nature, although it has implications for justice system responses to juvenile offending: How does survey-based identification of juvenile offenders compare with justice system identification of these offenders in terms of their distribution by gender and age? Addressing the fourth question reveals whether a subgroup of youth is repeatedly (high frequency) and chronically (persistence) involved in criminal offending; specifically, is repeated or high-frequency offending confined to a small percentage of youth, and do those youth persist in their offending patterns over time, unlike most, who stop or reduce their involvement as they move out of the teenage years and into adulthood? To answer the first question, we review recent reports on trends of juvenile offending, with an emphasis on violent criminal offending and homicide. The remaining questions are addressed using two primary sources described below.

Sources of Requisite National Data

Posing these four questions is seemingly straightforward, but addressing them through an analysis of existing national data is a bit more difficult. The reason is that such data typically come from one of two sources: (1) surveys in which youth are asked about their own involvement in crime as either an offender or victim (self-reported surveys), and (2) official records of juvenile offending, such as arrest records, court records, or confinement records. The challenge is that self-reported surveys and official records often yield different portraits of juvenile offending in the United States—they do not necessarily present the same national portrait (see any introductory criminology text, e.g., Barkan, 2006, for a discussion of the strengths and limitations of survey and official data on crime).

The advantage of self-reported data is that information is collected directly from youth involved (or not involved) in juvenile offending, independent of any action by the juvenile justice system. These data are typically considered more valid and reliable than data drawn from the official records of processing juvenile offenders through the system. Nonetheless, self-reported data have their own limitations. Youth may not consider what they did as a crime and thus may not report behavioral involvement in a survey. They may forget what they did in the past or refuse to divulge sensitive information even if they accurately remember it. They may confuse their role as the offender or the victim in a particular behavioral incident. For example, the "true" perpetrator of an aggravated assault believes he or she was the victim because the "true" victim threw the first punch. Whatever the reason, nonreporting or inaccurate reporting can produce bias in self-reported data.

The advantage of data from official records is that they are readily available and thus a convenient source of information on juvenile offending. However, the prevalence of such behavior will undoubtedly be underestimated, to some extent, by official records. Consider a cascading sequence of events that support this claim. Some behaviors, although technically criminal, may not be defined as such by those involved, whether perpetrators, victims, or witnesses. Even if defined as criminal, such behaviors may not be reported to the police. If police are notified or are witnesses to the behavioral incidents, they may or may not make an arrest. Upon arrest, youth may or may not be referred to juvenile court, and depending on the seriousness of the offense, they may or may not be confined. Cases of crime at each juncture in the sequence are lost, resulting in an undercount. Moreover, if some cases are more likely to be lost than others (e.g., low-income youth are more likely to be arrested, referred to court, and confined than their wealthier counterparts), the resulting portrait is likely to be distorted. The likelihood of distortion increases the more official records are removed from the scene of the crime, which is to say that data on confinement are more likely to be distorted than data from court records, but those data are more likely to be distorted than data from arrest records. The fundamental issue is whether the portrait revealed from an analysis of official records at any juncture resembles the reality of juvenile offending or merely reflects the juvenile justice system's response to it. One approach to assessing this distinction empirically is to compare results from an analysis of official data with those from self-reported data, which is the approach applied in this chapter.

A Portrait of Juvenile Offending
Using Self-Report Data from Add Health

Self-reported survey data are drawn from two of three waves of the National Longitudinal Study of Adolescent Health (Add Health). Add Health is a nationally representative, probability-based survey of youth in the United States. Wave I was conducted in 1995 and included youth from grades 7 through 12. Wave II covered the same grades in 1996, and wave III was conducted with the same participants in 2001–2002, when the youth interviewed in wave I were 18–26 years of age. The Add Health data are well suited for this analysis because they provide information on self-identified juvenile offenders, covering violent and nonviolent offenses and more minor forms of crime. Moreover, recent assessments of juvenile offenders and victims have drawn information from other surveys of youth (e.g., Snyder & Sickmund, 2006; U.S. Department of Health and Human Services, 2001), but Add Health data have not been analyzed for this purpose. Hence, these data provide a new addition to presenting a portrait of juvenile offending in the United States.

Add Health is based on a multistage cluster design in which the clusters were sampled with an unequal probability (Harris et al., 2003). At the first stage, 26,666 high schools were sorted into five categories, including school size, school type (public, Catholic, private), level of urbanization, and percent white. High schools were randomly ordered in these categories, and 80 were randomly selected. Of these 80 schools, 52 agreed to participate, with 28 replacement schools selected from these clusters. A replacement school was the school that followed the initially selected school on the randomly sorted list. A single-feeder school (middle or junior high school) was also selected for each of the 80 high schools. The feeder's probability of selection was proportional to the percentage of the incoming class attributable to the feeder. Four high schools did not have an eligible feeder because incoming students came from numerous sources, and 20 high schools basically were their own feeder because they included seventh and eighth grades.

A total of 90,118 students in the participating schools completed an in-school survey. At the second stage of sampling, youth and parents were sampled from stratified school rosters from all the schools. The strata included gender, grade level, and school level, with simple sizes being roughly equal for all strata. Participants were administered a 1½-hour in-home interview. In 1996, the wave II in-home question-naire was administered to youth only. In wave III, in-home interviews were conducted between July 2001 and April 2002, with participants moving from adolescence into young adulthood (ages 18–26).

Data for the present analysis were drawn from youth who par-ticipated in waves I and III (N = 14,322) and self-reported their involvement in different forms of crime. Wave I data are used to cal-culate prevalence rates for the entire youth sample and to show the distribution of those rates by gender, ethnicity, and age. Wave III data are used to estimate persistence in criminal offending into late ado-lescence and early adulthood. Three categories of offending are ana-lyzed: violent offenses, nonviolent offenses, and more minor forms of crime. Violent offending is measured through responses to the fol-lowing questions:

- How often did you get into a serious physical fight?
- How often did you hurt someone badly enough to need ban-dages or care from a doctor or nurse?
- How often did you use or threaten to use a weapon to get some-thing from someone?
- How often did you take part in a fight where a group of your friends was against another group?

The referent period for these questions, as well as those for nonviolent offenses and minor crimes, is "in the past 12 months," and response categories for all questions bearing on all types of criminal offending included *never, one or two times, three or four times,* and *five or more times.* An additive composite index was constructed by summing responses across these four categories (alpha = .74 for wave I and .63 for wave III). Similarly, an additive composite index was formed for nonviolent offenses by summing responses to the following questions (alpha = .66 for wave I and .60 for wave III):

- How often did you deliberately damage property that didn't belong to you?
- How often did you drive a car without its owner's permission?
- How often did you steal something worth more than $50?
- How often did you go into a house or building to steal some-thing?

Minor crime offending was measured through an additive composite index constructed from these questions (alpha = .68 for wave I and .57 for wave III):

- How often did you paint graffiti or signs on someone else's property or in a public place?
- How often did you take something from a store without paying for it?
- How often did you steal something worth less than $50?
- How often were you loud, rowdy, or unruly in a public place?

The alpha coefficient for wave III is low because only two items were available in this wave of data collection, and one of them was not identical to the wave I items (buying, selling, or holding stolen property).

Given these composite indices, prevalence rates of criminal offending are represented as the percentage of age, gender, or ethnic-specific populations that self-identify as violent, nonviolent, or minor criminal offenders (i.e., scored above zero on each of the indices).

A Portrait of Juvenile Offending Using Uniform Crime Report Arrest Data from *Crime in the United States*

Official data on juvenile offending are taken from "persons arrested" in the Federal Bureau of Investigation (FBI) Uniform Crime Report (UCR), specifically *Crime in the United States* (CIUS). This annual publication (available online, *www.fbi.gov/ucr/ucr.htm*) reports the number and rate of "crimes known to the police" for eight major felonies, four of which are violent crimes (murder, forcible rape, aggravated assault, and robbery), three that are property crimes (burglary, larceny–theft, and auto theft), and arson. CIUS also provides data on clearance rates and law enforcement employees. Relevant to the present analysis, the number and percent distribution of persons arrested by age and gender are provided for 29 offenses.

These data allow the calculation of percent distributions of juvenile offenders by age for each of the three offense categories: violent offenses, nonviolent offenses, and minor crimes. Percent distributions can also be constructed by gender and age, but the CIUS does not provide arrest data by ethnicity and age; therefore, ethnic distributions for juvenile offenders cannot be presented. This limitation with the CIUS data underscores the importance of self-reported surveys for presenting a more complete portrait of juvenile offending in the United States. For comparative purposes, arrest data are obtained for the same time period for which prevalence rates are calculated from the Add Health survey data (Federal Bureau of Investigation, 1995).

Comparing the Two Sources of Data on Juvenile Offenders

An important conceptual distinction must be maintained when comparing Add Health survey data with UCR arrest data from the CIUS annual report. Each source of information answers a slightly different question. Add Health data allow us to address the extent to which violent, nonviolent, or minor offending is a problem in the youth population. The CIUS arrest data address this question: Among youthful offenders, how much of their offending is a violent, nonviolent, or minor crime problem? Stated in statistical terms, the denominator of Add Health prevalence rates is the number of youth of a specific age, gender, or ethnicity in the sample, with the numerator being the number within those categories reporting involvement in some form of criminal offending (e.g., males 12–13 years of age who reported committing violent offenses, divided by the number of males 12–13 years of age in the sample). For CIUS arrest data, the denominator is the number of arrested juvenile offenders in a specific gender or age category, with the numerator being the number of those offenders who were arrested for a specific type of criminal offending (e.g., the number of males 12–13 years of age arrested for committing violent offenses, divided by the number of arrested males 12–13 years of age).

Given this distinction, the rates derived from the two data sources are not directly comparable. To address this comparability issue, alternative rates are calculated. Specifically, juvenile offenders are identified from self-reports of youth in the Add Health survey data, and percentage distributions by gender and age are calculated based on this subgroup. These distributions are more directly comparable to UCR arrest distributions because both are based on subgroups of juvenile offenders, not youth in the general population.

Evidence Bearing on the Four Questions

Drawing on Add Health survey data and the UCR official arrest data from the CIUS annual report, the discussion now moves to addressing empirically the four fundamental questions of this chapter.

- *Question 1: What have been the recent trends in juvenile offending?* Empirically documenting trends requires tracking juvenile offending over time, ideally with annual estimates of prevalence over an extended time period. Trends have been previously estimated using longitudinal designs, particularly panel studies of youth. Although they are tremendously rich in detail and have yielded considerable insight into the sources of juvenile offending, they have not been national in scope, being limited to local samples (see Thornberry & Krohn, 2003, for a comprehensive review). Other survey-based longitudinal studies are national in scope but tend to focus on specific types of offending, such as alcohol, drug, and tobacco use (e.g., Johnston, O'Malley, Bachman, & Schulenberg, 2006), school crime (e.g., Centers for Disease Control and Prevention, 2006), and gang presence and activity (e.g., Egley, Howell, & Major, 2006), or they have been limited to the number of years covered (e.g., Bureau of Labor Statistics, 2002). Nonetheless, these national surveys have been used effectively in recent reports on trends and patterns in juvenile offending and victimization (e.g., Snyder & Sickmund, 2006; U.S. Department of Health and Human Services, 2001).

However, considerable attention has been given to tracking and accounting trends in lethal violence involving juvenile offenders (e.g., Blumstein, 1995; Blumstein & Rosenfeld, 1998; Cook & Laub, 1998, 2002; Cork, 1999; Fingerhut, Ingram, & Feldman, 1998; Fox & Zawitz, 2006; Messner, Raffalovich, & McMillan, 2001). The trend since the mid-1980s is well known. Youth homicide rates accelerated rapidly to epidemic proportions between 1984 and 1993–1994. At that point in time, youth 18–24 years of age had the highest homicide rates in the country, followed by 14- to 17-year-old youth, which was a historic elevation for this latter age group. Moreover, homicide rates for all other age groups declined during this period. Since 1993–1994, youth homicide rates for all groups have declined precipitously, although an upturn in arrests for homicide involving youth under 18 years of age between 2001 and 2005 has been reported (Federal Bureau of Investigation, 2005). Whether this recent increase in youth homicide is the beginning of a new pattern of escalation or a temporary spike in the time trend remains to be seen.

Concerning trends in nonlethal youth violence, Snyder and Sickmund (2006) recently compared UCR arrest data and National Crime Victimization Survey (NCVS) data for youth 12–17 years of age between 1980 and 2003. The NCVS is an ongoing survey of a nationally representative sample of 77,200 households including nearly 134,000 persons. Data on a wide variety of criminal victimization experiences are collected from all household members 12 years of age or older. The annual survey has been ongoing in the United States since 1973, with a redesign occurring in 1992.

Even though the focus of the NCVS is on victimization, respondents reporting violent victimization are asked to estimate whether the age of at least one offender (or the only offender) involved is between 12 and 17. Snyder and Sickmund (2006) found that the number of victimizations is substantially greater than the number of arrests for every year in the 24-year time period, meaning much more victimization occurs nationally than appears in UCR arrest records. Nonetheless, they made the numbers comparable by plotting percent differences of each year in the interval from the 24-year average for arrests and for victimizations, respectively. The standardized trends show comparable patterns of variation between 1980 and 2003. Specifically, both the arrest trends and the perceived offender to violent victimization trends slightly declined between 1980 and 1985–1987, but then they increase sharply until 1993–1994, with a sharp downturn from that point in time through the end of the period. In short, nonlethal violent juvenile offending appears to have followed a similar trend to lethal juvenile violence. Whether nonlethal youth violence will show an increase in more recent years, as reported for lethal violence, also remains to be seen. That said, an increase in arrests of youth under 18 has been reported for robbery, but arrests for nonviolent property crimes have continued to decline (Federal Bureau of Investigation, 2005).

• *Question 2: What is the prevalence of juvenile offending, and how is it distributed?* According to the Add Health survey data, violent juvenile offending is quite prevalent, with an estimated 41.3% of the 14,322 youth in grades 7–12 reporting having engaged in some form of violence one or more times during the preceding 12 months, as of 1995. Youth involvement in nonviolent offenses is not as prevalent. An estimated 26.6% of those youth reported engaging in such offenses one or more times in the past year. Not surprisingly, the most common type of juvenile offending involves minor crimes. Of all youth in wave I of the Add Health survey data, more than half (58.6%) indicated that they had committed a specific minor crime one or more times during the 12-month referent period.

Although the prevalence rates of juvenile offending vary across types of criminal offenses (i.e., violent, nonviolent, and minor crimes), the distribution of these rates within each type of criminal offense by gender and ethnicity is virtually identical. As shown in Table 1.1, the prevalence rates for males are quite similar to those of females for each category of crime. That pattern holds true for ethnicity as well. The prevalence rates for each type of criminal offending are comparable across ethnic categories, including non-Hispanic white, African American, Latino, and other ethnicities. Stated in statistical terms, the small variations by gender or ethnicity for each type of criminal offending are statistically insignificant, with the exception of nonviolent offending. For this category of crime, Asian–Pacific Islanders have a slightly elevated prevalence rate (31.7%).

TABLE 1.1 Prevalence of Offenses by Gender and Ethnicity Using Add Health

	Offense		
	Violent	Nonviolent	Minor
Gender			
Male	40.9	26.1	58.2
Female	41.8	27.1	59.0
Ethnicity			
Non-Hispanic white	40.8	26.4	58.0
African American	43.6	25.3	57.9
Latino	40.1	26.5	59.3
Asian–Pacific Islander	40.2	31.7	62.1
Other	41.1	26.8	59.1

A different pattern emerges concerning the relation between age and criminal offending. As shown in Figure 1.1, the prevalence rates are relatively similar from ages 13 to 18, but they decline significantly from 19 to 21 years of age. Irrespective of the type of criminal offending, these shifts by age are statistically significant, as indicated by the likelihood ratio chi square statistic, with 10 degrees of freedom (violent offending, 57.5, $p = .00$; nonviolent offending, 23.5, $p = .01$; minor criminal offending, 18.2, $p = .05$). This distribution corresponds to the well-documented pattern of desistance in crime by age (e.g., Thornberry, 2004).

• *Question 3: How do Add Health survey data compare with UCR arrest data from the CIUS annual report?* Now, consider comparisons between Add Health survey data and the UCR official arrest data. Once again, self-identified offenders in the Add Health survey were compared to arrested offenders in the FBI's CIUS report. Table 1.2 displays the distribution of offenders by gender from both sources of data by type of criminal offense. Observe that the gender differences of juvenile offenders from Add Health are again virtually identical regardless of the type of criminal offending. Approximately half are male and half are female across criminal offense categories. Conversely, sharp gender differences are apparent and persistent across those categories concerning the CIUS arrest data. The ratio of males to females in the gender distribution of arrests is almost six-to-one (5.75) for violent offenses, three-to-one (2.77) for nonviolent offenses, and two-to-one (1.79) for minor crimes. These varying gender patterns between the two sources of data on juvenile offenders suggest that

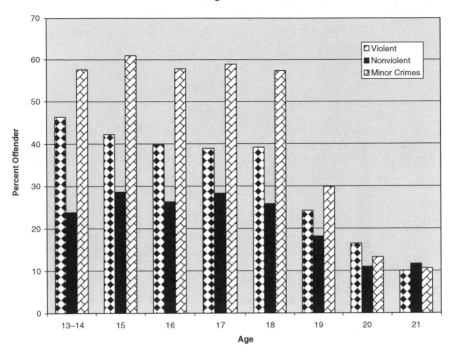

FIGURE 1.1. Prevalence by age using Add Health.

TABLE 1.2. Offender Distribution by Gender Comparing Add Health and CIUS Arrests

Gender	Minor crimes		Violent		Nonviolent	
	CIUS arrest data	Add Health data	CIUS arrest data	Add Health data	CIUS arrest data	Add Health data
Male	85.1	50.1	73.5	49.6	64.2	50.3
Female	14.8	49.9	26.5	50.4	35.8	49.7

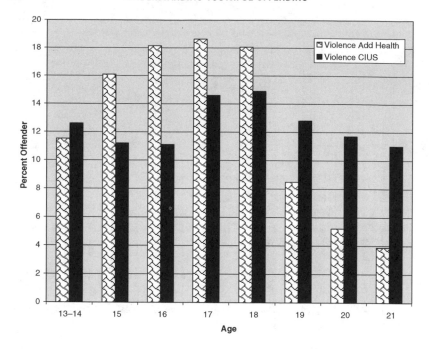

FIGURE 1.2. Offender distribution by age comparing Add Health and CIUS arrests for violent offenses.

males are more likely than females to be arrested for their criminal offending, particularly when it comes to violent crimes.

Comparisons of the offender distributions by age for Add Health survey data and CIUS arrest data are shown in Figures 1.2–1.4. For violent offending, the pattern of desistance by age is more pronounced for the Add Health data than the CIUS arrest data. Among youth arrested for violent offending (see Figure 1.1), 17- and 18-year-olds are most common, representing about 15% of those arrested. The distributions for the other age categories hover between about 11% and 13%, with no sharp desistance pattern to age 21, the last of the single-year age categories reported in the CIUS report. Concerning the Add Health data, the age of violent offenders gradually rises and peaks between 16 and 18, with a clear pattern of desistance through age 21.

These disparities between Add Health survey and UCR official data are not marked for nonviolent offenses and minor crimes. As presented in Figure 1.3, the age of nonviolent offenders increases to 17 and drops sharply for the subsample of offenders from the Add Health sur-

vey, whereas the distribution of nonviolent arrested offenders is greatest in the younger age categories and declines steadily to age 21. However, both sources of data on offenders reveal a pattern of desistance by
age. For minor crimes, Add Health survey data and UCR official data
reveal a similar portrait of juvenile offenders. Both show an increase
with age up to about 17 (although the peak for Add Health data is 15)
and then a clear decrease to the end of the age range, as displayed in
Figure 1.4.

- *Question 4: How common is repeated and chronic juvenile offending?*
High-frequency juvenile offenders were identified in the Add Health
data by selecting those that were one standard deviation above the
mean for each of the composite indices reflecting the frequency of violent, nonviolent, and minor criminal offending. This cut score would
result in the identification of 16% of the sample in the upper tier
of offending, assuming that violent, nonviolent, and minor criminal
offending are normally distributed. That is not the case. The distributions for all three criminal offense categories are positively skewed,

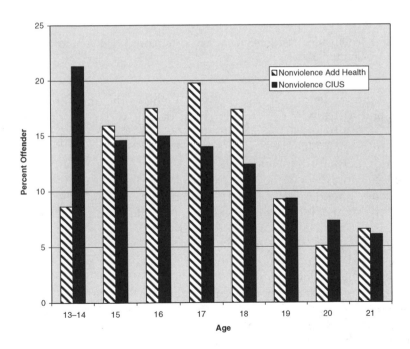

FIGURE 1.3. Offender distribution by age comparing Add Health and CIUS
arrests for nonviolent offenses.

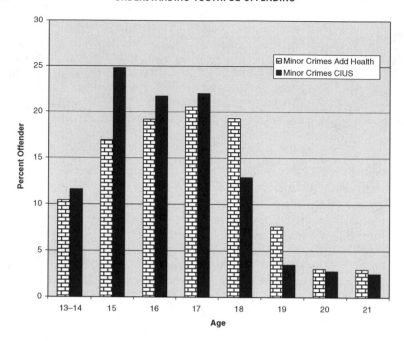

FIGURE 1.4. Offender distribution by age comparing Add Health and CIUS arrests for minor crimes.

with a preponderance of cases at the low end of the offending continuum and a steady and relatively sharp decline in the distribution of cases as the frequency of offending increases. Using this procedure, high-frequency offenders constitute 8.9% of the sample for violent offenses, 6.9% for nonviolent offenses, and 10.6% for minor criminal offenses. Only 2.3% of the 14,322 youth in grades 7–12 comprise high-frequency offenders across all three offense categories. These findings are consistent with previous research reporting a small percent of youth in the category of serious and frequent offenders (Moffitt, 2004). Moreover, although some statistically significant differences were found, the magnitude of those differences was not substantial. For example, females were significantly higher than males in high-frequency offending for nonviolent crimes, but the difference was only one percentage point (7.4 vs. 6.4%). Statistically significant differences were found by ethnicity for violent offending and minor criminal offending, but again, the differences were small, ranging from 7.4 to 10.4% for violence crimes and 9.8 to 13.6 % for minor crimes across the five ethnic categories (non-Hispanic whites, Hispanic, African American, Asian–Pacific Islander, and other ethnicities).

Apart from high-frequency offenders, how prevalent is persistent offending in the adult years? This question was addressed by determining the percentage of the 14,322 youth in the Add Health sample who self-identified as offenders in wave I and then again in wave III, when the age range was 18–26. Similar to high-frequency offenders in the adolescent years, only a small percentage of survey participants persists in offending: 12.0% of the sample persisted into the adult years for violent offenses, 11.4% persisted in nonviolent criminal offenses, and 9.6% persisted in minor crimes. Only 2.2% of the Add Health sample had patterns of persistence across all three types of criminal offending. Moreover, no significant differences in persistence were found by gender or ethnicity across all three categories of criminal offending.

Are high-frequency offenders in adolescence more likely to persist in their offending as they transition to adulthood? The answer is no. Cross-tabulating the two dummy variables for each category (i.e., did or did not qualify as a high-frequency offender by did or did not qualify as a persistent offender) yielded no statistically significant chi square statistics and weak measures of association (gamma coefficients never exceeding .06). The cross-tabulations showed a strong pattern of desistance even for high-frequency offenders; specifically, 86.9% of the high-frequency violent offenders in adolescence desisted in young adulthood, 87.5% of high-frequency nonviolent offenders desisted, and 90% of those involved in minor crimes during adolescence desisted as they aged into their young adult years. Among those who were high-frequency offenders across all three criminal offense categories ($N = 328$), 76.5% did not persist in their offending patterns, as reported in wave III of the Add Health survey. Hence desistance with increasing age remains the dominant pattern, even for high-frequency offenders.

Summary and Conclusion

The results of this descriptive analysis showed that survey-based prevalence rates (juvenile offenders in the general youth population) are undoubtedly higher than those derived from official arrest data, but both sources of data show similar trends over time. Specifically, lethal and nonlethal youth violence crested in the early 1990s and declined from that point into the new millennium, with a slight upturn in recent years. Rates of nonviolent property crime have continued to decline.

Additionally, the Add Health survey data revealed that prevalence rates in adolescence are rather high and vary across type of offending, being highest for minor crimes (almost 59%), followed by violent offending (about 41%), and then nonviolent offending (approximately 27%). However, no significant evidence was found in these data of differential involvement in violent, nonviolent, or minor criminal offending by gender or ethnicity.

Comparisons between self-identified offenders and arrested offenders documented substantial gender differences among the arrested, with males arrested at higher rates than females, especially for violent crimes. The age–juvenile offending distribution was similar between the two sources of information for nonviolent and minor criminal offending, although the pattern for violent offending was more evenly distributed across age groups for the official arrest data.

Nonetheless, both Add Health survey and official arrest data showed a clear pattern of desistance with age across all categories of criminal offending, and although small percentages of youth self-identified as repeat (high-frequency) offenders, desistance from offending was also the dominant pattern even among this subgroup. The result, of course, is that only small percentages of youth persisted in their offending behavior (approximately 10–12%).

In short, the analysis of Add Health survey data and official arrest data from the FBI's CIUS annual report produced a portrait of juvenile offending characterized by a distinct feature: For most youth, offending is prevalent and subsides with age, but for a small minority of youth, it persists into adulthood. This portrait is certainly not new. In fact, it has been the point of departure for much developmental theory and research on crime over the life course (Benson, 2002; Farrington, 2005; Sampson & Laub, 2005; Thornberry, 2004).

The analytical results reported in this chapter corroborate those of previous research on the prevalence and incidence of juvenile offending and have a common implication. Given the widespread nature of juvenile offending, the behavior is more normative than "abnormal" and, for most youth, quite possibly adaptive to developmental demands of an increasingly prolonged adolescence (Moffit, 2004). Criminalization of "adolescent-limited" behavior, culminating in detention and incarceration, has been shown to compromise transitions into conventional adult roles (e.g., Sampson & Laub, 2004). Instead of potentially jeopardizing our adolescents' futures, strength-based approaches should be used to augment positive developmental trajectories for the majority of those in adolescence. Scarce juvenile justice resources should be directed to the minority who persist in criminal offending, recognizing that even among those who persist, such offending ultimately declines with age (Sampson & Laub, 2005).

References

Barkan, S. E. (2006). *Criminology: A sociological understanding.* Upper Saddle River, NJ: Pearson Prentice Hall.

Bennett, W. J., DiLulio, J. J., & Walters, J. P. (1996). *Body count: Moral poverty and how to win America's war against crime and drugs.* New York: Simon & Schuster.

Benson, M. L. (2002). *Crime and the life course.* Los Angeles: Roxbury.

Blumstein, A. (1995). Youth violence, guns, and the illicit-drug industry. *Journal of Criminal Law and Criminology, 86,* 10–36.

Blumstein, A., & Rosenfeld, R. (1998). Explaining recent trends in U.S. homicide rates. *Journal of Criminal Law and Criminology, 88,* 1175–1216.

Bureau of Labor Statistics. (2002). *National longitudinal survey of youth 1997 cohort, 1997–2001.* Washington, DC: U.S. Department of Labor.

Centers for Disease Control and Prevention. (2006). Youth risk behavior surveillance—United States, 2005. *Morbidity and Mortality Weekly Report, 55,* 1–108.

Cook, P. J., & Laub, J. H. (1998). The epidemic of youth violence. In M. Tonry & M. H. Moore (Eds.), *Youth violence* (pp. 27–64). Chicago: University of Chicago Press.

Cook, P. J., & Laub, J. H. (2002). After the epidemic: Recent trends in youth violence in the United States. In M. Tonry (Ed.), *Crime and justice: A review of research* (Vol. 29, pp. 1–37). Chicago: University of Chicago Press.

Cork, D. (1999). Examining space–time interaction in city-level homicide data: Crack markets and the diffusion of guns among youth. *Journal of Quantitative Criminology,15* 379–406.

Egley, A., Howell, J. C., & Major, A. K. (2006). *National youth gang survey: 1999–2001.* Washington, DC: Office of Juvenile Justice and Delinquency Prevention, Office of Justice Programs, U.S. Department of Justice.

Farrington, D. P. (2005). *Integrated developmental and life-course theories of offending.* New Brunswick, NJ: Transaction Publishers.

Federal Bureau of Investigation. (1995). *Crime in the United States.* Washington, DC: Author.

Federal Bureau of Investigation. (2005). *Crime in the United States.* Washington, DC: Author.

Fingerhut, L., Ingram, D., & Feldman, J. (1998). Homicide rates among U.S. teenagers and young adults: Differences by mechanism, level of urbanization, race and sex, 1967 through 1995. *Journal of the American Medical Association, 280,* 423–427.

Fox, J. A., & Zawitz, M. W. (2006). *Homicide trends in the United States.* Washington, DC: Bureau of Justice Statistics, Office of Justice Programs, U.S. Department of Justice, available at *www.ojp.usdoj.gov/bjs/homicide/teens.htm*

Glassner, B. (2003). *The culture of fear: Why Americans are afraid of the wrong things.* New York: Basic Books.

Harris, K., Florey, F., Tabor, J., Bearman, P. S., Jones, J., & Udry, J. R. (2003). *The national longitudinal study of adolescent health: Research design* [Electronic version]. Retrieved July 10, 2006, from *www.cpc.unc.edu/projects/addhealth/design*

Johnston, L., O'Malley, P., Bachman, J., & Schulenberg, J. (2006). *Monitoring the future: National survey results on drug use, 1975–2005: Vol. I. Secondary school students 2005.* Bethesda, MD: National Institute on Drug Abuse.

Messner, S. F., Raffalovich, L. E., & McMillan, R. (2001). Economic deprivation and changes in homicide arrest rates for white and black youth, 1967–1998: A national level time-series analysis. *Criminology, 16,* 21–44.

Moffitt, T. E. (2004). Adolescence-limited and life-course persistent offending: A complementary pair of developmental theories. In T. P. Thornberry (Ed.), *Developmental theories of crime and delinquency* (pp. 11–54). New Brunswick, NJ: Transaction Publishers.

Newman, K. S., Fox, C., Harding, D., Mehta, J., & Roth, W. (2004). *Rampage: The social roots of school shootings.* New York: Basic Books.

Reiman, J. (2004). *The rich get richer and the poor get prison.* Boston: Pearson.

Sampson, R. J., & Laub, J. H. (2004). A life-course theory of cumulative disadvantage and the stability of delinquency. In T. P. Thornberry (Ed.), *Developmental theories of crime and delinquency* (pp. 133–161). New Brunswick, NJ: Transaction Publishers.

Sampson, R. J., & Laub, J. H. (2005). Developmental criminology and its discontents: Trajectories of crime from childhood to old age. *The Annals of the American Academy of Political and Social Sciences Series, 602,* 12–45.

Snyder, H. N., & Sickmund, M. (2006). *Juvenile offenders and victims: 2006 national report.* Washington, DC: National Center for Juvenile Justice, Office of Juvenile Justice and Delinquency Prevention, Office of Justice Programs, U.S. Department of Justice.

Thornberry, T. P. (Ed.). (2004). *Developmental theories of crime and delinquency.* New Brunswick, NJ: Transaction.

Thornberry, T. P., & Krohn, M. (Eds.). (2003). *Taking stock of delinquency: An overview of findings from contemporary longitudinal studies.* New York: Kluwer Academic/Plenum.

U.S. Department of Health and Human Services. (2001). *Youth violence: A report of the surgeon general.* Washington, DC: Author.

Zimring, F. E. (1998). *American youth violence.* New York: Oxford University Press.

Chapter 2

Theoretical and Research Advances in Understanding the Causes of Juvenile Offending

Nancy G. Guerra
Kirk R. Williams
Patrick H. Tolan
Kathryn L. Modecki

Why did I get into trouble? I wanted attention, to be in the spotlight. I made bad decisions and didn't listen to my mom after my dad left. I also saw a lot of violence all around me, like my mom getting beat up when I was 6 years old, so I learned to react with violence. Then I just started kicking it with the homies—they were in a gang, so I joined too.[1]

—16-year-old incarcerated male

The development and implementation of responsive treatment programs for serious juvenile offenders requires a clear understanding of the causes and correlates of delinquency and related problem behaviors. Although low levels of offending are relatively typical during adolescence, a smaller group of offenders has more serious criminal involvement (Elliott, 1994). It is this group of offenders described by Williams, Tuthill, and Lio in Chapter 1 who are the primary focus of this volume and whose delinquency is linked to a multitude of causes. As illustrated by the all-to-common experiences of one young man, highlighted above, these causes include individual factors (e.g., "bad decisions"), family relationships (e.g., paternal absence), peer influences (e.g., "kickin' it with the homies"), and exposure to violence in the community and the home.

Although there is some debate regarding the most important causes of serious juvenile offending and associated mechanisms of influence, a general consensus prevails that no single cause is sufficient; rather, it is the accumulation of risk factors over time and across contexts that most directly leads to offending (Agnew, 2005; Chung & Steinberg, 2006). A general consensus also prevails that offending is the result of the complex interplay of nature and nurture—whatever predispositions toward violence or criminality may be written on an individual's biological birth certificate, these unfold within a specific environment that both shapes and is shaped by them (Guerra & Knox, 2002; National Research Council, 2000; Niehoff, 1999).

The scope and complexity of this back-and-forth process of development and how it can lead to serious patterns of offending would seem to make it difficult, at best, to delineate clear guidelines for treatment linked to specific causes. Yet, this mandate has shaped juvenile justice practice at least since the early 1990s, when Andrews and colleagues articulated the *need principle* of effective juvenile justice practice; that is, treatment should focus on risk factors associated with offending behavior, labeled *criminogenic* needs (for a review see Andrews & Bonta, 2006). An important contribution of this approach was to focus efforts directly on risk for offending rather than risk for any type of problematic developmental outcome (although, as Siggins and Seidlitz note in Chapter 6, even this may be difficult in systems tasked with the overall well-being of youth in custody). Further, a distinction was made between *static* risk factors that could not be changed (such as parental criminality) and *dynamic* risk factors that could be changed, and, if changed, should reduce subsequent offending. From a practical standpoint, this framework requires precise specification and assessment of malleable risk factors for offending and the development of corresponding treatment programs.

Fortunately, just as juvenile justice practice was emphasizing risk for offending as the basis for treatment, research on the causes and correlates of delinquency was also on the upswing. In addition to a host of cross-sectional studies looking at risk factors and delinquency, several major longitudinal studies were yielding important results (see Thornberry & Krohn, 2003, for reports from several of these studies). A number of meta-analytic reviews also were conducted, highlighting the relative salience of individual and contextual risk predictors across childhood and adolescence (e.g., Lipsey, 1992; Lipsey & Derzon, 1998). Corresponding efforts examined protective factors that buffered risk, although it was often unclear if protective factors were measured as independent effects (i.e., predicting lower levels of offending) or as indirect moderators of risk (i.e., decreasing the likelihood of delinquency, given an identified risk). In any case, lists of risk and protective factors for offending were developed and circulated among researchers, practitioners, and juvenile justice agencies as guides for the design and implementation of interventions.

As risk and protective factor models of antisocial behavior matured, increasing emphasis was placed on the ecology of development and the need to develop multicomponent programs to address multiple risk factors across multiple contexts simultaneously (Metropolitan Area Child Study, 2002; Kerns & Prinz, 2002; Tolan, Guerra, & Kendall, 1995). Still, although ecological models emphasized both personal and contextual predictors of risk, they did not specifically consider "person in context" interactions focused on how behavior unfolds over time as part of the regular and ongoing interplay between individual action and social intervention in daily life (Raudenbush, 2005). They also did not distinguish adequately among risk for different aspects of delinquent careers, including onset, course, and desistance.

Over the last decade or so, developmental life-course (DLC) theories of delinquency have integrated the risk-factor prevention and treatment paradigm with research on features of criminal career trajectories as well as the effects of life transitions on offending (Farrington, 2005). As Thornberry (2005, p. 157) notes, "Driven in part by the empirical insights of descriptive longitudinal studies, in part by theoretical dissatisfaction with traditional models, and in part by a burgeoning interdisciplinary approach to the study of crime and delinquency, developmental models have greatly expanded the reach of our understanding of crime and delinquency." What has emerged is a rich portrait of how delinquency is intertwined with human development, with implications for treatment that go beyond the delineation of risk and protective factors.

Building on the last several decades of research on delinquency and antisocial behaviors, we begin this chapter with an illustrative review of the causes of juvenile offending using a risk- and protective-factor framework. We also briefly address the treatment implications of this framework. Next we turn to a discussion of DLC theory, noting how this approach highlights the reciprocal nature of person–environment influences on offending over time. As we point out, DLC theories emphasize the importance of moving beyond considerations of prevalence and frequency to a careful analysis of predictors of early delinquency (onset), length of delinquent career (duration), increases in delinquency over time (escalation), and moving away from criminal activity (desistance). We conclude with a discussion of the next steps— that is, moving beyond a traditional risk framework to integrate the assumptions of DLC theories into treatment programs for juvenile offenders.

A Risk- and Protective-Factor Framework for Understanding Juvenile Offending

As discussed throughout this volume, it has generally been acknowledged that treatment should be geared particularly toward the relatively small group of juveniles that commits the most significant proportion of serious offenses. Knowledge of the characteristics that distinguish this group of offenders from other youth is essential for the development of programs to alter these characteristics (as well as to identify, for targeted prevention programs, groups of youth most likely to offend). A large volume of research has examined the correlates and predictors of offending, often labeled risk and protective factors, in cross-sectional and longitudinal studies. This research examines prediction of delinquency onset or delinquent behavior at a specific point (or points) in time.

Risk factors are characteristics that increase the likelihood that a young person will engage in delinquent behavior. In contrast, protective factors decrease the likelihood of engaging in delinquent behavior and/or buffer the effects of known risk. A risk- and protective-factor approach is consistent with public health models of disease and prevention. For example, looking at heart disease, children of parents with heart disease are more likely to develop it themselves; however, exercise can buffer the correlation between family history and heart disease as well as decrease the likelihood of heart disease without considering family history (American Heart Association, 2007). Relevant to juvenile offending, association with antisocial peers is one of the most robust risk factors for delinquency (Brendgen, Vitaro, & Bukowski, 2000; Chung & Steinberg, 2006; Haynie, 2002). On the other hand, parental monitoring is a protective factor because it is associated with a decreased likelihood of offending and may also serve to buffer the effects of antisocial friends (Crosnoe, Erickson, & Dornbush, 2002; Gorman-Smith, Tolan, Loeber, & Henry, 1998). In practice, many risk and protective factors are simply opposite ends of a continuum; for instance, high parental monitoring can reduce delinquency, whereas low parental monitoring can increase it.

Most listings of risk and protective factors include dozens of predictors. For example, Agnew (2005) lists more than 30 risk factors that have relatively moderate-to-large direct effects on delinquency and crime. At the individual level, modifiable risk factors for delinquency include impulsivity, hyperactivity, attention deficits, low ability to learn from punishment, sensation seeking, irritability, low empathy, poor social problem-solving skills, and beliefs supporting crime. At the family level, these include family conflict, child abuse, negative parent–child bonding, low supervision and monitoring, and low social support. At the school level, risk factors include poor academic performance, negative bonding to school, and low educational goals. At the peer level, these include association with delinquent peers, gang membership, and unstructured and unsupervised activities with peers.

In Chapter 12 of this volume, Hoge and Robertson discuss individual and contextual predictors of risk in more detail, with particular reference to gender differences in the prevalence of risk factors and the processes by which they influence delinquency. In this chapter, we focus on how knowledge of risk and protective factors can be integrated into treatment for offenders, including new developments in theory that emphasize a life-course perspective and the corresponding implications for practice.

Summarizing the risk- and protective-factor research in order to make recommendations for "best bets" for treatment has proved challenging. It is often difficult to compare findings from studies with diverse samples, differences in timing of measurement, and inclusion of outcome measures of delinquency that range from less serious forms of problem behavior (e.g., initiation of smoking) to extremely serious forms of violence (e.g., homicide). Nevertheless, these efforts have culminated in relatively long lists of risk and protective factors, as illustrated above, that have been infused into juvenile justice assessment and practice. As discussed by Hoge in Chapter 3 of this volume, commonly used assessments for juveniles include risk- and protective-factor profiles designed to guide treatment planning. The literature on risk factors has also been used to guide the development of interventions targeting one or more potentially changeable risk or protective factors within individuals (e.g., cognitive-behavioral programs targeting individual cognitions) or contexts (e.g., family interventions designed to facilitate more effective family functioning and parental involvement).

Our understanding of risk for delinquency and related implications for treatment has been further refined through reviews and meta-analyses that have identified and provided a rank ordering of the most robust predictors of specific types of offending (e.g., serious and violent delinquency; Lipsey & Derzon, 1998). An important advance has been the inclusion of age comparisons to examine the relative strength of the main predictors at different ages. This advance is particularly relevant for treatment because programs must not only be age-appropriate in content, but must target risk factors for a given age group most linked to adolescent delinquency.

One line of investigation that is centrally important to understanding delinquency has emphasized the contribution of early antisocial behavior to later delinquency during the adolescent and young-adult years. A substantial body of research suggests that youth who begin their offending careers at an early age are more likely to become persistent, serious offenders during adolescence and beyond. For example, based on the Dunedin Multidisciplinary Health and Development Study of 1,000 persons from New Zealand over a 30-year time period, Moffitt (2004) identified an early-starter, "life-course persistent" group who tended to offend more frequently, with greater behavioral diversity, and whose offending lasted well into adulthood. This pattern is hypothesized to be due, in part, to time-invariant neuropsychological traits typically manifested in cognitive deficits, difficult temperament, and hyperactivity, with the influence of these traits exacerbated by other characteristics of social contexts, such as poor parenting, disrupted social bonds, or disadvantaged social circumstances (Piquero & Moffitt, 2005).

The link between early antisocial behavior and future offending has been supported in several studies—and when compared to other predictors, it comes to the forefront. For instance, in their meta-analysis of delinquency predictors, Lipsey and Derzon (1998) found that general offenses and substance use between the ages of 6 and 11 were the two best predictors of violent or serious delinquency between the ages of 15 and 25, followed by gender (male), low socioeconomic status, and parental criminality (ranked in the second group of predictors). This finding suggests a clear prevention mandate to target early antisocial behavior and its correlates prior to adolescence. However, in practice it is often difficult to accurately identify this group for focused services (Loeber et al., 1993; Tolan, 1988). A related problem is that although child antisocial behavior is one of the best predictors of adult offending, most antisocial children still do not grow up to be antisocial adults (Robins, 1978). Nevertheless, for treatment programming it is important to bear in mind that the most serious offenders are likely to have a prior pattern of habitual antisocial behavior.

A second, late-starter "adolescent-limited" group tends to confine offending to the adolescent years. Such offending is associated with a maturity gap in which youth experience a disjunction between their biological maturation and access to more adult roles and responsibilities. It is also associated with a peer context in which offending serves to demonstrate autonomy from adults, establish status and connections with friends, and provide alternative venues to social maturation (Piquero & Moffitt, 2005). This group of offenders is believed to have fewer enduring (and often unchangeable) risk factors, such as temperamental difficulties, with risk linked more to the circumstances of contemporary adolescence. The picture of late-onset offending is one of normative exploration rather than heightened risk. Still, although their crimes may be less serious than their early-starter counterparts overall, they do account for more than 25% of the most serious crimes, suggesting the importance of identifying the most proximal risk factors for both types of offenders (Elliott, 1994). It is also likely that these risk factors will increase the likelihood of delinquent offending for all youth, regardless of whether they began their careers early or are just getting started (Sampson & Laub, 2005).

Indeed, the risk factors at ages 12–14 that best predicted violent or serious delinquency at ages 15–25, as reported in the Lipsey and Derzon (1998) meta-analyses, were lack of social ties and involvement with antisocial peers, followed by a history of offenses (ranked in the second group), followed by aggression/physical violence, poor school attitude/performance, psychological difficulties, parent–child problems, and male gender (ranked in the third group). Interestingly, social influences provided the most significant contribution to future risk; these influences should be important for both early- and late-starter groups, and may be particularly important for early starters, who are more likely to be rejected by mainstream youth and gravitate toward delinquent peers (Patterson, Reid, & Dishion, 1992). In any event, because treatment programs cannot undo past behavior but can only focus on preparing youth for the future, and because the scientific basis for developing unique treatments based on age of onset is limited, it may be most prudent for treatment programs to emphasize risk factors that are most proximal (i.e., close in time) and most amenable to change. However, as we shall now discuss, risk- and protective-factor models have not emphasized the development of, and desistance from, offending over time, which is particularly relevant for treatment programs that attempt to "redirect" youth rather than prevent the onset of antisocial behavior. Let us now turn to a discussion of the DLC perspective.

DLC Perspectives on Juvenile Offending

The application of a risk- and protective-factor framework to prevention and intervention stressed the need to focus on dynamic risk factors (Andrews & Bonta, 2006). The term "dynamic" was used to describe the nature of a risk factor, specifically whether it could be changed, based on an association with potential for change or progress. However, we can also consider offending itself as a dynamic process involving individual development over the life course and factors that promote or interfere with criminal as well as conventional behavior. Rather than focus on variations *between* individuals (*inter*individual differences) in their frequency of offending, a more dynamic approach seeks to account for variation *within* individuals (*intra*individual change) as they age, or put more generally, as they move through age-graded, developmental stages of the life course.

This shift in emphasis vis-à-vis understanding the causes of offending has been reflected in a burgeoning literature on DLC criminology spanning the last decade or so. This recent tradition of theoretical and empirical work builds on the risk- and protective-factor framework and also incorporates research on trajectories of criminal involvement and the role of life transitions. As such, the DLC framework has made several contributions to understanding the etiological pathways into crime as well as events along the way that can redirect those pathways into more conventional lifestyles. DLC theories have been reviewed in several recently edited books (e.g., Farrington, 2005; Thornberry, 2004), and our discussion draws from that work.

The DLC perspective emphasizes trajectories of criminal offending over time, which essentially involves tracing behavioral involvement by age. This approach marks a major shift of emphasis in criminological research that historically has been more static or fixed in nature. This recent tradition also seeks to identify the personal and contextual characteristics associated with these intraindividual changes in behavioral trajectories. The research and theoretical applications in this tradition have produced many new insights about criminal offending, but five key contributions to the understanding of such behavior are particularly relevant because of their implications for the treatment of juvenile offenders.

First, analyses of intraindividual changes in behavioral trajectories over time have highlighted important dimensions of criminal offending previously shrouded by more static accounts of interindividual differences in the frequency of criminal offending. Tracing offending over time allows the identification of behavioral onset (when it starts), duration (how long it lasts), escalation or deescalation in the frequency and seriousness of offending, and desistance from offending (when it stops). These dimensions are important because they can be linked to different risk or protective factors involved in the generation, escalation, and persistence of criminal offending as well as those connected to the prevention, deescalation, and desistance of such behavior (Farrington, 2005).

For example, family factors such as harsh and inconsistent discipline, parental neglect, or abuse may be dominant aspects associated with the onset of offending during adolescence, but their direct influence wanes in significance as youth age into adulthood, with such factors playing virtually no role at all in the reduction or termination of criminal behavior. Other life events may slow down or stop the offending behavior, such as building stakes in conformity through education, job acquisition, or integration into highly valued intimate relationships. The point is that the trend in offending can be associated with life-course developments that shift trajectories in positive or negative directions. Such issues cannot be recognized, let alone addressed, without examining criminal offending dynamically—that is, as it unfolds over the life course of individuals. An important issue for treatment of adolescent offenders thus becomes the identification of specific risk and protective factors that increase or decrease the likelihood of desistance from offending and how best to support desistance.

Second, as evidenced by the work of Moffitt (2004) and others, DLC models have sought to identify distinct groups of offenders with distinct trajectories. A correlative contribution of focusing on groups of offenders has been the utilization of sophisticated statistical methodologies for the systematic analysis of behavioral trajectories (i.e., empirically documenting offending patterns over time). For example, Nagin and Land (1993) developed an analytical technique called "group-based trajectory modeling." The technique allows the tracking of criminal offending as youth age, but as the name implies, it also allows age-graded trajectories in such behavior that have common temporal patterns to be identified and consolidated into groupings or clusters. This statistical methodology has been used recently to identify categorical groupings of offenders in addition to the two groups discussed by Moffitt and colleagues (Nagin & Tremblay, 2005; Sampson & Laub, 2005; Thornberry, 2005).

Moreover, these analyses have also demonstrated that regardless of the intraindividual changes in criminal offending over time (i.e., when it begins, when the frequency of offending peaks, how long it lasts), all identified groups ultimately show temporal patterns of desistance from all types of serious and less serious offending. Thornberry (2005) offered one exception to this important finding. He identified a small group of "late bloomers" whose offending escalated after the age of 18 and continued until age 23, the last year for which he had data (see also Thornberry & Krohn, 2003).

Third, analyzing behavioral trajectories through the life course permits an investigation of factors that foster or inhibit the acquisition of human capital at specific times over the course of development. The notion of human capital is used here to denote "strengths" related to the attainment of personal competencies, such as a positive identity, a sense of personal agency, self-regulation skills, social problem-solving skills, a system of prosocial normative beliefs, a hopeful future goal orientation, academic excellence, and vocational skills. Lack of these markers of human capital has been associated with increased risk for criminal behavior; at low levels, many of these characteristics have been included in lists of individual risk factors. Although a DLC perspective builds on the risk-factor research, a critical distinction is the emphasis on how and why these characteristics are associated with adjustment (at high levels) and delinquency (at low levels).

The acquisition of human capital is seen as part of the overall process of development in context, whereby successfully building human capital is critical for individuals to meet the normative expectations of their developmental stage, as defined across a range of social settings. Doing so enhances the chances of meeting the performance demands of social situations and adequately preparing for the transition into new situations and/or new stages of development in the life course. Failing to do so can result in maladaptation and insufficient preparation for the demands facing youth as they move into the next stage of the life course. For example, inadequate preparation for the transition into high school may result in poor academic performance and dropping out of school, which, in turn, can potentially restrict opportunities for further education and conventional employment. The resulting restricted opportunities may push youth into illicit activities. In some sense, a DLC model provides a developmental framework for how risk and protective factors operate over time and across settings.

Moreover, the timing of transitions in the life course is seen as crucial, with some being normative in that life events occur in an age-appropriate manner, whereas other events can be "off-time." Normative timing can be protective, whereas being off-time can increase risk. For example, transitioning into marriage and having children or acquiring a job can be positive accomplishments in adulthood, fostering stakes in conformity or prosocial behavior (e.g., Sampson & Laub, 2005). However, if such events occur too soon in life, as in early adolescence, the off-time developments can have a reverse effect, restricting access to venues of personal growth and accomplishment and inhibiting rather than fostering the acquisition of human capital and the building of stakes in conformity. Thus specific events can be either risk factors or protective factors depending on developmental timing.

Fourth, DLC places emphasis on person-in-context interactions. Granted, some accounts of persistent offending tend to minimize the influence of social context and focus more on time-invariant personal traits such as difficult temperament or low self-control (e.g., Moffitt, 2004; Gottfredson & Hirschi, 1990). However, even among DLC investigators who acknowledge the influence of time-invariant personal traits on persistent offending, the emphasis remains on how others within social contexts respond to those traits and how those responses may undermine prosocial bonding and promote the pursuit of criminal opportunities through connections with "deviance service industries" (Hagan, 2004) and the transition into criminal lifestyles (e.g., Sampson & Laub, 2004; Matsueda & Heimer, 2004). Conversely, youth headed down the road to increasing criminal involvement can experience "turning points" that result in deescalation or termination of offending. For example, they may pursue conventional venues for prosocial lifestyles such as marriage or employment or have a window of opportunity fortuitously open in their life (Sampson & Laub, 2004, 2005).

Fifth, DLC models allow for the active role of the individual in constructing his or her social reality. Criminal activity is part of an emergent process rather than solely an outcome of identified risk, and this process hinges on personal agency. *Personal agency* refers to the conscious process by which people create their own lives though the choices and actions they take, given specific opportunities and constraints. In terms of offending, the implication is that individuals do not fall into crime but make conscious decisions to follow this path. Similarly, they do not fall out of crime but actively participate in the process of desistance, or at least invest so much in conventional goals that they do not want to risk jeopardizing their investment (Sampson & Laub, 2005).

Thus DLC theories build on the risk- and protective-factor framework but also go beyond the delineation of discrete individual and contextual "variables" that correlate with, or predict, offending. This wider purview is accomplished, in part, by incorporating the notion of life-course trajectories. As we shall now discuss, DLC theories offer a new framework that can address some of the limitations of risk- and protective-factor models and provide new directions for treatment.

Contributions and Limitations of a Risk- and Protective-Factor Framework for the Treatment of Juvenile Offenders

The risk- and protective-factor framework and associated principles of juvenile justice practice (e.g., the need principle) have made significant contributions to the development of treatment programs for offenders. In particular, the inclusion of both individual and contextual risk factors and related studies demonstrating the significant influence of context during childhood and adolescence have served to underscore the role of social and community conditions in offending, providing a solid foundation for the rehabilitation philosophy emphasized throughout this volume. Further, the recognition that delinquent behavior is the result of multiple risk factors that coalesce rather than a single cause has fostered the development of programs focused on multiple risk factors within individuals (e.g., aggression replacement training; Goldstein, 2004) or specific contexts (e.g., multisystemic family therapy for family risk; Henggeler, Melton, & Smith, 1992), as well as the emergence of multicomponent, multicontext programs designed to prevent and mitigate risk across contexts (e.g., Metropolitan Area Child Study [MACS] for individual, peer, school, and family risk; Metropolitan Area Child Study Research Group, 2002).

Just as this approach has produced significant contributions in understanding factors that increase the likelihood of offending and how they can be prevented or ameliorated through prevention and treatment, important limitations remain, particularly for translation of this framework into treatment programs for juvenile offenders. These limitations include (1) the lack of a broad evidence base for effective treatment programs addressing individual and contextual risk and protective factors; (2) the infeasibility of impacting contextual risk for identified individual offenders; and (3) the lack of identified risk and protective factors specifically associated with desistance.

In Chapter 4 of this volume, Guerra, Kim, and Boxer provide clear guidelines for treatment grounded in evidence-based principles linked to identified risk for delinquency; however, the evidence base for effective *programs,* particularly for treatment of juvenile offenders, is relatively scant. As they note, applying strict standards for effectiveness reduces the field to a handful of programs, most of which involve both delinquents and their families. Family interventions also require that families are willing and able to participate—which may not be the case, for instance, when youth are incarcerated several hundred miles from their homes or families are simply uninterested in treatment. They are also increasingly less appropriate during the transition into adulthood, when youth are moving towards independence and starting new families of their own.

In contrast to prevention programs that address risk at the population level (primary or universal prevention) or within a group of identified at-risk participants (secondary or selective prevention), treatment programs are, by definition, designed to impact an identified offender or those tasked with his or her care (i.e., families). The emphasis is on helping specific individuals change, in some cases by helping their families do better. The risk- and protective-factor framework has made a significant contribution by also highlighting the importance of contextual influences beyond families (e.g., peers, schools, neighborhoods, and even society as a whole), but it is beyond the scope of treatment programs to address these multiple influences directly.

The primary goal of treatment programs is to help offenders learn how to manage their own behavior within specific contexts rather than to change the contexts themselves. For example, when a low-income juvenile offender from a high-crime neighborhood is referred for treatment, it is impractical (and impossible) to focus treatment on changing neighborhood conditions; such interventions can only be part of larger, system-level changes. Although understanding how contexts shape behavior is vitally important for identifying social influences on offending and how they operate, in truth, contexts are difficult and costly to change, especially when the focus is on treatment programs for identified offenders. Rather, comprehensive treatment programs must build on knowledge of risk and protective factors across these contexts but ultimately help youth learn how to better navigate these settings to minimize risk and promote healthy adaptation.

Helping juvenile offenders learn to navigate developmental contexts in order to redirect their energies towards conventional pursuits requires a more precise understanding of characteristics implicated in desistance from offending. One of the most glaring limitations of the risk- and protective-factor model for treatment programs is the lack of distinction between prediction of onset (or delinquency at certain time points) and the prediction of desistance. As DLC theorists have noted, it is unclear whether the causes of onset and the causes of desistance are simply opposite ends of a spectrum, whether there is a completely different set of influences on desistance, or whether there are some shared and distinct causes of onset and desistance (Farrington, 2005). However, research grounded in a DLC orientation is beginning to shed light on some potential areas for treatment designed to encourage desistance. Let us now turn to a discussion of the specific treatment implications of this emergent perspective.

Implications of DLC Theories for the Treatment of Juvenile Offenders

As we have discussed previously, DLC theories incorporate research on risk and protective factors for offending, but also emphasize the importance of trajectories of criminal involvement and the role of life transitions and turning points. Because delinquency unfolds in real time, key life events can sustain or shift the course of behavior toward continued criminal involvement or a more conventional lifestyle. Rather than ask which factors are correlated with or predict delinquency, a central question for treatment of referred offenders thus becomes: *What individual factors, life experiences, and contextual supports are most likely to foster desistance from offending?*

Although research on desistance during late adolescence and early adulthood is scant, some potential candidates for intervention can be identified. For example, recent studies have found that strong adult social bonds, as evidenced by a marital attachment and job stability, are significantly related to lower levels of crime among groups previously identified as both delinquent and nondelinquent (Sampson & Laub, 2005). These experiences can redirect behaviors embedded in childhood propensities just as they can redirect the risky acts of adolescent experimentation, suggesting that programs to strengthen social ties during early adulthood can be important in reducing recidivism, irrespective of age of onset or offense history. Adult social bonds also provide opportunities for structured routines and new social networks that can replace unstructured time with delinquent peers. However, as mentioned previously, these accomplishments are time sensitive, in that they can increase risk when they occur during the teenage versus the young-adult years.

DLC theories emphasize the acquisition of strengths or human capital. These strengths include attitudes, beliefs, and skills that are frequently cited in listings of risk and protective factors. The emphasis shifts somewhat in DLC theories, however, toward factors that help foster personal competency and prepare individuals to maneuver life's ups and downs successfully. These factors include a positive identity, a sense of personal agency, self-regulation skills, social problem-solving skills, a system of prosocial normative beliefs, empathy, a hopeful future goal orientation, academic success, and job skills. Still, human capital is also bound by reality—individuals who cannot access job opportunities or who do not have a voice in their future are unlikely to sustain a positive outlook.

By concentrating on requisite strengths needed to navigate the transition to adulthood successfully within a context of identified constraints, DLC theories provide a slightly different way of thinking about treatment of offenders. Risk and protective factors become important as they contribute to or interfere with an offender's ability to shift his or her life path from criminal to noncriminal involvements. For example, a risk factor such as low self-control can limit an individual's ability to take advantage of available opportunities for successful engagement. It can also interfere with the resolution of conflicts and problems, with the end result being continued aggression or delinquency.

A DLC perspective thus allows us to reconsider the risk- and protective-factor framework, focusing specifically on the requisite social capital needed for adolescent offenders to make the transition to becoming law-abiding adults. Most programs derived from risk- and protective-factor models focus primarily on skill development without considering motivation to continue offending or change course or an individual's ability to bring about and sustain changes. For example, many individual-level treatment programs emphasize cognitive-behavioral (e.g., reframing, stop and think, social problem solving) and vocational skills. Yet, most practitioners who work with youth or with writers who tell their stories know that some youth seem to favor a criminal lifestyle over a more conventional one, often because of perceived rewards, defiance of the system, or the already entrenched status of their deviant social network (e.g., for youth who are second- or third-generation gang members). This preference for criminality is particularly likely for the smaller group of more chronic and serious offenders, for whom delinquency is not the result of time-limited experimentation but rather an emergent lifestyle.

From a DLC perspective, skills are important for healthy adaptation but must be consistent with an individual's identity, lifestyle, and future goals if they are to be used. Desistance from offending thus requires *motivation* to change, *agency* to purposely follow a path toward change, as well as the *skills* to bring about change. As one young offender put it, "No matter what, some people don't want to change, so nothing you can do, no program or skills you can give them, is going to change them until they truly want to change themselves."[2]

A focus on the centrality of motivation is consistent with recent efforts in juvenile justice to integrate principles of motivational interviewing (MI) into practice (Miller & Rollnick, 2002). This approach acknowledges that individuals often have multiple and sometimes conflicting goals, so an important goal of treatment is to enhance intrinsic motivation to change by exploring and resolving this ambivalence. MI is a process rather than a specific treatment. It can enhance the effectiveness of treatment when it precedes such treatment (Brown & Miller, 1993) or can be used as a counseling and communication style throughout a treatment program (Miller & Rollnick, 2002).

Beyond the importance of specific techniques to enhance motivation to change, we can also consider specific topics that should be included in treatment programs to address motivation. For instance, aggression replacement training (ART; Goldstein, 2004), which is primarily a skills-based anger management program, also includes a moral reasoning component designed to help youth consider the harmful consequences of aggressive and antisocial behavior and strengthen empathy. Indeed, most cognitive-behavioral programs derived from evidence-based principles (discussed in more detail in Chapter 4 of this volume) include components on changing norms about aggression and delinquency, understanding the feelings of others, and acknowledging the harmful consequences of criminal behavior.

In addition to motivation, change requires confidence in one's ability to make a difference. Consistent with the principles of MI, a counselor can convey confidence in the client's ability to change, but the ultimate responsibility lies with the person's own beliefs that change lies within. This self-confidence has been referred to over the years using various terms, including internal locus of control, self-efficacy, and personal agency. The term "agency" is used here because it is consistent with the DLC approaches guiding the present discussion.

As reviewed previously, "personal agency" refers to the active involvement of individuals in creating their own lives through conscious choices and related actions within a context of ongoing constraints. The concept of active participation is especially relevant for juvenile offenders, who are moving from the restrictions of childhood and adolescence into the multiple options of adulthood. A cornerstone of adolescent development is the achievement of an autonomous and coherent identity, a process that can culminate in conventional values and a commitment to pursue prosocial future goals, just as it can culminate in a commitment to criminal and nonconforming goals (Erikson, 1968). This emergent identity can shape behavior as well as the persons and contexts individuals seek out to display this behavior. Peer affiliations become a prominent feature in this quest for autonomy, particularly if there is tension or conflict with parents. As part of this process, adolescents often seek out like-minded youth who provide a type of identity verification (Swann, 1999). For example, an adolescent whose identity is grounded in being tough and aggressive is more likely to gravitate to gang culture and the opportunities for violence it offers (Kim & Guerra, 2007). This is akin to the concept of "niche seeking"—that is, the ability of individuals to find and engage contexts with features that are well-matched to their individual characteristics (Martin & Swartz, 2000).

Although the availability of contexts for offenders may be closed off somewhat because of personal characteristics or early behavioral patterns, individuals at this stage still have the capacity to learn from their experiences, set future goals, and move into contexts (e.g., a new family, a good job) that provide opportunities to accomplish more conventional goals. A primary focus of intervention thus becomes helping offenders construct their own noncriminal identities and corresponding life course by believing in their ability to do so, making choices, learning skills, and taking purposeful action toward this goal.

Rather than modifying contexts, per se, the focus is on helping youth learn to manage contexts by avoiding situations likely to increase risk for offending (e.g., spending unstructured time with delinquent peers) and seeking out contexts likely to decrease risk for offending (e.g., gainful employment). This focus can be particularly important for incarcerated offenders who must frequently return to the same communities with the same set of risk factors that contributed to their criminal involvement, but must now learn to avoid risky situations and develop a conventional lifestyle (e.g., Fagan, 1990). In some sense, this is similar to the approach of multisystemic therapy (Henggeler et al., 1992), one of the most effective treatment programs for juvenile offenders, where a key goal is helping participants learn how best to manage interconnected systems in their social ecology in order to reduce youth delinquency risk.

Summary and Conclusion

A central premise of this chapter is that effective treatment programs for offenders must be based on a clear understanding of the causes of delinquent behavior. As we have discussed, over the last several decades a risk- and protective-factor framework has guided much of juvenile justice assessment and practice, and an array of correlates have been identified. A major contribution of the risk- and protective-factor framework has been to highlight the importance of the multiple individual and contextual causes of offending. Still, much of the research looking at prediction of adolescent offending has concentrated on the enumeration, rather than the integration, of risk factors, resulting in a large number of empirically based predictors with less emphasis on how these risk factors interact over time.

More recently, the risk- and protective-factor framework has been integrated into a DLC perspective on offending. A DLC approach emphasizes individual development over the life course and factors that promote or interfere with criminal as well as conventional behavior. How individuals change over time is more important than why individuals are different from each other (e.g., comparisons of offenders and nonoffenders). As such, DLC theories have directed our attention toward the importance of moving beyond correlates and predictors of offending to a greater understanding of trajectories of offending, including onset, course, and desistance. Of particular importance for treatment of the more serious and chronic offenders is why they desist or stop offending. A corresponding focus of interventions thus becomes how to promote strengths and build human capital in order to maximize the likelihood that offenders will veer away from a delinquent lifestyle toward more conventional goals. Still, less is known about the specific factors that lead to desistance, how they vary by demographic characteristics, and whether they are similar or different across varied risk profiles.

We have suggested that shifting developmental pathways from criminality to conventionality requires more than a diverse skill base. Drawing on the DLC perspective, we emphasized the importance of motivation to change and personal agency to bring about change. Even when constraints loom large, individuals still have a hand in constructing their own identities and their own future. Treatment programs must help offenders develop a new sense of purpose and identity as hard-working citizens rather than lifelong criminals, and provide personal and vocational skills that allow this identity to unfold. In other words, skills should not be taught in isolation, but rather as part of efforts to help offenders see their future self as engaged in healthy relationships and purposeful activities as constructive members of society.

Notes

1. From interviews described in Chapter 4 of this volume.
2. As Note 1.

References

Agnew, R. (2005). *Why do criminals offend?* Los Angeles: Roxbury Publishing.
American Heart Association. (2007). *Risk factors and coronary heart disease.* Retrieved April 7, 2007, from *www.americanheart.org*

Andrews, D. A., & Bonta, J. (2006). *The psychology of criminal conduct—fourth edition.* Cincinnati, OH: Anderson.

Brendgen, M., Vitaro, F., & Bukowski, W. M. (2000). Stability and variability of adolescents' affiliation with delinquent friends: Predictors and consequences. *Social Development, 9,* 205–225.

Brown, J. M., & Miller, W. R. (1993). Impact of motivational interviewing on participation and outcome in residential alcoholism treatment. *Psychology of Addictive Behaviors, 7,* 211–218.

Chung, H. L., & Steinberg, L. (2006). Relations between neighborhood factors, parenting behaviors, peer deviance, and delinquency among serious juvenile offenders. *Developmental Psychology, 42,* 319–331.

Crosnoe, R., Erickson, K. G., & Dornbusch, S. M. (2002). Protective functions of family relationships and school factors on the deviant behavior of adolescent boys and girls. Reducing the impact of risky friendships. *Youth and Society, 33,* 515–544.

Elliott, D. S. (1994). Serious violent offenders: Onset, developmental course, and termination. The American Society of Criminology 1993 presidential address. *Criminology, 32,* 1–21.

Erikson, E. H. (1968). *Identity: Youth and crisis.* New York: Norton.

Fagan, J. (1990). Treatment and reintegration of violent juvenile offenders: Experimental results. *Justice Quarterly, 7,* 233–263.

Farrington, D. P. (2005). (Ed.). *Integrated developmental and life-course theories of offending.* New Brunswick, NJ: Transaction Publishers.

Goldstein, A. P. (2004). Evaluations of effectiveness. In A. P. Goldstein, R. Nensen, B. Daleflod, & M. Kalt (Eds.), *New perspectives on aggression replacement training* (pp. 230–244) Chichester, UK: Wiley.

Gorman-Smith, D., Tolan, P. H., Loeber, R., & Henry, D. B. (1998). Relation of family problems to patterns of delinquent involvement among urban youth. *Journal of Abnormal Child Psychology, 26,*319–333.

Gottfredson, M. R., & Hirschi, T. (1990). *A general theory of crime.* Palo Alto, CA: Stanford University Press.

Guerra, N. G., & Knox, L. (2002). Violence. In J. Dressler (Ed.), *Encyclopedia of crime and justice* (pp. 1649–1655). New York: MacMillan.

Hagan, J. (2004). Crime and capitalization: Toward a developmental theory of street crime in America. In T. P. Thornberry (Ed.), *Developmental theories of crime and delinquency* (pp. 287–308) New Brunswick, NJ: Transaction.

Haynie, D. L. (2002). Friendship networks and delinquency: The relative nature of peer delinquency. *Journal of Quantitative Criminology, 18,* 99–134.

Henggeler, S. W., Melton, G. B., & Smith, L. A. (1992). Family preservation using multisystemic therapy: An effective alternative to incarcerating serious juvenile offenders. *Journal of Consulting and Clinical Psychology, 60,* 953–961.

Kerns, S. E. U., & Prinz, R. J. (2002). Critical issues in the prevention of violence-related behavior in youth. *Clinical Child and Family Psychology Review, 5,* 133–160.

Kim, T. E., & Guerra, N. G. (2007). *Identity development and aggression in ethnic minority youth.* Manuscript submitted for publication.

Lipsey, M. W. (1992). Juvenile delinquency treatment: A meta-analytic inquiry into the variability of treatment effects. In F. Mosteller (Ed.), *Meta-analysis for explanations* (pp. 83–128). New York: Russell Sage Foundation.

Lipsey, M. W., & Derzon, J. H. (1998). Predictors of violent and serious delinquency in adolescence and early adulthood. In R. Loeber & D. Farrington (Eds.), *Serious and violent juvenile offenders* (pp. 86–105). Thousand Oaks, CA: Sage.

Loeber, R., Wung, P., Keenan, K., Giroux, B., Stouthamer-Loeber, M., VanKammen, W. B., et al. (1993). Developmental pathways in disruptive child behavior. *Development and Psychopathology, 15,*101–133.

Martin, W. D., & Swartz, J. L. (2000). (Eds.). *Person–environment psychology: Clinical and counseling applications for adolescents and adults.* Mahway, NJ: Erlbaum.

Matsueda, R. L., & Heimer, K. (2004). A symbolic interactionist theory of role-transitions, role-commitments, and delinquency. In T. P. Thornberry (Ed.), *Developmental theories of crime and delinquency*(pp. 163–213). New Brunswick, NJ: Transaction.

Metropolitan Area Child Study Research Group. (2002). A cognitive–ecological approach to preventing aggression in urban settings: Initial outcomes for high-risk children. *Journal of Consulting and Clinical Psychology, 70,* 179–194.

Miller, W. R., & Rollnick, S. (2002). *Motivational interviewing: Preparing people for change* (2nd ed.). New York: Guilford Press.

Moffitt, T. E. (2004). Adolescence-limited and life-course persistent offending: A complementary pair of developmental theories. In T. P. Thornberry (Ed.), *Developmental theories of crime and delinquency* (pp. 11–54) New Brunswick, NJ: Transaction.

Nagin, D. S., & Land, K. C. (1993). Age, criminal careers, and population heterogeneity: Specification and estimation of a nonparametric, mixed poisson model. *Criminology, 31,* 327–362.

Nagin, D. S., & Tremblay, R. E. (2005). What has been learned from group-based trajectory modeling? Examples from physical aggression and other problem behaviors. *Annals of the American Academy of Political and Social Science, 602,* 82–117.

National Research Council. (2000). *From neurons to neighborhoods: The science of early child development.* Washington, DC: National Academy Press.

Niehoff, D. (1999). *The biology of violence.* New York: Free Press.

Patterson, G. R., Reid, J. B., & Dishion, T. J. (1992). *Antisocial boys.* Eugene, OR: Castalia.

Piquero, A. R., & Moffitt, T. E. (2005). Explaining the facts of crime: How the developmental taxonomy replies to Farrington's invitation. In D. P. Farrington (Ed.), *Integrated developmental and life-course theories of offending* (pp. 51–72). New Brunswick, NJ: Transaction.

Raudenbush, S. W. (2005). How do we study "what happens next?" *Annals of the American Academy of Political and Social Science, 602* 131–144.

Robins, L. N. (1978). Sturdy childhood predictors of adult antisocial behavior: Replications from longitudinal studies. *Psychological Medicine, 8,* 611–622.

Sampson, R. J., & Laub, J. H. (2004). A life-course theory of cumulative disadvantage and the stability of delinquency. In T. P. Thornberry (Ed.), *Developmental theories of crime and delinquency* (pp. 133–161). New Brunswick, NJ: Transaction Publishers.

Sampson, R. J., & Laub, J. H. (2005). A life-course view of the development of crime. *Annals of the American Academy of Political and Social Science, 602,* 12–45.

Swann, W. (1999). *Resilient identities.* New York: Basic Books.

Thornberry, T. P. (2004). (Ed.). *Developmental theories of crime and delinquency.* New Brunswick, NJ: Transaction Publishers.

Thornberry, T. P. (2005). Explaining multiple patterns of offending across the life course and across generations. *Annals of the American Academy of Political and Social Science, 602,* 156–195.

Thornberry, T. P., & Krohn, M. D. (2003). (Eds.). *Taking stock of delinquency: An overview of findings from contemporary longitudinal studies.* New York: Kluwer/Plenum.

Tolan, P. H. (1988). Socioeconomic, family, and social stress correlates of adolescents' antisocial and delinquent behavior. *Journal of Abnormal Child Psychology, 16,* 317–322.

Tolan, P. H., Guerra, N. G., & Kendall, P. H. (1995). A developmental–ecological perspective on antisocial behavior in children and adolescents: Toward a unified risk and intervention framework. *Journal of Consulting and Clinical Psychology, 63,* 577–584.

Chapter 3

Assessment in Juvenile Justice Systems

Robert D. Hoge

Reliable and valid assessments are critical for effective decision making at all levels of the juvenile justice process. These include decisions relating to competency to waive rights, consent to treatment, and fitness to plead or stand trial. These legally relevant actions require assessments of various competencies in the youth (see Grisso, 1998; Grisso, Vincent, & Seagrave, 2005). However, the primary concern of this book is therapeutic intervention, and therefore the focus is on assessment procedures and instruments relevant to decisions about services provided for the juvenile offender in community and institutional settings. The chapter begins with a discussion of terms and conceptual issues relevant to the conduct of assessments in juvenile justice systems. This is followed by a review of selected assessment tools and procedures and, finally, a discussion of general recommendations for the conduct of forensic assessments.

Terminology and Conceptual Issues

Assessments conducted in juvenile justice systems display considerable variety in their objectives and formats. As well, a number of cautions should be observed in the selection and interpretation of the assessment tools. These and other issues are addressed in this section.

Some instruments and procedures discussed below are designed for evaluating risk for continuing contact with the judicial system. The focus may involve risk for any criminal action, serious crime, or violent crime. These risk instruments are relevant to decisions about pretrial detention, level of supervision provided in community or institutional settings, and the intensity of services provided the youth. The latter consideration is particularly important in the context of the current book because of its relevance for decisions about the level of therapeutic intervention to be provided. The risk principle of case classification states that high-risk cases should be provided with intensive levels of service, whereas lower-risk cases can be afforded lower levels (Andrews, Bonta, & Hoge, 1990). Observing this principle helps ensure that we concentrate our resources on cases really in need of intervention and, further, encourages us to avoid overinvolvement in the lives of lower-risk youth. However, as a word of caution, within populations of relatively high-risk youth (e.g., incarcerated offenders), the risk principle may be less relevant (because all youth are at relatively high risk) and assessments may need to consider other factors, such as motivation to change.

Other instruments and procedures are designed for assessing criminogenic needs. The latter are risk factors that can be changed, and, if changed, reduce the likelihood of continued antisocial activity. These are also referred to as dynamic risk factors. Dysfunctional parenting and antisocial peer associations are examples. The importance of assessing needs is expressed in the need principle of case classification: targets of service should reflect the needs of the client as related to risk for offending (Andrews et al., 1990). If dysfunctional parenting and negative peer associations are the primary risk–need factors of the youth, they should be the targets of any intervention. Observing the need principle will help to ensure that interventions are effective and that agency resources are used in an appropriate manner. However, as Guerra et al. discuss in Chapter 2, more is known about the extent to which these risk factors predict the onset of offending rather than escalation or desistance. It may be necessary to complement traditional risk assessments with an evaluation of important life transitions to be mastered in order to develop interventions that can build requisite strengths for adjustment (e.g., vocational skills to secure gainful employment; interpersonal skills to engage in healthy intimate relationships).

Instruments and procedures for assessing risk and need factors may be comprehensive, attempting to encompass a range of characteristics of any youth and his or her circumstances. System improvements have been associated with implementation of a comprehensive

approach to screening and needs assessments that can guide placement, supervision, and treatment decisions at all phases of processing
(Hsia & Beyer, 2000). On the other hand, a large number of useful
instruments provides for a focus on more specific issues. For example,
personality tests can be helpful in evaluating mental health or other
personality disorders, and various aptitude measures such as IQ tests
can be useful in assessing educational needs. These assessment tools
are useful in juvenile justice assessments to the extent that they aid in
case planning and management.

Forms of Assessment Instruments and Procedures

One important distinction to note is between clinical and standardized
assessments. Many assessments conducted in juvenile justice systems
are clinical in nature; that is, they rely on the more-or-less informal collection of information from interviews and file reviews, and the integration of that information through an informal judgmental process.
This procedure is often used by psychologists and psychiatrists in
forming a mental health diagnosis. It is often used as well by probation
officers in forming disposition recommendations. However, a considerable body of research indicates that clinical assessments demonstrate
limited reliability and validity (Grisso & Tomkins, 1996; Grove &
Meehl, 1996; Grove, Zald, Lebow, Snitz, & Nelson, 2000). This limitation is particularly true where clinical assessments are compared with
those based on standardized instruments or procedures.

Standardized instruments provide a structured format for the collection and synthesis of information. Items within the measures are
generally empirically derived, and an algorithm for scoring is provided, with the latter based in some cases on sample norms. The
Weschler Intelligence Scale for Children—Fourth Edition (WISC-4;
Weschler, 2004) is an example of a standardized instrument. Items and
scoring formats are structured, as are the scoring procedures. It is also
possible to derive predictions of educational performance from the
scores. A third category of measures, standardized clinical procedures,
will also be described below. This chapter focuses on standardized
measures, although guidance in the conduct of more clinical assessments is also provided.

Three advantages are associated with standardized measures
(Hoge, 1999a, 1999b; Wiebusch, Baird, Krisberg, & Onek, 1995). First,
they help guarantee some consistency across clinicians and situations.
Clinical judgments based on informal opinions about the cognitive

competence of the child will vary widely, whereas we know that an assessment based on performance on the WISC was formed in a consistent manner. Second, and related, we can determine the reliability and validity of scores yielded by the standardized measures—a more difficult task with clinical conclusions because of variations in the way scores are expressed. Third, and as we saw above, empirical research supports the superior efficacy of standardized, relative to clinical, assessments.

Several cautions apply in the use of standardized measures. First, clinical decisions are sometimes involved in administering the instruments. For example, the examiner often must exercise some judgment in scoring items on the WISC. Similarly, and as we will see, items on some of the risk–need assessment instruments call for the exercise of judgment (e.g., "Is parental supervision inadequate?"). However, these instruments generally provide detailed guidelines regarding scoring that help to address reliability issues.

A second caution relates to the margin of error that is always present. Instruments require at least a minimum level of reliability and validity (see Sattler & Hoge, 2006), and the psychometric properties of the measure must always be considered in its application. This point relates to the professional override principle: The standardized instruments may be useful in forming opinions about the client, but final decisions must be made by the responsible professional.

The third caution relates to a situation where the standardized measure does not provide a complete basis for a decision about the client. For example, we may be asked by the court to provide recommendations of appropriate levels of supervision and treatment strategies for a youth assigned probation. We may interview the client, review file information, and administer personality and aptitude measures. However, the final recommendation will require a clinical judgment in which we integrate these different sources of information. Standardized clinical procedures or structured professional opinions represent efforts to introduce some structure into this process. Some of the risk–need assessment tools described below illustrate this approach.

Finally, ethical guidelines must always be considered in using forensic assessment measures (Grisso & Vincent, 2005). Any agency will undoubtedly have policy guidelines regarding the conduct and uses of assessment, but psychologists are also bound by professional guidelines such as Ethical Principles of Psychologists and Code of Conduct (American Psychological Association, 2002), Standards for Educational and Psychological Testing (American Educational Research Association, 1999), and Specialty Guidelines for Forensic Psychologists (Committee on Ethical Guidelines for Forensic Psychologists, 1991).

Assessment Dimensions and Categories

Two formats are used in expressing scores from psychological assessment instruments. The categorical approach expresses scores in terms of discrete categories. In this case the youth is labeled as gifted, developmentally delayed, attention-deficit/hyperactivity–disordered, at high risk for violent re-offending or some other categorical construct.

The most prominent of the mental health categorization systems is based on the *Diagnostic and Statistical Manual of Mental Disorders, 4th Ed., Text Revision* (DSM-IV-TR; American Psychiatric Association, 2000). This system is widely used in forensic situations. DSM-IV-TR categories particularly relevant to juvenile forensic contexts include those relating to learning disabilities, attention-deficit disorders, disruptive behaviors, substance abuse, and mood and anxiety disorders. Some issues have been raised regarding the validity of this categorization system, but it nevertheless remains an important diagnostic system in forensic decision situations.

Dimensional constructs represent the second format for expressing scores from standardized measures. In this case scores are expressed as points on a quantitative dimension. For example, we talk about the degree of severity of depression or degree of risk for future offending. In many cases dimensional scores are expressed as a standardized measure, wherein an individual's score is expressed relative to a normative group. For example, the youth may obtain a *T*-score of 50 on a measure of risk for violent offending, indicating that his or her score was equal to the average score of a normative group.

Evaluating the Measures

Two of the most important bases for evaluating any psychological measure are reliability and validity (Hoge, 1999b; Sattler & Hoge, 2006). Reliability refers to the stability or consistency of a measure and can be evaluated through a number of procedures, including the test–retest, parallel forms (interrater agreement), and internal consistency methods. All are designed to evaluate the extent to which scores on a measure are affected by error variance. Reliability is an essential condition in a measure, and clinicians should pay close attention to evidence for reliability in choosing a measure.

Validity is also a critical consideration, although it is a somewhat more difficult construct because several different meanings are associated with the term. Table 3.1 provides definitions of the forms of validity most relevant for our purposes.

Although reliability and validity constitute the most important bases for evaluating a measure, several other considerations are relevant in selecting assessment tools and procedures. One of these is clinical utility. The measures selected must be appropriate to the goals of the assessment and characteristics of the youth being assessed. For example, there is little point in assessing cognitive aptitudes if this domain is not relevant to either placement or treatment decisions. Choice of assessment tools should focus closely on the purposes for which the assessment is conducted. When juveniles are assessed at multiple points in a system (e.g., at intake and again at placement), it is also critical that these assessments follow the youth and are integrated into case planning. Similarly, care has to be taken to ensure that measures are appropriate for the youth being assessed. Many instruments developed for adults cannot be used with youth without determining that they are reliable and valid for a younger age group. Gender, race, or ethnicity may also be relevant in choosing assessment tools.

Cost of the procedures and level of expertise required in conducting the assessments are also important considerations. It is unfortu-

TABLE 3.1. Major Forms of Validity

Content

Adequacy with which a measure represents the conceptual domain it is expected to encompass.

Construct

Theoretical meaning of scores from a measure; accuracy with which measure represents construct.

Criterion-related concurrent

Extent to which scores from a measure relate to concurrently collected indices of behavior or performance.

Criterion-related predictive

Extent to which scores from a measure relate to subsequent indices of behavior or performance.

Incremental predictive

Extent to which measure exhibits improvements in prediction relative to other procedures.

nate, but many systems provide limited funds for assessment services, which may, in turn, limit the activities that can be supported. Clinical expertise or competence is relevant because assessment instruments vary in the level of professional competence required in their administration and interpretation. Some instruments, such as the WISC and the Minnesota Multiphasic Personality Inventory—Adolescent (MMPI-A) require an advanced degree in a mental health profession and specialized training. Other measures do not require this level of professional qualification but do require specialized training. This is the case, as we will see, with some of the risk/need measures.

Cautionary Points in Assessing Adolescents

Several general concerns are relevant in the assessment of adolescents. It is important to keep in mind that they are different from adults; they differ in their cognitive processes, modes of emotional responding, and social needs (Scott, 2000; Vincent & Grisso, 2005). Furthermore, because young people between ages 10 and 20 may be at different stages of development, it is very important to maintain a developmental perspective in evaluating antisocial behaviors in children and adolescents.

Two aspects of the developmental process are particularly relevant in conducting assessments. First, the adolescent's capacity for reasoning and comprehending abstract concepts is limited. During an interview, for example, the client may have an understanding of the concept of "criminal responsibility" that is very different from that of the adult conducting the interview, and this discrepancy could lead to erroneous conclusions.

Second, because adolescence is a time of transition in personality, emotional functioning, and social relations, we must be cautious in forming conclusions or diagnoses. For example, symptoms of depression or anxiety may be a permanent and worrisome condition, or the symptoms may simply disappear over a relatively short period of time. Making this determination is not always easy. A related problem involves determining whether a condition is "normal" for this period of development or truly predictive of later negative outcomes. Most adolescents engage in risky behaviors, to one degree or another, but deciding at what point their experimentation exceeds the range of "normal behavior" may be problematic. Any psychologist engaged in assessing adolescents needs to have a solid background in developmental psychology and a sensitivity to the needs of youth in this age period.

Assessment Tools and Procedures for Evaluating Juvenile Offenders

The major categories of assessment instruments and procedures include personality tests, behavioral ratings and checklists, structured interview schedules, aptitude tests, attitude measures, and comprehensive risk and risk–need measures. Let us now consider these categories and their role in assessing juvenile offenders.

Personality Tests

Inferences about dimensions of personality are relevant to a broad range of forensic decisions, including waiver of rights, fitness to stand trial, and fitness to plead. They are also relevant to decisions about treatment. Depression, anxiety, aggressive tendencies, and amenability to treatment are personality dimensions relevant to choices about intervention strategies. As well, pathological categories such as conduct disorder, oppositional-defiant disorder, and attention-deficit/hyperactivity disorder can be useful in guiding treatment strategies.

In many cases inferences about personality states and traits are based on clinical judgments. However, and as we have seen, evidence suggests that the use of standardized measures can improve the assessment process. Personality tests generally involve a self-report format, and interpretation of the tests may require specialized training.

Many standardized personality tests are now available (see Hoge, 1999b; Sattler & Hoge, 2006), some of which provide for a broad focus on personality, whereas others deal with a narrower range of constructs (e.g., depression or anxiety). Examples of broad-based personality tests include the Adolescent Psychopathology Scale (APS; Reynolds, 1998) and the MMPI-A (Butcher et al., 1992). The Reynolds Adolescent Depression Scale—Second Edition (RADS-2; Reynolds, 2002) and Aggression Questionnaire (AQ; Buss & Warren, 2000) are examples more narrowly focused personality tests.

Behavioral Ratings and Checklists

Behavioral ratings and checklists provide information on maladaptive behaviors or behavioral patterns, and use parents, teachers, clinicians, or others familiar with the youth as respondents. These measures generally provide more direct information about behavioral adjustment than the personality tests. Scores may be expressed in terms of frequencies of very specific behaviors (e.g., acts of physical aggression) or as stable behavioral patterns (e.g., attentional disorders). Scoring and interpretation of these measures often require less specialized training than with personality tests, but some background in psychological assessment is normally required.

A wide range of checklist and rating scale measures is now available for assessing behavioral dimensions (see Grisso, 1998; Hoge, 1999b; Sattler & Hoge, 2006). These measures can be of great value in assessing juvenile offenders because in many cases, their risks and needs relate to dysfunctional behavior traits (e.g., impulsivity, aggressive tendencies, defiance), whereas other factors such as anxiety, attentional disorder, or poor self-concept may be important in case planning. Most of these measures also provide information about the overall severity of maladaptive behaviors, which may be relevant to decisions about the intensity of treatment. Information about these behavioral traits from standardized measures can form an important part of an assessment battery. Some examples of behavioral ratings and checklists relevant to assessing juvenile offenders include the Child Behavior Checklist (CBCL; Achenbach & Rescorla, 2001), Jesness Inventory—Revised (JI-R; Jesness, 2003), and Personality Inventory for Children—Second Edition (PIC-2; Wirt, Lachar, Seat, & Broen, 2001).

Assessments of Attitudes, Values, and Beliefs

Antisocial attitudes, values, and beliefs consistently emerge as risk factors for antisocial behavior (Gendreau, Little, & Goggin, 1996; Simourd & Andrews, 1994) and also play a role in some of the major theories of the causes of antisocial behavior (e.g., Andrews & Bonta, 2006; Bandura, Barbaranelli, Caprara, & Pastorelli, 1996; Guerra, Huesmann, & Hanish, 1994). Further, as discussed by Guerra, Kim, and Boxer in Chapter 4 of this volume, these social cognitions typically form the mainstay of cognitive-behavioral interventions for offenders. Some of the personality and behavioral measures discussed above provide for the assessment of attitudinal variables, whereas the How I Think questionnaire (HIT; Gibbs, Barriga, & Potter, 2001) is an example of a measure specifically designed to assess attitudes in juvenile offenders.

Cognitive and Academic Aptitude Measures

Intellectual functioning and academic aptitudes and achievement levels are often important elements of the assessment process. Academic failure is sometimes a correlate of juvenile delinquency, and cognitive competence may be an important responsivity factor in case planning. The psychologist dealing with juvenile offenders should have in his or her repertoire an individual test of intelligence (e.g., WISC-4; Weschler, 2004) and an achievement test (e.g., Diagnostic Achievement Test for Adolescents—Second Edition; Newcomer & Bryant, 1993). More specialized psychoeducational tests may be required under some circumstances. Sattler (2001) has provided a comprehensive overview of these measures.

Other Personality and Cognitive Measures

A variety of other standardized measures is available that may be of use in assessing juvenile offenders. These measures include standardized interview schedules, such as the Child and Adolescent Functional Assessment Scale (Hodges, 2000) and Diagnostic Interview Schedule for Children (Shaffer, 1996); measures of adaptive functioning, such as the Vineland Adaptive Behavior Scales—Second Edition (Sparrow, Cicchetti, & Balla, 2005); and screening instruments, such as the Massachusetts Youth Screening Instrument—Version 2 (MAYSI-2; Grisso & Barnum, 2003) and Eating Disorders Inventory–2 (EDI-2; Garner, 2005). Information about these measures is available from Dahlberg, Toal, Swahn, and Behrens (2005), Hoge (1999a, 1999b), Sattler (2001), and Sattler and Hoge (2006).

Comprehensive Risk and Risk–Need Measures

Over the past 10 or 15 years, considerable progress has been made in the development of standardized risk–need assessment tools. These are designed to evaluate youths' risk for antisocial behavior and to identify their needs (dynamic risk factors) to aid in case planning. Early risk instruments were limited by a narrow range of static risk factors, such as age at first arrest, number of prior convictions, and severity of the offense (Borum & Verhaagen, 2006; Hoge, 1999a; Hoge & Andrews, 1996; Le Blanc, 1998). These factors were not particularly useful; they led to a low level of predictability and provided no information relevant to interventions.

The more recent instruments are empirically based, attempt to identify both static and dynamic risk factors, and have been evaluated through psychometric research. Some of these can be characterized as actuarial instruments in that they yield empirically based estimates of risk and need. Other measures in this category are standardized clinical instruments, representing a structured professional judgment approach. All of these instruments are of value in helping to synthesize a range of information about the client and guide decisions about appropriate community or residential placements, levels of supervision, and interventions. These instruments are designed for use by psychologists, although some can be administered by probation officers, youth workers, and other such professionals with specialized training.

Although these measures can be valuable in assessing the juvenile offender, some cautionary points must be considered. First, completion of the instruments generally involves fairly extensive information-collection efforts, including interviews with the client, interviews with collaterals when available (e.g., parents, teachers), and reviews of files and other informational sources about the client. Second, professional expertise and training in administering and scoring the instrument are usually required, although this varies somewhat with the instrument. Third, although the validity of risk assessments yielded by the actuarial measures is greater than that yielded by clinical methods, some measure of error is always present. In other words, there will always be a certain percentage of false positives and false negatives. This area relates to a more general point that final decisions about the client should not be based on a single psychological measure or even a battery of such measures. Some provision for a professional override must be provided so that final decisions rest with the responsible professional.

Four measures are described below in some detail because they form an important category of assessment instruments in juvenile justice settings.

Estimate of Risk of Adolescent Sexual Offense Recidivism–2

The ERASOR-2 (Worling & Curwen, 2001) is an example of a structured clinical assessment tool focusing specifically on adolescent sexual offending. It is designed to evaluate risk for sexual re-offending on the part of individuals who have previously committed a sexual assault and to offer guidance in the development of treatment strategies.

Twenty-five risk factors are included in the ERASOR. Examples include "deviant sexual interest," "ever sexually assaulted two or more victims," and "antisocial interpersonal orientation." A specific scoring algorithm is not provided. Instead the assessor categorizes the level of risk as low, moderate, or high, based on the total number of items checked and the assessor's judgments about the pattern of risk observed.

Limited reliability and validity information are currently available for the measure. Guidelines for administering and scoring the instrument are available, as is a specialized training program. The authors emphasize the importance of utilizing multiple sources of information in scoring items.

Structured Assessment of Violence Risk in Youth

The SAVRY (Bartel, Borum, & Forth, 2000; Borum, Bartel, & Forth, 2005) provides for a structured clinical assessment of risk for violent actions. Items in the scale are empirically derived and specifically focused on adolescents.

The 24 risk items are divided into three categories: historical (e.g., "history of violence"), individual (e.g., "negative attitudes"), and social/contextual (e.g., "poor parental management"). Six items describing protective factors are also included (e.g., "strong social support"). Scoring is based on a summary risk rating of low, moderate, or high. An algorithm for calculating this is not provided; rather, the assessor determines the score based on his or her professional judgment.

Support for the reliability and validity of the SAVRY has been provided. Unlike the other comprehensive risk–need instruments described in this section, use of the SAVRY does not require special training. The authors indicate that a familiarity with the manual is sufficient.

Washington State Juvenile Court Assessment

The WSJCA (Barnoski, 2004; Barnoski & Markussen, 2005) is part of a two-step assessment process in which a short screening instrument is first administered. Youth who obtain a moderate- or high-risk score on that scale are then administered the full WSJCA. Only the latter instrument is discussed here.

The 132-item WSJCA provides for assessing both static and dynamic risk factors within 13 domains (e.g., criminal history, family, attitudes/behavior). "School misconduct" is an example of a dynamic risk factor and "belief in the value of an education," an example of a protective factor. Four types of scores are produced: static risk, dynamic risk, static protective, and dynamic protective. The scoring is designed to assist in developing a case plan.

Support for the reliability and validity of the measure is reported by the authors. Administration and scoring of the measure does require an intensive training program, and supporting training materials are available.

Youth Level of Service/Case Management Inventory

The YLS/CMI (Hoge, 2005; Hoge & Andrews, 2002) is a standardized actuarial measure providing estimates of risk for re-offending and a framework for developing case plans based on a risk–needs assessment. It also includes a professional override provision to allow the examiner discretion in identifying level of risk.

The first section of the YLS/CMI includes 42 items reflecting characteristics of the offender (e.g., "chronic drug use") or his or her circumstances (e.g., "parent provides inadequate supervision") identified in the literature as correlates of juvenile offending. The items are divided into the following subscales: Prior and Current Offenses/Dispositions, Family Circumstances/Parenting, Education/Employment, Peer Relations, Substance Abuse, Leisure/Recreation, Personality/Behavior, and Attitudes/Orientation. This section yields an overall risk–need score and a risk–need score within each of the above domains. An opportunity is also provided for indicating areas of strength. Subsequent sections include Summary of Risks and Needs, Assessment of Other Needs and Special Considerations, Professional Override, Contact Level, and Case Management Plan. The latter involves identifying a set of goals reflecting the risk–needs assessment and identification of means of achieving those goals.

A training program is associated with the YLS/CMI; trainees should have some background in child development and experience working with antisocial youth. Psychometric research has been conducted with the instrument, and support for criterion-related predictive validity has been reported for both genders and a variety of ethnic groups.

Other Comprehensive Risk and Risk–Need Measures

Other measures in this category include the Early Assessment Risk List for Boys–20B (EARL-20B; Augimeri, Koegl, Webster, & Levene, 2001), Psychopathy Checklist: Youth Version (PCL:YV; Forth, Kosson, & Hare, 2003), and the Wisconsin Juvenile Probation and Aftercare Assessment form (WJPAA; Baird, 1985). Reviews of these measures are available from Grisso et al. (2005).

Guidelines for Conducting Interviews with Juveniles

Assessments conducted in juvenile justice systems for any purpose necessarily involve an interview with the youth and, where feasible, collateral sources such as parents, teachers, or professionals associated with him or her. Highly structured interview schedules such as the Diagnostic Interview Schedule for Children (Shaffer, 1996) are available, particularly for the assessment of mental disorders. As well, comprehensive risk–need instruments such as the WSJCA and the YLS/CMI provide semistructured interview schedules to assist in collecting information required for completing the inventories. An interview is an essential part of any forensic assessment.

Miller and Rollnick's (2002) motivational interviewing program is a valuable resource in helping people improve their interviewing skills. Other resources for assisting in developing interview skills include Gratus (1988), Sattler (1998), and Sattler and Hoge (2006). The following are some general guidelines derived from those sources:

- *Establish rapport:* Dealing with antisocial youth is sometimes challenging, but it is our responsibility as professionals to treat each client with respect and to make every attempt to gain his or her trust. Expressing empathy for the client's situation will often help in establishing a relationship.
- *Listen carefully:* Eliciting good information from a client depends on listening carefully to what he or she has to say. It is important to enter the interview with an open mind rather than with an agenda.
- *Remain objective:* Although the interviewer should maintain a positive attitude and treat the youth's responses in a respectful manner, this does not necessarily mean that the interviewer endorses the youth's responses.
- *Facilitate communication:* There is little point in using language or concepts the youth does not understand. We should ensure that our questions and responses are clearly understood by the client.
- *Maintain control:* The youth should be treated with consideration during the interview, but not be allowed to direct or divert the questioning.
- *Avoid argumentation:* Engaging the youth in lengthy arguments and confronting any of the youth's positions in a hostile manner are usually counterproductive. Maintain a positive atmosphere as much as possible.

Assessment Centers

The Office of Juvenile Justice and Delinquency Prevention (Oldenettel & Wordes, 2000) has developed the community assessment center concept as part of a larger comprehensive strategy for serious, violent, and chronic juvenile offenders (Wilson & Howell, 1995). The following are the four main features of the assessment center concept, as it would be applied within a community or region:

- A single point of entry is provided for all juveniles who come into contact with the juvenile justice system.
- An immediate and comprehensive assessment is provided, which may involve an initial screening process and then a more intensive assessment for those identified as at moderate or high risk–need.
- A management information system is created to monitor the youths' needs and their progress through the system.
- An integrated case management system uses "information from the assessment process and the management information system to develop recommendations, facilitate access to services, conduct follow-ups, and periodically reassess youth" (Oldenettel & Wordes, 2000, p. 2).

Ideally, such an assessment center would also coordinate its services with those provided by the educational, mental health, and social service systems in order to avoid the fragmentation of services so often observed in our communities.

Some Practical Considerations

Both conducting and utilizing assessments are too often carried out in a casual manner in juvenile justice systems. This is unfortunate in light of the important role these assessments play in the decision process (Hsia & Beyer, 2000). A number of steps should be considered in planning assessment activities.

1. The context and purpose of the assessment should be major determining factors in this planning. This chapter has stressed the use of assessments in evaluating risk for continuing criminal activity and the identification of dynamic needs underlying the risk factors. However, assessments are sometimes employed for other purposes (e.g.,

evaluating risk for suicide or for violent acts in a residence or school setting), and the procedures would have to be adjusted accordingly. Care must also be taken that the assessment instruments or procedures are appropriate for the youth being assessed. It is a mistake, for example, to simply assume that a measure validated for adults would be relevant to an adolescent, or that norms developed for male offenders would be applicable for girls.

2. Ethical considerations in the use of assessments were discussed earlier in the chapter, but a comment should be made on the stage of processing where the assessment occurs. Sometimes the assessment is done at intake and prior to adjudication. In this case care may have to be taken to ensure that information provided in the assessment does not impact on the judicial process (Grisso & Vincent, 2005). The risk–need assessment procedures addressed in this chapter are primarily designed to guide postdisposition decisions about treatment interventions.

3. The qualifications of the individual conducting the assessment are an important consideration. We have seen that some of the standardized risk–need assessment tools are appropriate for use by probation officers, teachers, or other such professionals with special training in administering and scoring the instrument. Other tools, including personality and aptitude tests, must be used by a qualified mental health professional. In any case, the individual conducting the assessment must possess the required professional qualifications and training. In too many cases measures are inappropriately administered, scored, and interpreted because of a lack of expertise and qualifications.

4. The sources of information on which the assessment is based must also be considered. An interview with the youth is nearly always necessary. However, interviews with collaterals such as parents, teachers, and principals may also be desirable. As well, file information revealing past behaviors and results from psychological tests may also be involved. The issue then becomes integrating this sometimes contradictory information and producing meaningful conclusions. The latter may be expressed as an estimate of risk for re-offending, an identification of need factors that can be addressed and increase the probability of desistance, a mental health diagnosis, or specific intervention recommendations. Some of the standardized risk–need assessment instruments described in this chapter can assist in this process, but in some cases the final integration of the information will depend on clinical judgment. Borum and Verhaagen (2006) and Hoge and Andrews (1996) have offered guidance in forming these judgments.

5. Attention also should be paid to ways in which the assessments are integrated into the juvenile justice system and the larger system of youth services. Sometimes there are disconnects within the system itself, such that assessments conducted at intake are not communicated well to others in the system, including those responsible for delivering treatment to the youth. It is also sometimes the case that professionals receiving the assessments and responsible for executing their recommendations have little understanding of the process. In addition, procedures for reassessing youth for evaluating their progress (and the effectiveness of the system) are often lacking.

6. Sharing of assessments among juvenile justice, education, mental health, and social service systems is also poor in many cases. This lack of sharing is particularly unfortunate because many of our youth and their families are involved in several of those systems. There are sometimes issues of confidentiality associated with sharing information, but, as emphasized in the assessment center concept discussed above, multiple agencies often need to engage in more careful planning in their conduct and uses of assessments.

Summary and Conclusion

This chapter has stressed the importance of conducting careful assessments of youth and the value of using standardized psychological measures and procedures whenever possible. Assessments are important in the context of rehabilitation strategies because they help guide decisions about the intensity of the services to be provided as well as the target of those services. A youth with relatively minor behavioral and circumstantial issues should not be treated the same as one with serious personality disorders underlying his or her antisocial activities. Assessing risk factors with standardized measures and observing the risk principle of case classification ensures that each youth receives services appropriate to his or her needs and that services are used in an economical manner.

Similarly, observing the need principle of case classification by assessing the specific needs and circumstances of youth helps to ensure that appropriate services are delivered and that our resources are used in a rational fashion. The importance of identifying areas that will contribute to the youth's desistance from continued antisocial activities was emphasized in Chapter 2. These standardized measures that identify these areas, particularly the broad-based risk–need measures, can play an important role in achieving that goal.

We have cited several advantages associated with the use of standardized measures. First, a growing body of research demonstrates that higher levels of validity are associated with these measures in comparison with unstructured or clinical procedures and that standardized measures lead to better decisions (Grisso & Tomkins, 1996; Grove & Meehl, 1996; Grove et al., 2000).

Second, and related, it is easier to evaluate the reliability and validity of standardized measures. Third, using standardized measures ensures some consistency in the assessment and decision processes; the criteria for assessment and decisions are visible and concrete. Finally, standardized measures help provide a link with theoretical and research developments in the field. For example, all of the comprehensive risk–need instruments described above are based on the latest research regarding the correlates and causes of criminal activity in youth.

One final suggestion is offered: We should engage in greater efforts to educate others involved in juvenile justice and correctional systems with regard to the purpose and importance of the assessment process. This includes judges, prosecuting and defense attorneys, youth workers in community and institutional settings, and relevant politicians and policymakers. Increased understanding and support from the multiple players in the juvenile justice system should go a long way toward enhancing the value of our assessment efforts.

References

Achenbach, T. M., & Rescorla, L. A. (2001). *Manual for the ASEBA School-Age Forms and Profiles.* Burlington: University of Vermont, Research Center for Children, Youth, and Families.

American Educational Research Association. (1999). *Standards for educational and psychological testing.* Washington, DC: American Educational Research Association.

American Psychiatric Association. (2000). *Diagnostic and statistical manual of mental disorders* (4th ed., text rev.). Washington, DC: Author.

American Psychological Association. (2002). Ethical principles of psychologists and code of conduct. *American Psychologist, 57,* 1060–1073.

Andrews, D. A., & Bonta, J. (2006). *The psychology of criminal conduct—fourth edition.* Cincinnati, OH: Anderson.

Andrews, D. A., Bonta, J., & Hoge, R. D. (1990). Classification for effective rehabilitation: Rediscovering psychology. *Criminal Justice and Behavior, 17,* 19–52.

Augimeri, L. K., Koegl, C. J., Webster, C. D., & Levene, K. S. (2001). *Early*

Assessment Risk List for Boys: EARL-20B, Version 2. Toronto, ON: Earlscourt Child and Family Centre.

Baird, S. C. (1985). Classifying juveniles: Making the most of an important management tool. *Corrections Today, 47,* 32–38.

Bandura, A. C., Barbaranelli, C., Caprara, G. V., & Pastorelli, C. (1996). Mechanisms of moral disengagement in the exercise of moral agency. *Journal of Personality and Social Psychology, 71,* 364–374.

Barnoski, R. (2004). *Assessing risk for re-offense: Validating the Washington State Juvenile Court Assessment* (Report No. 04-03-1201). Olympia: Washington State Institute for Public Policy.

Barnoski, R., & Markussen, S. (2005). Washington State Juvenile Court Assessment. In T. Grisso, T. Vincent, & D. Seagrave (Eds.), *Mental health screening and assessment in juvenile justice* (pp. 271–282). New York: Guilford Press.

Bartel, P., Borum, R., & Forth, A. (2000). *Structured Assessment of Violence Risk in Youth* (SAVRY). Tampa, FL: Louis de la Parte Florida Mental Health Institute, University of South Florida.

Beck, J. S., Beck, A. T., & Jolly, J. B. (2001). *Beck Youth Inventories.* San Antonio, TX: Psychological Corporation.

Borum, R., Bartel, P. A., & Forth, A. E. (2005). Structured Assessment of Violence Risk in Youth. In T. Grisso, T. Vincent, & D. Seagrave (Eds.), *Mental health screening and assessment in juvenile justice* (pp. 311–323). New York: Guilford Press.

Borum, R., & Verhaagen, D. (2006). *Assessing and managing violence risk in youth.* New York: Guilford Press.

Buss, A. H., & Warren, W. L. (2000). *Aggression Questionnaire Manual.* Los Angeles: Western Psychological Services.

Butcher, J. N., Williams, C. L., Graham, J. R., Archer, R. P., Tellegen, A., Ben-Porath, Y. S., et al. (1992). *Minnesota Multiphasic Personality Inventory—Adolescent.* Minneapolis: University of Minnesota Press.

Committee on Ethical Guidelines for Forensic Psychologists. (1991). Specialty guidelines for forensic psychologists. *Law and Human Behavior, 15,* 655–665.

Dahlberg, L., Toal, S., Swahn, M., & Behrens, C. (2005). *Measuring violence-related attitudes, behaviors, and influences among youths: A compendium of assessment tools* (2nd ed.). Atlanta: Centers for Disease Control and Prevention, National Center for Injury Prevention and Control.

Forth, A. E., Kosson, D. S., & Hare, R. D. (2003). *The Hare Psychopathy Checklist—Youth Version.* North Tonawanda, NY: Multi-Health Systems.

Garner, D. M. (2005). *Eating Disorder Inventory—3.* Lutz, FL: Psychological Assessment Resources.

Gendreau, P., Little, T., & Goggin, C. E. (1996). A meta-analysis of the predictors of adult offender recidivism: What works! *Criminology, 34,* 401–433.

Gibbs, J. C., Barriga, A. Q., & Potter, G. B. (2001). *How I Think (HIT) questionnaire.* Champaign, IL: Research Press.

Gratus, J. (1988). *Successful interviewing*. Harmondsworth, UK: Penguin.

Grisso, T. (1998). *Forensic evaluation of juveniles*. Sarasota, FL: Professional Resource Press.

Grisso, T., & Barnum, R. (2003). *Massachusetts Youth Screening Instrument— Version 2: User's manual and technical report*. Sarasota, FL: Personal Resource Press.

Grisso, T., & Tomkins, A. J. (1996). Communicating violence risk assessments. *American Psychologist, 51*, 928–930.

Grisso, T., & Vincent, G. (2005). The context for mental health screening and assessment. In T. Grisso, T. Vincent, & D. Seagrave (Eds.), *Mental health screening and assessment in juvenile justice* (pp. 44–70). New York: Guilford Press.

Grisso, T., Vincent, G., & Seagrave, D. (Eds.). (2005). *Mental health screening and assessment in juvenile justice*. New York: Guilford Press.

Grove, W. M., & Meehl, P. E. (1996). Comparative efficiency of informal (subjective, impressionistic) and formal (mechanical, algorithmic) prediction procedures: The clinical–statistical controversy. *Psychology, Public Policy, and the Law, 2*, 293–323.

Grove, W. M., Zald, D. H., Lebow, B. S., Snitz, B. E., & Nelson, C. (2000). Clinical versus mechanical prediction: A meta-analysis. *Psychological Assessment, 12*, 19–30.

Guerra, N. G., Huesmann, L. R., & Hanish, L. (1994). The role of normative beliefs in children's social behavior. In N. Eisenberg (Ed.), *Social development* (pp. 140–158). Thousand Oaks, CA: Sage.

Hodges, K. (2000). *Child and Adolescent Functional Assessment Scale*. Ypsilanti: Eastern Michigan University.

Hoge, R. D. (1999a). An expanded role for psychological assessments in juvenile justice systems. *Criminal Justice and Behavior, 26*, 251–266.

Hoge, R. D. (1999b). *Assessing adolescents in educational, counseling, and other settings*. Mahwah, NJ: Erlbaum.

Hoge, R. D. (2005). Youth Level of Service/Case Management Inventory. In T. Grisso, T. Vincent, & D. Seagrave (Eds.), *Mental health screening and assessment in juvenile justice* (pp. 283–294). New York: Guilford Press.

Hoge, R. D., & Andrews, D. A. (1996). *Assessing the youthful offender: Issues and techniques*. New York: Plenum.

Hoge, R. D., & Andrews, D. A. (2002). *Youth Level of Service/Case Management Inventory user's manual*. North Tonawanda, NY: Multi-Health Systems.

Hsia, H. M., & Beyer, M. (2000, March). *System change through state challenge activities: Approaches and products*. [Bulletin]. Washington, DC: US Department of Justice, Office of Justice Programs, Office of Juvenile Justice and Delinquency Prevention.

Jesness, C. F. (2003). *Jesness Inventory—Revised*. North Tonawanda, NY: Multi-Health Systems.

Lachar, D., & Gruber, C. P. (1995). *Personality Inventory for Youth*. Los Angeles: Western Psychological Services.

Le Blanc, M. (1998). Screening of serious and violent juvenile offenders: Identification, classification, and prediction. In R. Loeber & D. P. Farrington (Eds.), *Serious and violent juvenile offenders: Risk factors and successful interventions* (pp. 167–193). Thousand Oaks, CA: Sage.

Miller, W. R., & Rollnick, S. (2002). *Motivational interviewing—second edition.* New York: Guilford Press.

Newcomer, P. C., & Bryant, B. R. (1993). *Diagnostic Achievement Test for Adolescents—second edition.* Austin, TX: PRO-ED.

Oldenettel, D., & Wordes, M. (2000). *The community assessment center concept.* Washington, DC: U.S. Department of Justice, Office of Juvenile Justice and Delinquency Prevention.

Rahdert, E. R. (1991). *The Adolescent Assessment/Referral System.* Rockville, MD: National Institute on Drug Abuse.

Reynolds, W. M. (1998). *Adolescent Psychopathology Scale.* Lutz, FL: Psychological Assessment Resources.

Reynolds, W. M. (2002). *Reynolds Adolescent Depression Scale—Second Edition.* Lutz, FL: Psychological Assessment Resources.

Sattler, J. M. (1998). *Clinical and forensic interviewing of children and families: Guidelines for the mental health, education, pediatric, and child maltreatment fields.* San Diego: Sattler.

Sattler, J. M. (2001). *Assessment of children: Cognitive applications* (4th ed.). San Diego: Sattler.

Sattler, J. M., & Hoge, R. D. (2006). *Assessment of children: Behavioral, social, and clinical foundations* (5th ed.). San Diego: Sattler.

Scott, E. S. (2000). Criminal responsibility in adolescence: Lessons from developmental psychology. In T. Grisso & R. G. Schwartz (Eds.), *Youth on trial: A developmental perspective on juvenile justice* (pp. 291–234). Chicago: University of Chicago Press.

Shaffer, D. (1996). *Diagnostic Interview Schedule for Children* (DISC-4). New York: New York State Psychiatric Institute.

Simourd, L., & Andrews, D. A. (1994). Correlates of delinquency: A look at gender differences. *Forum on Corrections Research, 6,* 26–31.

Sparrow, S. S., Cicchetti, D. V., & Balla, D. A. (2005). *Vineland Adaptive Behavior Scales—Second Edition.* Circle Pines, MN: American Guidance Service.

Vincent, G., & Grisso, T. (2005). A developmental perspective on adolescent personality, psychopathology, and delinquency. In T. Grisso, T. Vincent, & D. Seagrave (Eds.), *Mental health screening and assessment in juvenile justice* (pp. 22–43). New York: Guilford Press.

Weschler, D. (2004). *Weschler Intelligence Scale for Children—fourth edition.* San Antonio, TX: Psychological Corporation.

Wiebush, R. G., Baird, C., Krisberg, B., & Onek, D. (1995). Risk assessment and classification for serious violent and chronic juvenile offenders. In J. C. Howell, B. Krisberg, J. D. Hawkins, & J. J. Wilson (Eds.), *A sourcebook: Serious, violent, and chronic juvenile offenders* (pp. 171–212). Thousand Oaks, CA: Sage.

Wilson, J. J., & Howell, J. C. (1995). Comprehensive strategy for serious, violent, and chronic juvenile offenders. In J. C. Howell, B. Krisberg, J. D. Hawkins, & J. J. Wilson (Eds.), *A sourcebook: Serious, violent, and chronic juvenile offenders* (pp. 36–47). Thousand Oaks, CA: Sage.

Wirt, R. D., Lachar, D., Seat, P. D., & Broen, W. E., Jr. (2001). *Personality Inventory for Children—second edition.* Los Angeles: Western Psychological Services.

Worling, J. R., & Curwen, M. A. (2001). *Estimate of Risk of Adolescent Sexual Offense Recidivism* (ERASOR). Toronto, ON: Thistletown Regional Centre.

Part II

TREATMENT PROGRAMS AND POLICIES
FOR THE GENERAL OFFENDER POPULATION

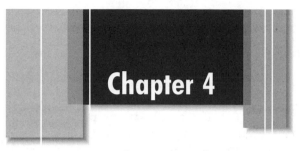

Chapter 4

What Works
Best Practices with Juvenile Offenders

Nancy G. Guerra
Tia E. Kim
Paul Boxer

The emphasis on rehabilitation of juvenile offenders throughout this volume suggests an obvious question: What works in the treatment of juvenile offenders? To answer this question and to guide programming, policymakers and practitioners increasingly rely on evaluations, reports, reviews, meta-analyses, and certified programs that prevent or reduce delinquency. In some cases, specific programs have been evaluated, replicated, and vetted as "proven" to be effective. In other cases, programs are selected that have been deemed "promising" and/or are consistent with principles of effectiveness. However, even with this push toward scientific evidence as the basis for program selection, programs are selected in other cases because of popular appeal (e.g., boot camps or get-tough programs) or effective marketing, regardless of whether there is corresponding and supportive scientific evidence, or even when they have been proven harmful.

Because we believe that treatment programs should be guided by the best evidence available, we begin this chapter with a summary and review of specific programs that have been rigorously evaluated and are considered effective in the treatment of juvenile offenders. Many of the programs for youth conduct problems that have been deemed effective (and are frequently cited in reviews of best practices) focus on early *prevention* of problem behaviors, often without regard to at-risk status, rather than *treatment* for youth who have entered the juvenile justice system. Indeed, there are very few proven treatment programs for delinquent youth and no proven program models in custodial settings (Greenwood, 2005). If we consider as proven only those programs that have been carefully evaluated with offenders (excluding non-serious status offenders) in multiple settings and include longer-term outcomes, those reviewed by a scientific advisory group, and those used widely (suggesting feasibility, cost-effectiveness), only three programs meet this standard: multisystemic family therapy, functional family therapy, and multidimensional treatment foster care, with the possible addition of aggression replacement training.

Given that the three most effective programs require family involvement—which may be unrealistic for incarcerated offenders or for those from the most seriously distressed families—we also discuss promising programs, including those with evidence based on a single program or limited replication that are used occasionally and may be listed in reviews or catalogs of effective or promising programs. We complement our review of these programs with a discussion of evidence-based principles,[1] building on meta-analytic results that consider simultaneously multiple features of effective programs and how these programs are implemented in different settings and for different populations. In addition, we also recognize the importance of carefully delineating evidence-based principles, given that one size does not fit all and that program adjustments and modifications are the rule rather than the exception.

We also consider the implications of generally modest effect sizes—even under optimal delivery conditions, treatment outcomes are typically only moderate at best. As Guerra, Williams, Tolan, and Modecki discuss in Chapter 2 of this volume, this is due, in part, to the multiple influences on delinquency that vary over time and across contexts. Given that most programs target a small set of risk factors or contexts, it is unlikely that they will have pronounced effects on reducing delinquency. As we point out, it may be important to focus on dynamic or changeable risk factors with the greatest influence. For instance, families are more enduring than peer groups and have a greater investment in their children's welfare (for younger offenders who are still under the supervision of their families), and individual skills and beliefs may impact behaviors across a wide range of situations and contexts. Programs may also be necessary but not sufficient to prevent further delinquency, particularly given the multiple influences on risk and the concentration of serious delinquency among a small group of the most troubled youth. A particular program may not work alone but may be effective in combination with other interventions.

It is also important to consider the perspectives of offenders themselves regarding their perceived treatment needs and strategies for how to prevent further delinquency. Juvenile offenders are a rich source of information on their own personal history of delinquency as well as their experiences and observations of other delinquents. To this end, we include excerpts from interviews we conducted with incarcerated youth and summarize their suggestions. As described in the literature and discussed by offenders, there are multiple pathways to delinquency and variations in receptivity to change likely to result in significantly different treatment needs and outcomes. We conclude with suggestions for principles of effective treatment that address both programmatic and implementation issues. Guerra and Leaf, in Chapter 5, provide a more in-depth discussion of the implications of these principles for juvenile justice practice.

Proven Treatment Programs for Offenders

Although lists of "proven" and "promising" programs for the treatment of offenders may vary as a function of outcomes chosen, criteria applied, and statistical methods (e.g., meta-analysis) employed, at the top of most lists is a very small number of rigorously evaluated programs that have consistently demonstrated significant positive effects on reducing offending and related behaviors. These include multisystemic therapy (MST), functional family therapy (FFT), and multidimensional treatment foster care (MTFC), which have all been vetted by the University of Colorado Blueprints for Violence Prevention project (Elliott, 1997). A fourth program, aggression replacement training (ART), generally is also considered a proven program based on multiple studies of impact on delinquent behavior, although it has been deemed only "promising" on other highly regarded listings (e.g., Blueprints).

Multisystemic Therapy

MST is a family-based therapeutic intervention for youth that focuses on helping the families deal more effectively with their children's behavioral problems and the risk factors contributing to delinquency (Henggeler, Schoenwald, Borduin, Rowland, & Cunningham, 1998). These risk factors include low levels of parental monitoring of activities, poor discipline practices, association with delinquent peers, and poor school performance. In addition to improving parents' abilities to address these causes of delinquency, MST also addresses barriers to family empowerment and effective functioning within the family ecology. MST is both intensive and expensive, providing round-the-clock support for families and locating other family members and adults who can supervise and support the youth. Trained teams of MST therapists typically have a caseload of four to six families and provide 50 hours of face-to-face contact over a 3- to 6-month time period. Cost is approximately $5,000 per family.

A number of well-controlled experimental studies have shown that MST is effective in treating the relatively serious problems of juvenile offenders and their families, resulting in decreased delinquency and incarceration of violent and chronic offenders several years post-treatment (Henggeler et al., 1998; Schaeffer & Borduin, 2005). However, recent effectiveness trials within juvenile justice systems have raised concerns about the difficulty of implementation in real-world settings, particularly when the central training agency, MST, Inc., is less involved, and the potential for no significant differences in impact or even increased recidivism arises when implementation is poor (Washington State Institute for Public Policy, 2004).

Functional Family Therapy

FFT is a family behavioral intervention designed several decades ago to work with less serious and generally younger delinquent youth (Alexander & Parsons, 1973). It is a structured intervention that combines family systems concepts, social learning theory, behavior management, and most recently, cognitive processes (Sexton & Alexander, 2000). A main focus of the program is to improve family functioning through increased family problem-solving skills, enhanced emotional bonds among members, and improved ability of parents to provide structure and guidance to their children. The program is relatively short-term, is delivered in the home by individual therapists, and is less intensive and less expensive than MST. Cost is approximately $2,000 per family. Positive effects on reduction of delinquency and recidivism have been demonstrated across a range of levels within the juvenile justice system, including diversion, probation, alternatives to incarceration, and reentry from custodial settings (Gordon & Graves, 1995; Sexton & Alexander, 2000). Like MST, there is also a central training agency, FFT, Inc. When administered by competent therapists in real-world settings, the program has also been shown to reduce felony recidivism for up to 18 months following intervention, as compared to a control group (Washington State Institute for Public Policy, 2004).

Multidimensional Treatment Foster Care

MTFC differs from MST and FFT because participating youth do not live at home but in a therapeutic living environment with foster parents. As such, MTFC is an alternative to group residential treatment for youth with more serious delinquency who need out-of-home placement. Families from the community are recruited and trained to provide structure and behavior management for these youth, and family therapy is also provided for the youths' biological families. Cost per youth (excluding foster care costs) is similar to that of FFT, approximately $2,000. Studies of youth who have been randomly assigned to group homes or MTFC have consistently demonstrated reduced arrests among MTFC participants (Chamberlain & Reid, 1997). This program is particularly noteworthy as an alternative to incarceration, given that custodial programs generally are less effective than community-based programs for any type of intervention (Lipsey, 2006; Lipsey & Wilson, 1998).

Aggression Replacement Training

ART is a multimodal program for aggressive juvenile offenders that emphasizes skill acquisition, impulse and anger control, and moral reasoning development. It is a 30-hour program, administered with groups of offenders three times per week for 10 weeks. The estimated cost is approximately $750 per youth. Unlike family interventions, ART is appropriate for incarcerated youth and those over age 18, and has recently been adapted for use with older youth and adults. Although it has not been vetted as a Blueprint program (Elliott, 1997), it has been evaluated as showing some positive effects for delinquent youth in a range of settings, including community-based programs, residential treatment facilities, and secure confinement (Goldstein, 2004). This flexibility can make it particularly appealing for juvenile justice systems. Indeed, it is often selected as a best-practice program because of easy adaptation across settings, and it can be effective in reducing recidivism in these settings when implemented by competent counselors (Washington State Institute for Public Policy, 2004). Because a primary focus of this program is on aggression reduction, ART may be particularly relevant for youth who manifest aggressive attitudes or behavior (see Boxer & Frick, Chapter 7, this volume).

Promising Treatment Programs for Offenders

In light of the increasing emphasis on evidence-based programs for prevention and treatment of delinquency, the small number and limited range of effective programs are quite striking. For youth who live with their families (or foster families) in communities, the news is relatively good. However, except for ART, for youth who are incarcerated, no longer live with their families, or do not have families who are motivated to participate in programming, there is less to draw from, at least in the way of well-documented, cost-effective, and practical programs that have been evaluated with different youth populations and in different settings. Rather, we must turn primarily to individual evaluations of programs most likely to reduce delinquency because of their specific focus on factors linked to delinquent behavior and juvenile justice involvement. Following this review of individual programs, we consider general standards of evidence-based principles, as gleaned from recent reviews and meta-analyses.

Beyond the family programs reviewed previously, effective programs focus primarily on individual offenders. These programs typically attempt to change the way offenders think about situations that may potentially involve delinquency, including how they interpret their social surroundings, relate to others, and solve interpersonal problems. They are alternately labeled *cognitive-behavioral* programs and *cognitive-behavioral skills* programs. Although social skills may be addressed, the focus is on the central role of cognition in skill acquisition and use. Indeed, there is robust literature linking attitudes, beliefs, and social-cognitive problem-solving skill deficits to aggressive and delinquent behavior (e.g., Guerra & Slaby, 1990). Most cognitive-behavioral programs include training participants in one or more of the following areas: (1) cognitive self-control, (2) anger management, (3) social problem solving, (4) social perspective taking, (5) empathy, (6) moral reasoning, and (7) changing attitudes and beliefs. Typically, they use a variety of intervention techniques, including role playing, modeling, and group discussions, to promote social-cognitive development.

In general, programs that focus on any one of these components in isolation (e.g., those that focus only on anger management or only on empathy) are less effective than more comprehensive and multicomponent cognitive-behavioral programs (Tolan & Guerra, 1994). It may be that changing one aspect of how an offender thinks, for instance, by teaching cognitive self-control skills, is less effective in preventing future delinquency if he or she still believes that violence and delinquency are acceptable behaviors and has little regard for their impact on others. It may also be that single-component cognitive-behavioral programs can be effective for youth who have specific deficits. For instance, anger management may be more helpful for decreasing relationship violence for youth with anger problems than for predatory delinquency or for youth with significant substance abuse or mental health problems (as discussed by Veysey, Chapter 10, this volume).

Comprehensive cognitive-behavioral programs have been found to yield significant improvements in associated cognitions and skills as well as corresponding improvements in antisocial and delinquent behavior for both incarcerated youth and those on probation. For example, Hawkins, Jenson, Catalano, and Wells (1991) randomly assigned incarcerated delinquent males and females in Washington State to either a control condition or a 10-week cognitive-behavioral skills training. The skills taught included self-control, consequential thinking, negotiation, and the ability to refuse drugs and alcohol. This program emphasized preparation for community reentry and aftercare. Aftercare included continued contact with case managers for 6 months following release. Because of the multiple components, effects on recidivism due only to the cognitive-behavioral training are difficult to extract. However, the program was effective in increasing targeted skills in the intervention group relative to the control group.

In another study with incarcerated male and female delinquents, Guerra and Slaby (1990) randomly assigned youth offenders in California to a cognitive mediation training program, an attention control group, or a no-treatment control group. The cognitive mediation training group received the Viewpoints program, a 12-session intervention designed to enhance interpersonal problem- solving skills and simultaneously change normative beliefs that support aggression. The intervention resulted in significant improvements in problem-solving skills and reductions in normative beliefs that support aggression as well as short-term changes in problem behavior within the institution. Furthermore, the changes in normative beliefs supporting aggression were directly related to changes in behavior.

In a more recent cognitive-behavioral program for incarcerated youth, Rohde, Jorgensen, Seeley, and Mace (2004) randomly assigned male offenders in Oregon to either an intervention condition or a usual-care condition. Youth in the intervention condition participated in the Coping Course, a 16-session cognitive-behavioral intervention designed to teach a variety of cognitive skills, including cognitive restructuring, relaxation, coping, and problem solving. The intervention yielded significant improvements, relative to controls, for a number of skills as well as for externalizing problems, which are most closely linked to antisocial behavior.

A similar but more intensive program for youth on probation, Time to Think, was developed and evaluated by Ross, Fabiano, and Ewles (1988). The program included 80 hours of group intervention focused on changing offender cognitions. High-risk juvenile offenders were randomly assigned to the intervention, a life-skills program (attention control), or a control group. Groups were led by trained and supervised probation officers. Recidivism rates for the three groups were 18%, 48%, and 70%, respectively. This finding suggests that life-skills training is more effective in reducing recidivism than no intervention, but that cognitive-behavioral programs are even more effective than skills programs that lack a cognitive component.

In addition to programs developed and evaluated by researchers, such as those described above, there have been several large-scale efforts to design and implement programs for offenders within a cognitive-behavioral skill model. For example, the State of California contracted with Change Companies to develop an intensive cognitive-behavioral journaling intervention, with individual modules focused on particular problem areas (e.g., gangs, anger management). Many states use the Thinking for a Change program developed by the National Institute of Corrections (Bush, Glick, & Taymans, 1997). This program includes 22 lessons focused on listening, giving feedback, self-control, perspective taking, anger management, and social problem-solving skills. Both programs are grounded in cognitive-behavioral principles. To date, there have been no carefully randomized evaluations of these programs, although they are clearly consistent with evidence-based principles for treatment of juvenile offenders in community or institutional settings.

Evidence-Based Principles for Treatment of Juvenile Offenders

Two factors have been primarily responsible for the delineation of evidence-based principles for treatment of offenders and their blending into policy and practice. First, as mentioned previously, the evidence base for effective programs is quite limited for juvenile offender populations, particularly for incarcerated youth. However, there have been many individual programs with reasonable evaluations that allow us to extract common elements linked to their success. Second, even when evidence-based practices are carefully specified, such as in the Blueprints programs, they are rarely implemented exactly as detailed. Note the implementation of MST in Washington State: When the central MST training agency was less involved in program oversight, the local implementation fell short, and MST was not related to reductions in recidivism (Washington State Institute for Public Policy, 2004). Further, even programs that have demonstrated effectiveness in multiple settings may not be relevant in all settings. For instance, youth institutions across the United States vary greatly in terms of the demographics of those served, including such issues as the extent of juvenile gang problems. These differences, however, may limit or require modification of existing programs beyond what is detailed in program guidelines. Specification of evidence-based principles thus can guide program selection, implementation, and modification when needed.

To date, there have been several reviews and meta-analyses of effective programs. Some reports suggest that many different types of interventions can be effective with offenders (beyond cognitive-behavioral programs and including individual and group counseling, life-skills training, behavior management, mentoring, employment-related programs, and remedial education), although some elements and configurations tend to have stronger effects (Lipsey, 1992, 2006; Lipsey & Wilson, 1998). To maximize the likelihood of positive outcomes, particularly with new programs that have little or no evaluation data, it is important to consider these common elements and the configurations linked to the strongest effects. These can be discussed in terms of critical components of program focus (*what* should be done), critical components of implementation (*how* and *where* it should be done), and youth most likely to benefit (*who* should receive a particular type of program).

Critical Components of Programs

The empirical evidence from multiple program evaluations leads us to consider four critical components of programming for juvenile offenders: (1) highly structured interventions rather than unstructured programs produce greater effects; (2) interventions that involve a cognitive component linked to specific skills are more effective; (3) interventions that engage families and reduce familial risk for delinquency are more effective; and (4) interventions that are more comprehensive and address multiple risk factors across different contexts are more effective than single-component programs.

Promising interventions tend to be highly structured, emphasizing individual skills and beliefs. Less structured interventions that rely exclusively on individual or group counseling generally have not been shown to be effective. In part, this may be due to the wide variation in activities that are considered as counseling, variations in staff training and skills, duration of counseling, and difficulties in evaluating unstructured programs. The recommendations, in general, suggesting that counseling is largely ineffective, have led to a certain amount of confusion in the field (e.g., Sherman et al., 1997).

Although counseling may not be effective alone, it can be an important component of more structured programs, and even increase the likelihood of success. In other words, counseling combined with intensive case management, cognitive-behavioral skills programs, or educational and vocational services may increase the likelihood of effectiveness (Lee & McGinnis-Haynes, 1978; Shore & Massimo, 1973). Individual counseling using mental health professionals as part of other more structured programs also has shown some promise, particularly in noninstitutional settings (Lipsey & Wilson, 1998). An intensive counseling component can even lead to effectiveness for programs previously deemed ineffective. For instance, the general lack of support for wilderness challenge programs has relegated them to the "doesn't work" category (Greenwood, 2005; Sherman et al., 1997). However, a careful examination of these interventions suggests they can be effective when they incorporate a distinct, well-structured therapy component (Wilson & Lipsey, 2000).

One of the most robust and widely cited findings from comparison of effective elements of programming emphasizes the central role of changing youth *cognitions* in order to change their delinquent behavior (Lipsey & Wilson, 1998). For example, Izzo and Ross (1990) conducted a meta-analysis of 46 delinquency intervention programs, noting that programs that included a cognitive component were more than twice as effective as programs that did not. One reason for this increased effectiveness is that internal factors such as cognition are more likely to generalize across situations as compared with strict behavioral programs that may be effective only when contingencies are maintained (Kazdin, Bass, Siegel, & Thomas, 1989). Less is known about the specific components of cognition most linked to behavior change, although the Viewpoints intervention study by Guerra and Slaby (1990) highlighted the importance of changing normative beliefs about the appropriateness of aggression in mediating subsequent behavior change.

In addition to the importance of including a cognitive component in individual interventions, the most compelling evidence for best practices suggests the importance of involving families, particularly with younger adolescents who are more likely to remain with, or return to, the same familial environment that influenced their initial delinquent behavior. Considering the proven effectiveness of family interventions such as MST and FFT, it is surprising that more efforts have not been made to develop such interventions for incarcerated youth and to address family issues in cognitive-behavioral interventions. In part, this absence may be due to logistic constraints, particularly with incarcerated offenders who may be far from their homes, neighborhoods, or families.

One exception is brief strategic family therapy (BSFT). This program is a time-limited, structured approach designed to improves adolescent behavior by improving family relationships most directly linked to the problem behavior, and to improve relationships between family members and other important systems in their social ecology (Robbins & Szapocznik, 2000). It has potential with incarcerated offenders when implemented as a *one-person family therapy*. The idea behind this approach is that a change in the behavior of the juvenile offender should lead to corresponding changes or adjustments in the behavior of other family members, such that family interactions can be changed even when the whole family does not participate in the intervention. Although there have been only limited evaluations with offenders, findings suggest that BSFT can be as effective as family-based interventions in changing the behavior of juvenile offenders (Perkins-Dock, 2001).

Another lesson learned from evaluations of proven programs such as MST is that programs that address the multiple determinants of delinquency are more likely to be successful than those that focus on a single area (e.g., anger management) within a single context. A principal feature of MST is that it helps families leverage support from other developmental contexts, including the school and community. As noted throughout this volume, delinquent behavior is the result of a complex interaction of individual propensities, situations, close interpersonal relationships, institutions, culture, and societal influences.

Given the complexity of risk, it is unlikely that intervening in any one area for a brief period will carry over and maintain effects over time. Yet, most interventions focus on changing one promising risk factor within a relatively short time frame, and most emphasize changing individual characteristics. This may also be a reason for the relatively modest effect sizes of treatment programs. Still, there is very little in the way of treatment programming that (1) simultaneously promotes the development of multiple individual skills, (2) shifts norms and practices of relevant proximal contexts (e.g., peers, families), and (3) increases opportunities within the community to utilize these skills.

In addition to these four critical components of effective interventions (highly structured, cognitive component, engage families, comprehensive), there is also a growing interest in shifting towards *strength-based* rather than *risk-focused* intervention programming. This does not mean turning risks into strengths, but rather leveraging youth strengths to address risk. For instance, a youth who struggles with family problems may also do very well academically. Rather than ignore academic functioning because it does not contribute to risk status, this strength can be leveraged in treatment planning, for instance, by working with the youth to mobilize this protective factor to counteract risk.

Finally, as discussed by Guerra et al. in Chapter 2 of this volume, the emergence of developmental, life-course perspectives (DLC) on offending provide another lens through which to conceptualize treatment programs, moving beyond reducing risk and building protective factors. A DLC framework stresses the importance of differentiating predictors of delinquency onset from predictors of desistance from offending. An important focus thus becomes identification and promotion of assets that can redirect youth from a delinquent lifestyle toward more conventional personal and social ties.

Critical Components of Implementation

A valuable lesson learned from reviews and meta-analyses of intervention programs for offenders is that *how* and *where* programs are implemented are just as important as *what* is done. Recall the outcome evaluation of Washington State's evidence-based programs for offenders discussed previously. The impetus behind this evaluation was to determine whether proven or promising programs could work statewide in a "real-world" setting. Findings suggested that these programs worked *only* when implemented in a competent manner. However, it proved quite difficult to attain competence—in the case of FFT, fewer than half of the implementation efforts were rated as competent, and low levels of competence in implementation actually predicted *increases* in recidivism of offenders. Implementation of MST varied widely across counties and across agencies tasked with implementation, rendering it impossible to determine effectiveness (Washington State Institute for Public Policy, 2004).

What factors are associated with successful implementation of treatment programs? Findings suggest that the integrity with which a program is implemented increases the likelihood of success. Integrity can be enhanced by involving the researcher (or agency set up to provide training) and by carefully monitoring the implementation process. Well-established programs also tend to have better mechanisms for training and oversight and appear to produce greater effects. This finding is somewhat problematic because there are very few well-validated programs with national organizations that provide such training. With or without such guidance, it is still beneficial to have program delivery and oversight by certified counseling staff, based on findings that treatment programs administered by mental health professionals have stronger effects than similar programs administered by correctional staff (Lipsey & Wilson, 1998).

Interventions that are implemented as group treatment programs also must take into account the potential impact for increased delinquency due to "deviant peer contagion" (Dodge, Dishion, & Lansford, 2006). Given that association with antisocial peers is among the most robust predictors of delinquency, it seems almost paradoxical to group offenders together for the purposes of treatment. Indeed, concerns that grouping antisocial youth together for treatment or placement would result in negative social influence among participants is anything but new—the history of the juvenile justice system in the United States reflects efforts to minimize these negative peer effects. Yet, treatment, supervision, funding, and public safety needs often necessitate aggregating youth in programs or facilities. Does this practice increase delinquency or counteract the effects of treatment?

To address this concern, some program evaluations have examined the potentially negative or iatrogenic effects of group treatment programs as well as variations in outcome for group versus individual interventions. The deviant peer contagion hypothesis followed from studies reporting increases in delinquency for youth who participated in group-based interventions. For example, Dishion and colleagues (Dishion & Andrews, 1995; Dishion, Andrews, Kavanagh, & Soberman, 1996) reported on the Adolescent Transitions Program (ATP), an intervention for high-risk boys and girls that compared the effects of parent focus, teen focus, combined, and attention control programs on subsequent antisocial behaviors and delinquency. Long-term follow-up of the 12-week program suggested that the teen focus group showed increased negative behaviors compared to controls; the effects of participating in the teen group even undermined the positive effects of the parent group for participants in the combined intervention. However, effects were generally marginally significant, suggesting that this influence is still relatively weak (Weiss et al., 2005).

Corroborating this finding in a recent meta-analysis of group versus individual treatment effects with delinquent youth, Lipsey (2006) found that group treatments did not produce smaller effects than individual treatments, although effects were smaller when groups were more heterogeneous (i.e., mixed serious and less serious delinquents) or consisted of less delinquent youth (i.e., prevention). This finding suggests that group treatments are less effective for younger and less delinquent youth, especially when they are mixed with more delinquent youth, but that overall, deviant peer influences in group treatment are small or negligible. This observation is consistent with a recent meta-analysis conducted by Weiss and colleagues (Weiss et al., 2005), who demonstrated a lack of support for contagion or deviancy training effects in group treatment. Further, recent analyses of data from the Metropolitan Area Child Study project shows that aggressive youth in small group treatment can socialize each other to become more or less aggressive over time, depending upon the average pretreatment levels of aggression across all group members (Boxer, Guerra, Huesmann, & Morales, 2005).

There are also examples of efforts to leverage the powerful influence of the peer group by intentionally trying to shift peer norms away from deviancy toward a "positive peer culture." A wide range of programs has been implemented under this rubric, beginning with the original tradition of "guided group interaction" (Empey & Erikson, 1974) and referred to by a variety of labels, including positive peer culture, peer group counseling, and youth leadership training. The central idea is that peers themselves are best able to turn around a negative subculture and mobilize the power of their group to promote prosocial, helping, and caring behaviors (Vorrath & Brendtro, 2005). Although there have been a number of evaluations of this approach over the years, they generally have suffered from significant limitations, including nonrandom assignment to condition, limited follow-up, and outcome assessments for some youth limited to the time when they were still incarcerated (i.e., limiting their opportunities to get arrested). At best, evaluations of positive peer culture suggest it has no measurable effects; at worst, it may have negative consequences, particularly in less restrictive settings (Gottfredson, 1987).

More recent efforts to improve peer culture have emphasized creating a positive normative climate that extends beyond the peer group. When applied in institutional settings, this approach can be seen in organizational structures that emphasize respect, support, caring, and close supervision to encourage positive behavior. For instance, when youth are assigned to smaller residential units with close supervision and a family atmosphere, as in the "teaching family model," results are encouraging (Lipsey & Wilson, 1998). Similarly, the residential program at Lookout Mountain in Colorado (discussed in more detail in Chapter 5) builds on principles of restorative justice that govern many aspects of daily life. In summary, it appears that implementing programs with groups of juvenile offenders requires sensitivity to potential for contagion, but this contagion can be counteracted by providing close supervision, creation of a positive climate, and commitment to a treatment and rehabilitation orientation.

A final note on implementation of treatment programs concerns the location of programming, specifically the relative benefits of community-based versus residential treatment. Placing offenders in residential settings should be the last resort, particularly when they are removed from their families and communities. It is difficult for youth to learn skills and behaviors that allow for institutional adjustment and subsequently utilize these skills in their home communities. Similarly, it is difficult to engage families in the treatment process—an obstacle that is particularly problematic if family risk factors contributed significantly to delinquency risk. In addition to the significantly increased costs of incarceration, programs are more effective in community settings. As Greenwood (2005) notes, "the most important reason for avoiding group placements is the clear evidence that all types of preventive programming produce better results in community settings rather than in institutions" (p. 289).

Youth Most Likely to Benefit

Summary judgments of "what works" fail to identify the potential differences in outcomes for different youth. In other words, if programs are deemed effective, does this mean that they work equally well for girls and boys of different ages, with different delinquent offense histories, and from different ethnic groups or community settings? Although the field has long acknowledged the importance of examining differential response to interventions, in truth, most evaluations examine differences in group means or averages between intervention participants and a comparison control group. Some of the more rigorously evaluated and widely used programs (such as MST) have examined program effectiveness with different samples of youth, for instance, girls and boys and youth from different ethnic and community backgrounds. In general, the more comprehensive programs have not shown wide variations in effects for different groups of offenders. Still, there is some concern about the unique needs of specific groups of delinquents within the general offender population. For instance, there has been considerable recent attention to issues surrounding girls' delinquency. As discussed by Hoge and Robertson in Chapter 12 of this volume, there is a growing recognition that a significant number of girls are involved in delinquent activities and that research on causes and treatments for males may not necessarily generalize to females.

There has also been relatively little research examining differences in effectiveness of interventions for youth from different ethnic and community backgrounds. To the extent that the relations between risk and offending are similar across ethnic groups, we would expect the effectiveness of interventions to reduce risk to be relatively constant (although some ethnic groups may experience elevated risk due to their life circumstances). However, there are also unique risk factors for offending associated with the experience of minority status in the United States (e.g., oppression and marginalization of some ethnic groups) as well as cultural practices of different ethnic groups that may impact intervention outcomes (Guerra & Phillips-Smith, 2005).

Another problem with considering only average differences in intervention outcomes is that we are unable to distinguish whether an intervention is differentially appropriate for youth with different levels of risk for re-offending. This area is particularly important for community-based programming, where participants are likely to vary greatly (as compared with offenders incarcerated in state institutions) as to their likelihood of re-offending. The "risk principle" of effective practice suggests the need to target intensive services on higher-risk youth; as a corollary to this principle we should also examine whether programs are equally effective for this group. On the other hand, within settings that serve all high-risk youth (e.g., institutions for serious offenders), targeting services to the "highest of the high-risk" group may be less productive, given that these youth are likely to have the longest histories of offending and behaviors most resistant to change. As Boxer and Frick discuss in Chapter 7, the cognitive and emotional characteristics of these very high-risk and often violent offenders present unique and quite difficult challenges to effective treatment.

Not only is program impact likely to vary as a function of risk of re-offending, it may also be that programs are differentially appropriate for offenders with different risk profiles. Until program evaluations examine key moderators of program effectiveness (based on both demographics and risk profiles) as well as overall effectiveness, this area will remain somewhat problematic. The field has long acknowledged the need to match styles and modes of services to the learning styles of offenders, labeled the "responsivity principle," but less emphasis has been placed on documenting the best principles and programming options to reflect the great amount of diversity within the juvenile offender population. The question must become, "What works for whom and under what conditions?"

Juvenile Offender Interviews

Because juvenile offenders are a heterogeneous group with multiple potential pathways to delinquency, the notion of "one size fits all" for treatment programs is problematic. Indeed, we have underscored the importance of developing and evaluating programs that address this diversity in terms of both offender needs and feasibility of implementation. Another important but frequently overlooked source of information comes from offenders themselves. To better understand treatment needs, we conducted interviews with six adolescent males incarcerated at a correctional institution serving the most serious offenders. We asked offenders four questions specifically related to treatment:

1. What specific prevention, intervention, or treatment programs did you participate in prior to being incarcerated and what impact did these programs have on you?
2. What specific intervention or treatment programs have you participated in since being incarcerated and what impact did these programs have on you?
3. If you were in charge of this institution, what type of intervention or treatment services would you provide and why?
4. If you were in charge of making sure that youth did not get involved in delinquency, what type of prevention programs would you provide in schools and communities?

To provide a context for these questions, we also asked offenders to provide a little information about what they saw as the factors that led to their offending behavior.

Program Involvement Prior to Incarceration

All of the youth interviewed had been involved in some type of tutoring, after-school sports, and community recreation activities prior to being incarcerated. They all felt that these programs were extremely helpful because they kept kids off the streets and engaged in constructive activities. Several youth mentioned that the main advantage of these programs was to "keep me off the streets and away from my homies" as well as to tire them out—"When I got home from Pop Warner football I was just too tired to do anything else." Tutoring was seen as helpful but often boring and frustrating. Further, these programs did not seem to deal effectively with underlying emotional and behavioral problems. As one youth noted, "I liked the math tutoring ɔgram, but in the end it didn't help me stay out of trouble because the other kids still annoyed me, so I fought with them."

Treatment Programs While Incarcerated

Offenders had also been involved in numerous treatment programs during their incarceration. Programs included remedial education, vocational training, gang awareness, substance use treatment, victim awareness, criminal thinking errors program, parenting classes, and group and/or individual counseling. All of the youth found that the victim awareness and counseling programs helped them better understand the harm they caused others and how it was often linked to harm caused to them. Most youth mentioned needing "someone to talk to" and the importance of "learning how to cope with feelings, to understand and manage anger better." Programs emphasizing cognitive change (such as the criminal thinking errors program) were seen as beneficial as well. As one offender put it, "This place rewires your brain, it changes the way you think."

According to the offenders interviewed, the gang awareness programs were the least effective. In part, this was due to the influence of gang culture and related ethnic tensions within the correctional system. One youth noted, "This place can't change you because all it does it put you around a lot of other gang members, and since I'm a gang member, I have to keep up appearances." He felt it would be a lot easier to benefit from treatment programs if he were not in a gang. Several youth also noted that treatment helps only those who really want to change. For some youth, motivation is directly linked to a desire never to be locked up again. As one youth put it, "I will never do anything wrong again because I never want to come back. I don't care if I'm on parole for 20 years, I just never want to be locked up again—once I'm out I won't even get a speeding ticket."

Treatment Programs Offenders Would Recommend

Consistent with our emphasis on the multiple potential pathways to offending and the diverse needs of youth, offenders noted the need to provide a range of services as well as including staff with diverse values, interests, and backgrounds. Regular counseling was routinely recommended—"a place where you are able to express feelings and get help with anger and rage." Opportunities to learn practical skills that would be useful in the real world were seen as more useful than idle time locked in rooms or cells. Several youth noted the importance of allowing youth to stay connected with their families and loved ones through regular visits, letters, and phone calls. Others noted the importance of peer hierarchies both on the streets and in correctional facilities. As one offender commented, "You should take the hardest gang member that is locked up in the facility and really get to him and try to change him. Because if you can change this person, others will follow in his footsteps because they will look up to him and realize they can change too." A common theme was a need for role models and guidance from others they looked up to—"you can't follow in your own footsteps."

Prevention Programs Offenders Would Recommend

The most frequent recommendation was to keep youth active and involved—"down time is trouble time." Beyond activities, the common theme for prevention was to help children understand the realities of crime and punishment, including effects on victims as well as the real world of probation and prisons. One youth suggested putting up "knowledge posters" in schools and community centers that tell youth how much time they would get for different types of crimes. Most youth mentioned that they didn't think clearly about the real effects of a criminal lifestyle and what daily life would be like once they entered the system. They also didn't think much about how their crimes would impact both their families and their victims; rather, they just lived day-to-day, "kicking it with the homies," rather than thinking about their future.

Summary and Conclusion

We have reviewed the evidence base for effective treatment programs and principles for juvenile offenders, delineating "best bets" for programming and implementation.

Best Bets for Programming

- For youth who live with, or will return to, their families of origin and whose families contribute significantly to their risk status, intensive family interventions that help families problem-solve, monitor their children, and engage other adults in providing guidance (MST is a specific example).
- For youth in foster placement or group homes, intensive training for assigned families emphasizing close supervision, guidance, and home-like atmosphere (MTFC is a specific example).

- For working with individual youth or small groups, cognitive-behavioral skill-building programs that emphasize multiple cognitive factors most closely connected to risk (ART is a specific example).
- For youth with psychological problems, individual counseling when part of highly structured programming.
- For youth with multiple causal factors linked to delinquency, comprehensive interventions that address risk (this may be a combination of interventions).
- For group and residential programming with offenders, programs and structures that expressly encourage prosocial rather than delinquent norms and leverage peer influences to build support for these prosocial norms.

Best Bets for Implementation

- Programs that can be implemented with fidelity—usually these are well-established programs with oversight by a lead training agency.
- Programs of longer duration rather than brief interventions.
- Community- versus institution-based programming.
- Programs that provide more individual than group counseling, particularly for younger offenders.
- Treatment programs administered by mental health professionals or well-trained counselors or probation officers.

How do these conclusions bear on overall efforts to promote effective treatment for juvenile offenders? We suggest that they can be integrated into a set of principles to guide effective treatment. These are distinct from the principles of effective practice that have been infused into juvenile justice programming for several years, although these principles may be seen as a more specific elaboration focused exclusively on optimizing treatment effectiveness.

Principles of Effective Treatment

Closer-to-Home Principle

Whenever possible, youth should receive treatment in the communities where they live, with incarceration in state institutions used as a last resort for purposes of community safety. When youth cannot live with their families of origin, they should be assigned to residential, community-based facilities that provide treatment in small cottages or homes with foster families or teaching family support. Incarcerated youth should still retain ties with their home communities in order to develop a positive support system.

Rehabilitation Principle

Treatment will be most effective if there is institutional and political support for a rehabilitation orientation in juvenile justice programming. This support must become part of the "culture" of practice, so that it is infused at all levels of the system and provides a set of organizing beliefs to guide services. Efforts should be directed toward "reframing" issues, for instance, so that offenders are seen as young persons who can become productive citizens rather than deviants who must be treated harshly.

Evidence-Based Principle

Treatment should follow evidence-based principles for programming and implementation. Because of the limited number of treatment programs for offenders with proven effectiveness and concerns about the appropriateness of these programs for girls and boys from different ages and ethnic groups, a range of programs should be considered. These programs should be structured and address dynamic risk factors that are most likely to change and most likely to generalize (e.g., family functioning, cognitive-behavioral skills).

Risk-Focused, Strength-Based Principle

Treatment programs for offenders must address multiple types of risk for re-offending and the different patterns of risk through comprehensive programming. Level of service should be matched primarily to specific risk profiles of offenders. (See Chapter 3 for a more detailed discussion of assessment.) Treatment must also identify and leverage youth strengths as an additional mechanism to reduce risk. Finally, emphasis should also be placed on building strengths to promote desistance from an offending lifestyle.

These principles are being utilized, to a certain degree, in juvenile justice and youth corrections in the United States. In Chapter 5, Guerra and Leaf provide examples of how these treatment principles can be integrated into statewide programming as part of a recent continuum-of-care initiative. They also discuss challenges to the implementation of treatment programs at the system and institutional levels and how these have been successfully addressed in Colorado.

Note

1. Here we use the term "evidence-based principles" to denote important elements or components of treatment programs. This is somewhat different from the principles of the effective practice commonly referenced in juvenile justice.

References

Alexander, J. F., & Parsons, B. V. (1973). Short-term behavioral intervention with delinquent families: Impact on family process and recidivism. *Journal of Abnormal Psychology, 81,* 219–225.

Boxer, P., Guerra, N. G., Huesmann, L .R., & Morales, J. (2005). Proximal effects of a small-group selected prevention program on aggression in elementary school children: An investigation of the peer contagion hypothesis. *Journal of Abnormal Child Psychology, 33,* 325–338.

Bush, J., Glick, B., & Taymans, J. (1997). *Thinking for a change: Integrated cognitive behavior change program.* Washington, DC: National Institute of Corrections, U.S. Department of Justice.

Chamberlain, P., & Reid, J. B. (1997). Comparison of two community alternatives to incarceration for chronic juvenile offenders. *Journal of Consulting and Clinical Psychology, 6,* 624–633.

Dishion, T. J., & Andrews, D. W. (1995). Preventing escalation in problem behaviors with high-risk young adolescents: Immediate and 1-year outcomes. *Journal of Consulting and Clinical Psychology, 63,* 538–548.

Dishion, T. J., Andrews, D. W., Kavanagh, K., & Soberman, L. H. (1996). The Adolescent Transitions Program. In R. D. Peters & R. J. McMahon (Eds.), *Preventing childhood disorders, substance abuse, and delinquency* (pp. 184–214). Thousand Oaks, CA: Sage.

Dodge, K. A., Dishion, T. J., & Lansford, J. E. (Eds.). (2006). *Deviant peer influences in programs for youth: Problems and solutions.* New York: Guilford Press.

Elliott, D. S. (1997). *Blueprints for violence prevention.* Boulder, CO: Center for the Study and Prevention of Violence, University of Colorado.

Empey, L. T., & Erikson, M. L. (1974). *The Provo experiment: Evaluating community control of delinquency.* Lexington, MA: Lexington Books.

Goldstein, A. P. (2004). Evaluations of effectiveness. In A. P. Goldstein, R. Nensen, B. Daleflod, & M. Kalt (Eds.), *New perspectives on aggression replacement training* (pp. 230–244). Chichester, UK: Wiley.

Gordon, D. A., & Graves, K. (1995). The effect of functional family therapy for delinquents on adult criminal behavior. *Criminal Justice and Behavior, 22,* 60–74.

Gottfredson, D. C. (1987). An evaluation of an organization development approach to reducing school disorder. *Evaluation Review, 11,* 739–763.

Greenwood, P. W. (2005). *Changing lives: Delinquency prevention as crime-control policy.* Chicago: University of Chicago Press.

Guerra, N. G., & Phillips-Smith, E. (Eds.). (2005). *Preventing youth violence in a multicultural society.* Washington, DC: American Psychological Association.

Guerra, N. G., & Slaby, R. G. (1990). Cognitive mediators of aggression in adolescent offenders: 2. Intervention. *Developmental Psychology, 26,* 269–277.

Hawkins, J. D., Jenson, J. M., Catalano, R. F., & Wells, E. A. (1991). Effects of a skills training intervention with juvenile delinquents. *Research on Social Work Practice, 1,*107–121.

Henggeler, S. W., Schoenwald, S. K., Borduin, C. M., Rowland, M. D., & Cunningham, P. B. (1998). *Multisystemic treatment of antisocial behavior in children and adolescents.* New York: Guilford Press.

Izzo, R. L., & Ross, R. R. (1990). Meta-analysis of rehabilitation programs for juvenile delinquents: A brief report. *Criminal Justice and Behavior, 17,* 134–142.

Kazdin, A. E., Bass, D., Siegel, T., & Thomas, C. (1989). Cognitive-behavioral therapy and relationship therapy in the treatment of children referred for antisocial behavior. *Journal of Consulting and Clinical Psychology, 55,* 76–85.

Lipsey, M. W. (1992). Juvenile delinquency treatment: A meta-analytic inquiry into the variability of treatment effects. In F. Mosteller (Ed.), *Meta-analysis for explanations* (pp. 83–128). New York: Sage.

Lipsey, M. W. (2006). The effects of community-based group treatment for delinquency. In K. A. Dodge, T. J. Dishion, & J. E. Lansford (Eds.), *Deviant peer influences in programs for youth: Problems and solutions* (pp. 162–184). New York: Guilford Press.

Lipsey, M. W., & Wilson, D. (1998). Effective intervention for serious offenders: A synthesis of research. In R. Loeber & D. Farrington (Eds.), *Serious and violent juvenile offenders* (pp. 86–105). Thousand Oaks, CA: Sage.

Perkins-Dock, R. E. (2001). Family interventions with incarcerated youth: A review of the literature. *International Journal of Offender Therapy and Comparative Criminology, 45,*606–625.

Robbins, M. S., & Szapocznik, J. (2000). *Brief strategic family therapy* [Bulletin]. Washington, DC: Office of Justice Programs, Office of Juvenile Justice and Delinquency Prevention, Department of Justice.

Rohde, P., Jorgensen, J. S., Seeley, J. R., & Mace, D. E. (2004). Pilot evaluation of the coping course: A cognitive-behavioral intervention to enhance coping skills in incarcerated youth. *Journal of the American Academy of Child and Adolescent Psychiatry, 43,* 669–676.

Ross, R. R., Fabiano, E. A., & Ewles, C. D. (1988). Reasoning and rehabilitation. *International Journal of Offender Therapy and Comparative Criminology, 32,* 29–35.

Schaeffer, C. M., & Borduin, C. M. (2005) Long-term follow-up to a randomized clinical trial of multisystemic therapy with serious and violent juvenile offenders. *Journal of Consulting and Clinical Psychology, 73,* 445–453.

Sexton, T. L., & Alexander, J. F. (2000). *Functional family therapy* [Bulletin]. Washington, DC: Office of Justice Programs, Office of Juvenile Justice and Delinquency Prevention, Department of Justice.

Sherman, L. W., Gottfredson, D., Mackenzie, D., Eck, J., Reuter, P., & Bushway,

S. (1997). *Preventing crime: What works, what doesn't, what's promising.* Washington, DC: National Institute of Justice.

Tolan, P. H., & Guerra, N. G. (1994). *What works in reducing adolescent violence: An empirical review of the field.* Boulder, CO: Center for the Study and Prevention of Violence, University of Colorado.

Vorath, H. H., & Brendtro, L. K. (2005). *Positive peer culture.* New Brunswick, NJ: Aldine.

Washington State Institute for Public Policy. (2004). *Outcome evaluation of Washington State's research-based programs for juvenile offenders.* Olympia, WA: Author.

Weiss, B., Caron, A., Ball, S., Tapp, J., Johnson, M., & Weisz, J. R. (2005). Iatrogenic effects of group treatment for antisocial youth. *Journal of Consulting and Clinical Psychology, 73,* 1036–1044.

Wilson, S., & Lipsey, M. W. (2000). Wilderness challenge programs for delinquent youth: A meta-analysis of outcome evaluations. *Evaluation and Program Planning, 23,* 1–12.

Chapter 5

Implementing Treatment Programs in Community and Institutional Settings

Nancy G. Guerra
Caren Leaf

Translating evidence-based programs into real-world applications requires careful attention to barriers to implementation and how these can be overcome. There are many reasons that findings from juvenile justice treatment research are not embraced in everyday practice, including political, economic, and practical challenges that are often interconnected. Even the most successful and widely used intervention programs, such as multisystemic therapy (MST), can be compromised by poor implementation (Washington State Institute for Public Policy, 2004). For this reason, it is not enough to identify effective programs or practices without also considering how to optimize implementation.

In this chapter we address barriers and challenges to providing effective treatment for juvenile offenders in community and institutional settings. We consider the implementation challenges related to each of the principles of effective treatment discussed in Chapter 4. These principles are consistent with the research literature that has focused primarily on how to optimize outcomes such as improvements in behavior and reductions in delinquency recidivism. However, using these principles to guide practice requires moving beyond a specification of "what" should be done to more careful consideration of "how" best to do it. To illustrate effective implementation strategies, we provide examples from a recent Continuum of Care Initiative in the state of Colorado as well as a model residential treatment program, Lookout Mountain Youth Services Center (LMYSC), and other relevant efforts. We begin by restating the principles of effective treatment, followed by a brief discussion of the Continuum of Care Initiative and an overview of the philosophy and practices at LMYSC.

Principles of Effective Treatment

In Chapter 4, Guerra et al. provided a review of the empirical literature on what works in the treatment of juvenile offenders. From this literature, the following four principles emerged:

- *Closer-to-home principle.* Whenever possible, youth should receive treatment in the communities where they live, with incarceration in state institutions used as a last resort for purposes of community safety. When youth cannot live with their families of origin, they should be assigned to residential, community-based facilities that provide treatment in small cottages or homes with foster families or teaching family support. Incarcerated youth should retain ties with their home communities in order to develop a positive support system.
- *Rehabilitation principle.* Treatment will be most effective if there is institutional and political support for a rehabilitation orientation in juvenile justice programming. This support must become part of the "culture" of practice, so that it is infused at all levels of the system and provides a set of organizing beliefs to guide services. Efforts should be directed toward "reframing" issues, for instance, so that offenders are seen as young persons who can become productive citizens rather than deviants who must be treated harshly.
- *Evidence-based principle.* Treatment should follow evidence-based principles for programming and implementation. Because of the limited number of treatment programs for offenders with proven effectiveness and concerns about the appropriateness of these programs for girls and boys from different ages and ethnic groups, a range of programs should be considered. These programs should be structured and should address dynamic risk factors most likely to change and most likely to generalize (e.g., family functioning, cognitive-behavioral skills).

- *Risk-focused, strengths-based principle.* Treatment programs for offenders must address multiple types of risk for re-offending and the different patterns of risk through comprehensive programming. Level of service should be matched primarily to specific risk profiles of offenders. Treatment must also identify and leverage youth strengths as an additional mechanism to reduce risk. Finally, emphasis should also be placed on building strengths to promote desistance from an offending lifestyle.

Colorado Continuum of Care Initiative

Juvenile offenders often receive fragmented, uncoordinated, insufficient, or inappropriate services from multiple agencies and systems (Hsia & Beyer, 2000). Placements in secure residential facilities may be less about public safety and offender needs and more about bed space, funding guidelines, or political currents. Offenders who could be well served by community options may not be afforded this opportunity, just as offenders in the community may not receive appropriate services to reduce risk of re-offending. To address these issues, several states have engaged in comprehensive planning and systems reform toward creating a more integrated, effective, and coordinated juvenile justice system.

For example, the Colorado Division of Youth Corrections recently embarked on a comprehensive systems improvement effort based on a "continuum-of-care" model. The central idea behind this reform effort is that youthful offenders comprise a diverse group needing a broad array of services in settings that range from least restrictive (e.g., diversion, natural supports) to moderately restrictive (e.g., community residential programs) to most restrictive (e.g., secure residential placement). Putting in place a continuum-of-care model requires the statewide availability of a variety of services that meet standards of effectiveness. It also requires a systematic process for matching youth with the most appropriate placements (in order to tailor the type, intensity, and duration of treatment for each youth, based on risk and needs). The overarching goal of this initiative is to match youth with the most effective services in the most appropriate settings to meet their rehabilitation needs. Emphasis is placed on utilizing community-based services when appropriate. Further, for youth who are in the most restrictive settings, efforts are made to transition them to community-based programs at the most optimal time, with a provision for continuing aftercare to facilitate reintegration while on parole.

Lookout Mountain Youth Services Center

Lookout Mountain Youth Services Center (LMYSC), run by the Colorado Division of Youth Corrections, was established in 1881 as a humane and progressive rehabilitation school for wayward boys between ages 7 and 16. Over the course of more than 100 years, it has undergone many changes and transformations, including a shift toward serving more serious and older delinquents in the 1980s, but has still retained its emphasis on rehabilitation, as evidenced by a comprehensive rehabilitation policy adopted in the 1990s. This policy provided for a broad range of clinical and educational services to respond to the multiple mental health, educational, and vocational needs of the offender population. A cornerstone of this approach was the development of a public–private partnership model between the state and established educational and mental health service providers. A partnership was developed with the University of Colorado Health Sciences Center to provide direct mental health services and consultation, which was shifted to Devereux Cleo Wallace in 2002. In 1994, Metropolitan State College of Denver contracted to provide educational and vocational services to LMYSC. Currently, the education and vocation programming is operated by Community College of Denver (CCD).

The rehabilitation philosophy of LMYSC emphasizes (1) effective educational, vocational, mental health (offense-specific), and drug and alcohol services designed according to evidence-based practices and principles; (2) stakeholder participation; (3) normative culture; and (4) restorative justice. As described above, emphasis is placed on public–private partnerships to enhance educational, vocational, and mental health services. To enhance communication and avoid fragmentation of services, all programming and initiatives are discussed and reviewed by a leadership team at LMYSC. This team is comprised of the director, leaders from each professional area, and student representatives from the honors group. Normative culture and restorative justice are principles aligned with the concept of "CommUnity"—a community based on unity requires acting in ways that promote respect, safety, and concern for self and others. The mission statement of LMYSC promotes the concept of community:

> We believe in the dignity and worth of all people. Our mission is to be a model of excellence providing treatment for youth in a safe, secure and healthy environment. We create opportunities for positive growth and change. Lookout Mountain Youth Services Center is a unique culture within the juvenile corrections system of young men and adults working

together to enhance the future of our youth, their families and our communities.

Ten community norms are emphasized by the value of normative culture: support for normative culture, positive language, respect, teamwork, dress code, supportive confrontation, goals, safety, impulse control, and no contraband. These norms are posted throughout the facility and are integrated into guided feedback sessions, counseling, and all aspects of daily life. The value of restorative justice emphasizes efforts to repair harm by giving back to others and the community. An individual who harms others also harms the community; restorative justice emphasizes repairing this harm and preventing future injury rather than simply punishing the offender.

Implementation Challenges Related to Principles of Effective Treatment

Let us now turn to a discussion of implementation challenges for each of the specific principles of effective treatment, using the Colorado Continuum of Care Initiative and LMYSC to provide specific examples (as well as other national efforts and programs).

Closer-to-Home Principle

We begin with the importance of keeping youth in or close to the communities where they live. In Chapter 4, Guerra et al. reviewed evidence that prevention and treatment programming produces better results and is more cost-effective in community settings than in institutions. Indeed, the majority of youth housed in secure correctional institutions pose little threat to communities. In one study of incarcerated juveniles in 14 states, violent offenders comprised a minority of youth in confinement, ranging from a low of 11% to a high of 44% (Krisberg, Onek, Jones, & Schwartz, 1993). In addition to harsh conditions and increases in mental health problems as a result of incarceration, removing youth from their community environments and local cultures increases their isolation, provides them with an exclusively delinquent peer group, and does little to facilitate productive engagement when they return home.

Both research and common sense suggest that youth will do better when they receive treatment services closer to home in real-world settings with opportunities to interact with law-abiding citizens and become meaningfully engaged in their communities. The problem then becomes one of implementation. In other words, what are the specific barriers to reducing incarceration and increasing community-based options? We may know what to do, but we must also craft policies and practices that specify *how* to do it, given a variety of political, economic, and practical challenges to implementation.

Political Challenges to Implementing the Closer-to-Home Principle

Perhaps the greatest political challenge to implementing community-based treatment programs and reducing youth incarceration stems from upswings in public fear of crime. Historically, this escalation in public fear has led to a perception that youth crime is out of control (fueled in recent years by high-profile school shootings and similar events), resulting in calls for stricter enforcement and punishment rather than enhanced prevention and rehabilitation in the community. In the United States since the 1980s, politicians have had a seemingly insatiable appetite for incarceration, even when rates of violent juvenile crime have gone up and then down during this period. Indeed, although there was a marked increase in violent juvenile crime until the mid-1990s, rates in 2001 were as low as in the early 1980s. Yet, the number of youth confined in secure residential institutions nearly doubled during this period. It is particularly troubling to note that although the rate of juvenile violent crime has declined 44% since the mid-1990s, the rate of confinement has remained relatively constant (Snyder, 2003). To further emphasize this intolerance of youth crime, the very nature of adolescence as a transitional stage between childhood and adulthood has been challenged. The public penchant for incarceration has been accompanied by a push to try violent juvenile offenders in adult court at increasingly younger ages, despite research showing that this action will have little impact on crime (Fagan, 1995).

Has this push toward incarceration of youth been driven more by the perceived political costs of being "soft" on juvenile crime rather than true public opinion? Politicians and the media may not always accurately portray the prevailing public beliefs, and resulting policies may be misguided. Several public surveys suggest that citizens overall are more reflective about youth crime and understand the importance of community-based educational and counseling programs. For example, in a comprehensive public opinion survey conducted in the 1990s, the overwhelming majority of respondents said that juveniles who commit serious crimes should be punished, but that they should also benefit from rehabilitation, if at all possible. Almost three-fourths of those surveyed said they preferred a system that provided community-based services rather than secure confinement in institutions (Schwartz, 1992).

It may also be that political currents are catching up with public opinion favoring rehabilitation, because there has been a recent upswing in support for community-based programming and a growing awareness of the costs (and disproportionate impact on minority youth) of secure confinement. In some cases, these costs have been made public through lawsuits challenging harsh conditions in state-run youth institutions (e.g., *Farrell v. Hickman* in California, as discussed in Safety and Welfare Remedial Plan, 2006). In other cases, there has been a surge in publicity and action from distinguished panels (e.g., National Research Council Panel on Juvenile Crime and Juvenile Justice); foundation initiatives and study groups (e.g., Annie E. Casey Juvenile Detention Alternatives Initiative; MacArthur Foundation Research Network on Adolescent Development and Juvenile Justice); federal reports; and research studies emphasizing the advantages of comprehensive, community-based programming tailored toward the specific developmental and treatment needs of youth. Further enhancement of community-based, "closer-to-home" approaches will require a continued effort to disseminate this information and lead reforms.

Economic Challenges to Implementing the Closer-to-Home Principle

Although secure confinement is the most costly treatment option for youth, costs per youth decrease when institutions run at maximum capacity. This fact creates a somewhat ironic economic incentive to send youth to these facilities and to maintain consistently high levels of commitment. A further incentive to incarceration in state facilities stems from the decreased costs to some counties for sending youth to state facilities. A longstanding policy was one of saddling counties with the costs of local programs while allowing them to send youth to state facilities at little cost. Counties also had relatively little money with which to develop high-quality, community-based programs. Fortunately, this policy has changed in recent years as states reshaped the funding landscape, providing incentives for counties to develop local programs and attaching costs for state incarceration. As Tyler, Ziedenberg, and Lotke (2006) note, "A number of states have shown that by rethinking how they fund their juvenile justice systems, states and localities can succeed in keeping more youth at home, reduce the number of youth incarcerated, and promote better outcomes for young people moving through these systems" (p. 2).

State funding formulas for serious offenders that rely on average daily population (ADP) of commitment (incarceration) also provide economic disincentives for community-based services. Otherwise put, reducing ADP sets in motion a downward funding spiral. For instance, the Colorado Continuum of Care Initiative was made possible through authorization from the General Assembly to flexibly utilize up to 10% of "general fund" appropriation funds from the "purchase of contract placements" line in order to provide treatment, transition, and wrap-around services for juveniles on parole or in community-based residential programs. However, overall funding levels are still based on a formula that uses ADP. If the initiative were successful in more rapidly transitioning youth from restrictive and expensive residential commitment to community-based placements, overall funding levels would decrease. As noted in their baseline evaluation report (Triwest, 2006):

> Given that community expenditures . . . are also funded as a percentage of the overall budget based on commitment ADP, successful community initiatives will undermine the budget on which they depend. Without a shift in funding allocation structures, as better community services become available and Client Managers become more effective in appropriately transitioning youth to community placements, the Division's resources for both commitment and community-based services could shrink to the point that youth are left without either commitment or community placements. (p. vii)

Using a different strategy, RECLAIM Ohio (Reasoned and Equitable Community and Local Alternative to Incarceration of Minors) began in the mid-1990s by giving counties a fixed state allocation based on average juvenile felony adjudication in the previous 4 years. Although counties with higher crime rates receive more funds, funding was also tied to a reduction in the state bed space used by counties in the previous year (for youth with lower public safety risk but not for certain types of serious and violent offenders who pose a threat to public safety). The fewer non-high-risk ("optional") youth sent to state facilities, the more monies would be received in the following year. This funding structure encouraged counties to develop local options instead of sending youth to state facilities.

As this example suggests, implementation of closer-to-home programming can be facilitated by funding allocations based both on juvenile crime rates and incentives for developing community-based programs instead of daily population rates in state facilities. This strategy is further supported by studies that have found that community-based residential programs, such as multidimensional treatment foster care

(MTFC), are more cost-effective and produce greater impact on recidivism than incarceration (Chamberlain & Reid, 1997; Greenwood, 2005; Lipsey, 2006).

Practical Challenges to Implementing the Closer-to-Home Principle

Comprehensive treatment strategies built around the concept of community-based services require that appropriate opportunities and programs be available. In other words, it is impractical to refer youth to a specific type of program (e.g., MST or other evidence-based family treatment programs) if there are no community agencies providing this service. Given the different needs of youth as related to risk for re-offending, community-based programming requires a menu of available services consistent with best practices. To the extent that agencies or programs follow evidence-based principles (but do not provide specific evidence-based programs), it is also important to establish that programs are indeed consistent with current research evidence. This effort becomes even more problematic when considering the relevance of available programming for youth from diverse ethnic and socioeconomic backgrounds. One mechanism for stimulating agency programming in selected areas and utilizing evidence-based practices is for states and counties to issue requests for proposals (RFPs) for these services. In Colorado the RFP mechanism has been used to further promote partnerships between private residential facilities and community agencies in order to facilitate youth transitions back into the community.

There are a number of other practical challenges related to the reintegration of youth into communities following residential placements, particularly those outside the community and in secure facilities. In many states, incarcerated youth are not allowed to leave institutions under any circumstances until they are released, so they have no exposure to community norms and opportunities or familiarity with new situations they will face. Further, they are often incarcerated far from their home communities, limiting the involvement of their families and the development of opportunities in their communities. Yet allowing youth to build positive community supports requires that they be connected to, rather than isolated from, their families, mentors, and communities, suggesting at the very least policies that allow for off-site programs and opportunities. At LMYSC, youth participate in a number of community activities while they are incarcerated, including sports leagues, community field trips, and home visits, according to their behavior and progress. Further, planning for release begins well before the release date and includes visits to new living facilities and/ or agencies that will assist youth during this transition.

Rehabilitation Principle

Implementing juvenile justice treatment, by definition, requires adoption of a rehabilitative approach. That is, a basic premise of treatment is that offenders can change and redirect their behavior toward noncriminal and productive ends. However, as discussed in the introductory chapter of this volume, although juvenile justice in the United States may have gotten its start as a treatment provider, it has never been clear whether its primary intent was to provide care, support, and rehabilitation or to prosecute and punish children and adolescents who commit crimes (Fagan, 1990). These organizational tensions are rarely considered in the implementation of treatment programs, yet they can result in considerable ambiguity of purpose and interfere with continuity of practice. Consider, for example, a secure detention facility where some staff members believe that they can help youth become productive citizens, whereas other staff members believe that these youth are deviants who must be treated harshly. Clearly, rehabilitative treatment is more likely to be effective if there is consistent and widespread support for its importance and effectiveness.

Let us now turn to a discussion of the political, economic, and practical challenges to adoption of a rehabilitation model for juvenile justice treatment. That is, how can we implement policies and practices that engage citizens and staff in supporting the importance of treatment and rehabilitation, underscore their economic benefits, and overcome practical challenges?

Political Challenges to Implementing the Rehabilitation Principle

The forces that impact public opinion and political will regarding incarceration are also likely to shape beliefs about rehabilitation. Perceptions that troublesome youth should be locked up in secure facilities are likely to go hand-in-hand with beliefs that punishment is a central goal of juvenile justice. Rehabilitation is also constrained by the notion that positive support for delinquents essentially sanctions or reinforces their behavior. Critics have charged that any "hug-a-thug" approach essentially rewards the undeserving—Greenwood (2005) has referred to this approach as the "paradox of perverse rewards" (pp. 168–169). However, although delinquents often receive additional educational, vocational, and counseling services, in truth, high-risk youth who are more likely to become delinquent typically receive an extended array of government services long before they commit a crime. Further, incarceration without services is more costly than community-based services without incarceration, and it is less effective than rehabilitation. It would be foolish to forgo the benefits of community-based treatment programs that are also less costly simply to serve a collective desire for vengeance, but this desire for vengeance must be acknowledged nonetheless.

Political challenges to rehabilitation also come from the beliefs of those inside juvenile justice systems. It is important to recognize how the beliefs of those who manage and staff juvenile justice services can impede or facilitate rehabilitation efforts. For example, California's recent efforts to emphasize treatment as part of the Department of Corrections and Rehabilitation, Division of Juvenile Justice Safety and Welfare Remedial Plan (2006) notes, "An overall shift in practices is needed to move from a punitive model to a rehabilitative model. . . . It is recognized that there will be a substantial learning curve for staff as the components of the new model are implemented" (p. 10). This shift requires not only a change in practices but a change in the *culture* of juvenile corrections. Accomplishing this shift is particularly difficult for states that locate their juvenile corrections agency within the state corrections agency, because the juvenile authority can be easily overwhelmed and transformed into a mini-adult system. Although some states that maintain this organization have managed to avoid this "takeover," California youth facilities have clearly become prisons. As noted in the California Department of Corrections and Rehabilitation (CDCR) Safety and Welfare Remedial (2006) plan, "The challenge is to transform an operational culture that has become 'adultified' into something quite different" (p. 11). Again, the clear message is that the culture of juvenile corrections provides the foundation for implementation of programming so that efforts to enhance rehabilitation require a parallel investment in creating a responsive cultural climate. This climate must also permeate all residential and nonresidential programs that are part of the juvenile justice system.

One of the most impressive accomplishments at LMYSC, which is also woven into the Continuum of Care Initiative, is a systemwide emphasis on rehabilitation. This emphasis is framed by the "3 Rs" of rehabilitation—relationship building, respect, and responsible behavior. An over-arching goal of relationship building is to provide youth with a connection to an adult they may not have had before, although it can be challenging to maintain these connections when youth leave a facility or the system. At LMYSC the number of youth who regularly call or ask to come back and visit after they have left is a testament to the importance of these connections. The emphasis on respect and responsible behavior covers the total environment, from physical space to social interactions, in order to demonstrate to residents that they are "good enough to succeed." The facility is well maintained, pleasant, even cheerful, and youth walk freely around the scenic grounds. They are taught to be proud of where they live and to take personal responsibility to keep it nice. For instance, instead of staff removing tagging, youth are tasked with making sure that the facility is well maintained and that tagging does not occur. Respect between residents and staff is also mutual, and both are accountable for their actions. In a recent (2007) youth climate survey, more than 80% of youth at LMYSC said that staff "always" or "sometimes" show respect. Walking the grounds of LMYSC, one cannot help but notice the friendly faces, smiles, and general atmosphere of good will.

Even simple changes can promote a culture of rehabilitation. At LMYSC one of the most dramatic shifts came about after the program was reframed as a CommUnity (emphasizing unity) rather than an institution, a simple word change with a much deeper meaning. This change led to questions for both staff and residents regarding how individuals should act in the community and what responsibilities they should have. It should be relatively easy for juvenile justice programs to consider what a language of rehabilitation looks like and make appropriate changes. Terms such as *institution, wards, warden, inmates, feedings,* and *movements* reflect a culture of control, whereas terms such as *community, residents, director, and mealtimes* suggest a culture of participation and engagement more supportive of rehabilitation.

Economic Challenges to Implementing the Rehabilitation Principle

Many of the economic challenges to providing effective rehabilitation programs for juvenile offenders are part of the same funding issues discussed in the previous section. Funding formulas that provide little incentive to develop local treatment programs and minimize the costs of incarceration in state facilities are not conducive to the development of community-based rehabilitation programs. As economic policies shift (e.g., as illustrated in Colorado and Ohio), we can expect that a broader array of rehabilitation options will become available.

Rehabilitation and treatment are clearly more cost-effective than incarceration and punishment. There is little doubt that it is less costly to provide intensive treatment to youth living at home (e.g., MST costs approximately $5,000–$7,000 per youth). Cost–benefit analysis has also examined the actual monetary benefit to society of such programs in terms of preventing crime and reducing victim suffering. For example, the Washington State Institute for Public Policy estimated that the net benefit of MST to taxpayers and victims is more than $130,000 (Aos, Phipps, Barnoski, & Lieb, 2001). The challenge is thus how best to communicate the economic benefits of rehabilitation and to promote the use of cost–benefit analysis for making juvenile justice program allocation decisions.

Practical Challenges to Implementing the Rehabilitation Principle

Rehabilitation also takes more work because it is based on positive expectations for success, skill building, and change. In a punitive culture, a positive outcome is that "nothing happens," that is, no incidents are reported; but a culture of rehabilitation involves positive change. It is also important not to minimize the importance of providing a safe and secure environment so that rehabilitation does not compromise safety and security. This is a clear implementation challenge of the rehabilitative approach because it takes more energy, requires more staff, and involves more work. It also requires a particular type of staffing, with a focus on counseling rather than control. Not all staff are well suited to this approach, suggesting a need for careful screening and ongoing training. However, in systems with entrenched staffing infrastructures and strong unions, it may be extremely difficult to change staff culture, particularly with a culture that is more demanding. Youth also see it as more work, so they must be convinced of the benefits of this approach as well.

Another important practical implementation concern is how best to achieve a consistent philosophy and orientation across state and private services. This consistency issue has been a particular challenge for the Continuum of Care Initiative. With approximately 1,400 youth committed to the Department of Youth Corrections in 2005–2006, Colorado currently has 11 state-operated facilities, with 65% of beds contracted in privately operated programs. Youth regularly go in and out of state and private programs, suggesting a need to coordinate policies and practices across the public and private sector. To this end, the initiative directs energy toward building consensus around rehabilitation so that there is consistency in core values, standards of care, and key practices. This consensus building is achieved through a variety of mechanisms, including statewide trainings and targeted funding opportunities.

Finally, rehabilitation in practice is often accompanied by unrealistic expectations for success and rigid consequences for failure. Most adolescents engage in normative rule testing and risk taking from time to time, with some cushion or margin of error (e.g., warnings, lectures). However, for youth in the juvenile justice system there is virtually no slippage allowed, particularly after youth are released from institutions into the community. Parole revocation can occur for the slightest infraction—a standard which is hard for any teenager to maintain. There is also little respite or "time out" for youth on parole and in crisis who need a brief intervention to help them stay on course. Implementation could be enhanced by providing at least some degree of flexibility and tolerance for occasional missteps when progress is being made.

Evidence-Based Principle

Over the past decade, considerable attention has been focused on documenting and disseminating evidence-based programs for juvenile justice (and a host of other social and health programs). Funding guidelines regularly require adoption of evidence-based programs or consistency with evidence-based principles and approaches. However, in practice, evidence-based programs have not been broadly or consistently implemented, and it is even more difficult to determine what constitutes an acceptable evidence-based principle or approach. For instance, because cognitive-behavioral therapy is considered a best practice in treating youth offenders, should any and every program that targets offender cognitions be recommended? As we discuss, implementing evidence-based practices in juvenile justice presents several political, economic, and practical challenges.

Political Challenges to Implementing the Evidence-Based Principle

Amid increasing needs and decreasing funding for juvenile treatment services, the mantra of evidence-based programming has clearly generated political support. Indeed, it is common practice for RFP and funding streams to require selection of prevention and intervention programs based on high-quality evidence. What is more problematic is whether political will translates into high-fidelity implementation or appropriate adaptation in "uncontrolled" real-world settings. The implementation challenge is not one of generating political support for the evidence-based principle, but rather of generating support for follow-through in order to achieve broad and consistent implementation (suggesting an economic challenge that is discussed later). Overall, the alignment of science and politics has created a general sense of encouragement in the field, with relatively few political challenges to adoption of evidence-based programs.

More perplexing and also relevant to the practical reality of implementing evidence-based programs is why some programs continue to garner political support and persist despite evidence that they do not work. In the juvenile justice literature there are three clear examples of programs that don't work but have persisted: boot camps, "shock" programs such as Scared Straight, and waiver of juveniles to adult court. For instance, several evaluations have demonstrated that boot camps, particularly mainstream, military-style programs, do not affect recidivism. A "second generation" of programs developed in the mid-1990s added more treatment and rehabilitation components, but still had a lackluster impact on recidivism (Austin, 2000). Although these programs have subsequently declined, they persisted (and still persist) despite a lack of empirical support. Shock programs such as Scared Straight have not only failed to impact offending, but in some cases participants have done worse than those in comparison probation groups that did not participate in this type of programming (Lewis, 1983). Similarly, despite evidence that waiver of juveniles to adult court has a negative impact on both youth and public safety (Fagan & Zimring, 2000), virtually every state in the United States has enacted legislation supporting this process.

In some sense, these programs benefited from the same political momentum that generated a series of get-tough policies in juvenile justice. They are all high-profile programs with some degree of dramatic appeal that can easily line up with political agendas designed to accommodate public fear of youth crime. Promotional efforts and salesmanship also facilitate adoption. Lack of clear evidence from a few studies has been attributed to just that—there are still very few studies—when political and economic conditions favored implementation. In addition, these programs were relatively low cost when compared to alternatives, suggesting the need to consider carefully the economic realities of implementation.

Economic Challenges to Implementing the Evidence-Based Principle

Many evidence-based programs are derived from studies of the causes and correlates of behaviors or outcomes. The primary emphasis is on developing programs that address relevant risk and protective factors and promote desired changes. Funded by research grants that provide required funds for high-quality implementation and evaluation, there generally is less emphasis on developing and evaluating low-cost programs. As a consequence, evidence-based programs tend to be intensive, demanding, and costly. In practice, few settings have the funding and resources to adequately implement these programs, particularly with the same degree of fidelity and monitoring. Otherwise put, high-fidelity implementation of evidence-based programs can be obtained but only when there are sufficient resources and technical support. When resources and technical support are lacking, poor implementation and adaptations are more common. Poor implementation, in turn, compromises program outcomes, resulting in a loss of program effectiveness.

As new treatment programs for juvenile offenders are developed and evaluated, they should be informed by the economic realities of the juvenile justice enterprise. Even with a focus on comprehensive programming, it is still possible to consider the minimal intensity needed for change. Research funding streams should emphasize not only the theoretical and empirical bases of programs but also comparisons of approaches that range in intensity and costs. For instance, it may be possible to replace intensive interventions with more extensive interventions that rely on multiple contacts over time, using lower-cost strategies. There may be a minimum threshold needed to effect change, but the added benefits beyond this threshold may not justify the additional costs. It also may be possible to experimentally evaluate core components of evidence-based interventions and determine their relative contribution to overall effectiveness. At the very least, comparisons of intervention components and competing approaches based on cost should be encouraged.

Practical Challenges to Implementing the Evidence-Based Principle

In addition to economic concerns, there are a number of practical challenges to implementing evidence-based juvenile offender treatment programs. To begin with, programs with clear treatment and implementation guidelines and associated technical support still may not be implemented effectively. It is often difficult to attain competence, even with this support, as evidenced by the uneven implementation of MST in Washington. In this case, the state responded by establishing adherence and outcome standards to ensure quality implementation of juvenile justice research-based programs (Washington State Institute for Public Policy, 2003, 2004). However, adherence standards hinge on carefully developed manuals and implementation protocols. Yet in truth, very few research-based treatments for juvenile offenders have been replicated and translated into packaged or manualized programs.

Even fewer programs specify which modifications are or are not permissible (in part, because it is unlikely that programs have been evaluated with specific modifications).

It is also likely that the most careful delineation of program components and implementation guidelines still would not translate into 100% adherence in the real world. First, many treatment studies use small and potentially unrepresentative samples of youth, such that results may not generalize across gender, ethnicity, and context. It requires a leap of faith to assume that evidence of treatment effectiveness from carefully controlled trials on small samples can generalize to a wide variety of populations (Green, 2001). Second, there are several instances where program evidence is inconclusive—for example, some studies demonstrate effectiveness and others do not, or early evidence of effectiveness is refuted by additional replications.

The Quantum Opportunities program illustrates this point. This program is a comprehensive multiyear program for high-risk youth that includes skills training, service opportunities, mentoring, and financial incentives for participation and completion. Results of early evaluations show that participants were less likely than controls to be arrested during high school, and it was designated as a model "blueprint" program (Elliott, 1997). However, subsequent evaluations from the Department of Labor did not report positive outcomes, and it was demoted to "promising."

Packaged interventions also provide little room for active participation or ownership in developing the treatment and implementation strategy. Yet, research suggests that perceived ownership increases the likelihood of effective implementation. As Backer (2005) comments:

> No matter how good the intervention or the science behind it, no matter how good the implementation strategy, efforts to promote change in any complex system are very likely to fail unless the change effort has the support and active involvement of the people who live in that system. In particular, those who will be implementing the intervention need to feel some sense of ownership for it, and some degree of active participation in developing the implementation strategy. (p. 4)

An awareness of community conditions and drive for ownership thus sets the stage for program adaptation. If adaptation is the rule rather than the exception, research must keep pace by determining which program elements are core components and should not be changed and which elements can be implemented with greater flexibility. This research focus can be facilitated through greater collaboration and partnerships between researchers and juvenile justice practitioners.

Risk-Focused, Strengths-Based Principle

The risk-focused, strengths-based principle specifies that interventions should seek to modify dynamic (changeable) risk factors of juveniles related to their risk of offending, building on strengths or protective factors. However, not all youth experience the same set of risk and protective factors. For example, some offenders may come from relatively stable families but have strong associations with delinquent peers and poor academic performance. In contrast, other offenders may do well academically but come from extremely dysfunctional families and live in high-crime neighborhoods. To address this diversity across individual offenders, comprehensive programming must be available. As Hoge discusses in Chapter 3, a cornerstone of this strategy is the development and use of reliable and valid assessments.

In recent years, justice systems have increased their reliance on assessments that include both a severity of offense/re-offending risk score (primarily to inform placement decisions) as well as detailed descriptions of the risk and protective factors linked to specific youth profiles (primarily for treatment planning). Still, there are implementation challenges for assessment as well as implementation challenges to link assessments with treatment planning and delivery. Beyond the political and economic challenges of providing adequate funding for treatment options (similar to issues raised in the discussion of challenges to rehabilitation), most of these challenges involve practical issues. Therefore, in this section we limit our discussion of implementation challenges to these practical concerns.

Practical Challenges to Implementing the Risk-Focused, Strength-Based Principle

An important component of systems improvement in juvenile justice treatment is the utilization of comprehensive needs assessments to plan services most likely to reduce recidivism (Hsia & Beyer, 2000). Much progress has been made both in development of comprehensive screening tools and integration of these assessments into treatment planning. In many states, these assessments are also used to identify particular needs beyond risk for re-offending, such as mental health, special education, or specific substance use problems, so that focused treatments or specialized assignments can be made. In practice, there are often weak links in the chain.

First, assessment data may not follow a youth through various stages in system involvement. For example, in reviewing the use of assessments at the California Youth Authority, the California Department of Corrections and Rehabilitation Remedial Plan (2006) notes that the Youth Authority employs an exemplary assessment approach involving extensive assessments and significant staff time, but that these assessments are not adequately incorporated in day-to-day custody, treatment, and training decisions:

> Assessment data is not simply translated or summarized for those staff who supervise the ward on current living units. There is virtually no passing on of these assessment data to the YA parole staff who prepare the youth for return home, or to those field staff who must supervise the ward on release. Because the detailed Reception Center assessments are not routinely repeated, there are concerns expressed that these data are badly outdated for those youths who remain in the YA for substantial terms. (pp. 13–14)[1]

Clearly, assessments must be repeated appropriately in order to detect change, and utilization of assessments must occur during all phases of treatment.

Second, careful screening to identify specific areas of risk assumes that treatment programs to address this risk are available either in the community or in residential and detention facilities. As discussed previously, given the different needs of youth in relation to risk for re-offending, comprehensive treatment programming requires a menu of services, available within residential and detention facilities as well as at the community level, consistent with best practices. Yet in a climate of relatively scarce resources there are few examples of juvenile justice systems that are able to provide this breadth of programming. Systems are more typically characterized by "inadequate risk assessment procedures, lack of alternative programs, inadequate special programs (e.g., mental health, gender-specific) and poor supervision in probation and aftercare" (Zavlek, 2005, p. 4).

This area becomes even more problematic when we consider the availability of evidence-based programming for offenders in general (i.e., independent of particular resources in a state or county system). In truth, there is a relatively scant evidence base that has been translated into standardized treatment protocols—and this is limited primarily to family interventions such as MST, with more general support for cognitive-behavioral strategies. To the extent that an offender's risk is linked to family problems or patterns of thinking, and assuming that evidence-based programs are available in a particular setting, treatment can follow assessment. However, there are many clear risk factors for delinquency and re-offending that have not been amenable to treatment thus far.

A prime example is the influence of antisocial and delinquent peers, one of the most robust predictors of concurrent and subsequent delinquency. When we consider association with peers in the context of the influence of youth gangs, we are hard pressed to find an adequate number of evidence-based programs or even any clear principles for working with gang-involved youth, particularly for youth in correctional settings. Yet as Parker et al. discuss in Chapter 8, gangs present significant problems in communities, treatment settings, and juvenile detention facilities. Most surveys have reported that approximately 75% of incarcerated youth have some gang affiliation, although rates vary by states (Knox, 1991). Youth who are gang involved on the streets often solidify their attachments in correctional facilities, only to return to the streets with even stronger gang alliances. Yet there are few programs that have been effective in breaking the cycle of street-gang membership, gang involvement in youth correctional facilities, and continued gang involvement in communities to which incarcerated youth return. Identifying youth risk in relation to affiliation with antisocial peers or gang memberships means little if we do not develop and evaluate programs to address this need.

Third, although juvenile justice practice generally embraces the principle of targeting the most intensive services to those most at risk (labeled the risk principle), this may be more applicable to the lower ends of the continuum. In other words, youth with relatively low levels of risk (for whom delinquent behavior may be more adolescent-limited or occasional) are likely to desist from offending without any treatment services. However, for youth at the high end, for instance, those incarcerated in secure detention, it is unclear whether variations in risk within this group warrant more extensive services. It may be that the highest-risk youth who are most entrenched in a delinquent lifestyle would be most resistant to change, and that slightly lower-risk youth within this group might be more responsive to treatment efforts. The challenge for implementation is to provide services for those most likely to benefit, beyond consideration of risk level—a point that has not been carefully delineated (in other words, characteristics of youth within a high-risk group most associated with positive change and characteristics most associated with resistance to change).

Finally, the field generally has embraced the notion of strengths-based programming, without clear guidelines for implementation. In practice, strengths-based nomenclature has been translated into a focus on "building" protective factors or turning risk factors into strengths or protective factors. A youth who is not doing well academically (risk factor) is encouraged to participate in educational activities so that he or she can develop this particular strength. Following this logic, it is unclear how a focus on strengths is different from a focus on risks, assuming that the goal of any risk-focused approach is to turn risks into strengths. Helping youth "build strengths" sounds less negative than helping "reduce risks," but it is still a deficit-based model (although possibly masquerading as something less negative). A different strategy, consistent with many community development approaches (e.g., Kretzmann & McKnight, 1993), is to use assessments to identify strengths and to build on these strengths as a strategy to reduce risk. Rather than "check off" an area because the youth is already doing well, these strengths could be mobilized to help the youth do even better. For example, some offenders may have good grades and academic credits, whereas others may have concerned and involved families. The question then becomes how these strengths can be identified both to provide a positive context for youth and to become a foundation for treatment planning.

Summary and Conclusion

In this chapter we have discussed several political, economic, and practical challenges to implementing treatment programs for juvenile offenders. As we have illustrated, in order to optimize translation of evidence-based programs and principles, we must also examine potential barriers to implementation and how these can be overcome. We conclude with three overarching themes that are critical for effective program implementation.

First, we must build a broad foundation of support for rehabilitation and community-based treatment. The research and practice literature provide clear evidence that youth do better with comprehensive treatment programming in their communities rather than secure confinement in institutions. Yet, political pressures and beliefs about punishment can interfere with support and funding for treatment, despite evidence that it is more effective (or even generate enthusiasm for ineffective programs such as boot camps and waiver to adult court). Support for rehabilitation must not only be garnered from citizens and politicians but also from those within the justice system who work directly with youth. The experience at LMYSC provides compelling evidence of the importance of creating a culture of rehabilitation within treatment settings.

Second, we must expand the evidence base of treatment programs for offenders in order to address additional risk factors (e.g., influence of antisocial peers, gang involvement) with different populations (e.g., gender, ethnic differences). It is also important to consider the relative merits of programs with differing costs (e.g., from least expensive to most expensive). Researchers have ignored the costs of intervention for too long—yet this is often a primary barrier to implementation in real-world settings with limited resources. Very few jurisdictions are able to foot the bill for 24-hour on-call therapists working with small case-loads, even if the evidence for this strategy is compelling. We must also develop strategies for strengths-based programming that identify and use individual strengths in order to redirect youth toward a more conventional and law-abiding lifestyle.

Third, we must develop clear implementation protocols for evidence-based programs that identify critical core components and those that can be modified. Given that strict compliance with treatment protocols is unlikely and that implementation can actually be enhanced through local ownership, flexible programs are more likely to take hold than those requiring rigid adherence. Yet we know relatively little about specific components of evidence-based programs that are essential for change. For instance, cognitive-behavioral programs often target a multitude of attributions, beliefs, and problem-solving skills, yet it is unclear whether these are all equally important in preventing subsequent antisocial and delinquent behavior.

It is encouraging that the research community is also paying attention to the importance of implementation in the translation of evidence-based programs. A number of recent federal and state funding initiatives have focused on methods for dissemination, adoption, and implementation of interventions, rather than the effectiveness of the interventions themselves on outcomes. Community participatory research that encourages collaborations between practitioners and researchers can facilitate the design and evaluation of interventions that more easily translate to real-world settings. Dialogue between justice professionals and academic researchers can generate a new generation of juvenile offender treatment studies designed to optimize both outcomes and feasibility of implementation.

Note

1. In the remedial plan filed in response to the *Farrell v. Hickman* lawsuit, the state also has delineated specific actions to address this problem.

References

Aos, S., Phipps, P., Barnoski, R., & Lieb, R. (2001). *The comparative costs and benefits of programs to reduce crime.* Olympia, WA: Washington Institute for Public Policy.

Austin, J. (2000). *Multisite evaluation of boot camp programs: Final report.* Washington, DC: Institute on Crime, Justice, and Corrections, George Washington University.

Backer, T. (2005). *Implementation of evidence-based interventions: Key research issues.* Los Angeles: Human Interaction Research Institute.

California Department of Corrections and Rehabilitation Division of Juvenile Justice. (2006). *Reforming California's juvenile corrections system: Farrell v. Hickman (Safety and Welfare Remedial Plan).* Sacramento, CA: Author.

California Department of Corrections and Rehabilitation Division of Juvenile Justice. (2006). *Safety and welfare remedial plan.* Sacramento, CA: Author.

Chamberlain, P., & Reid, J. B. (1997). Comparison of two community alternatives to incarceration for chronic juvenile offenders. *Journal of Consulting and Clinical Psychology, 6,* 624–633.

Elliott, D. (1997). *Blueprints for violence prevention.* Boulder: Center for the Study and Prevention of Violence, University of Colorado.

Fagan, J. (1990). Treatment and reintegration of violent juvenile offenders: Experimental results. *Justice Quarterly, 7,* 233–263.

Fagan, J. (1995). Separating the men from the boys: The comparative advantage of juvenile versus criminal court sanctions on recidivism among adolescent felony offenders. In J. C. Howell, B. Krisberg, J. D. Hawkins, & J. J. Wilson (Eds.), *A sourcebook: Serious, violent, and chronic juvenile offenders* (pp. 238–260). Thousand Oaks, CA: Sage.

Fagan, J., & Zimring, F. (Eds.). (2000). *The changing borders of juvenile justice.* Chicago: University of Chicago Press.

Green, L. W. (2001). From research to "best practices" in other settings and populations. *American Journal of Health Behavior, 25,* 15–178.

Greenwood, P. W. (2005). *Changing lives: Delinquent prevention as crime-control policy.* Chicago: University of Chicago Press.

Hsia, H. M., & Beyer, M. (2000, March). *System change through state challenge activities: Approaches and products.* [Bulletin]. Washington, DC: Office of Justice Programs, Office of Juvenile Justice and Delinquency Prevention, Department of Justice.

Knox, G. W. (1991). *An introduction to gangs.* Barren Springs, MI: Vande Vere Publishing.

Kretzmann, J. P., & McKnight, J. L. (1993). *Building communities from the inside out.* Chicago, IL: Northwestern University Institute for Policy Research.

Krisberg, B., Onek, D., Jones, M., & Schwartz, I. (1993). *Juveniles in state custody: Prospects for community-based care of troubled adolescents.* San Francisco: National Council on Crime and Delinquency.

Lewis, R. V. (1983). Scared Straight—California style: Evaluation of the San Quentin squire program. *Criminal Justice and Behavior, 10,* 209–226.

Lipsey, M. W. (2006). The effects of community-based group treatment for delinquency. In K. A. Dodge, T. J. Dishion, & J. E. Lansford (Eds.), *Deviant peer influences in programs for youth: Problems and solutions* (pp. 162–184). New York: Guilford Press.

Schwartz, I. M. (Ed.). (1992). *Juvenile justice and public policy: Toward a national agenda.* New York: Lexington Books.

Sherman, L. W., Gottfredson, D., Mackenzie, D., Eck, J., Reuter, P., & Bushway, S. (1997). *Preventing crime: What works, what doesn't, what's promising.* Washington, DC: National Institute of Justice.

Snyder, H. N. (2003). *Juvenile Arrests 2002.* [Bulletin] Washington, DC: Office of Justice Programs, Office of Juvenile Justice and Delinquency Prevention, U.S. Department of Justice.

Triwest (2006). *First year evaluation report for the Continuum of Care Initiative.* Boulder, CO: Author.

Tyler, J., Ziedenberg, J., & Lotke, E. (2006). *Cost effective corrections: The fiscal architecture of rational juvenile justice systems.* Washington, DC: Justice Policy Institute.

Washington State Institute for Public Policy. (2003). *Recommended quality control standards: Washington State research-based juvenile offender programs.* Olympia, WA: Author.

Washington State Institute for Public Policy. (2004). *Outcome evaluation of Washington State's research-based programs for juvenile offenders.* Olympia, WA: Author.

Zavlek, S. (2005). *Planning community-based facilities for violent juvenile offenders as part of a system of graduated sanctions.* Washington, DC: Office of Justice Programs, Office of Juvenile Justice and Delinquency Prevention, U.S. Department of Justice.

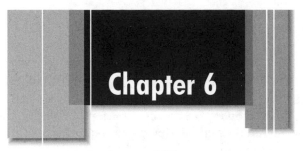

Chapter 6

How Policy Affects Practice in the Treatment of Juvenile Offenders
The California Experience

Elizabeth Siggins
Amy Seidlitz

Juvenile justice policies provide the foundation for the implementation of treatment programs. For example, as discussed in the introduction to this volume, policies supporting a rehabilitation emphasis are more likely to lead to funding and support of treatment programs for offenders than policies emphasizing punishment and control. For this reason, one of the challenges faced when selecting and implementing treatment programs is that they must be integrated into existing (or changing) juvenile justice systems. As such, the policies that guide these systems can have a significant effect on which programs are most likely to be adopted and how they will be implemented. Enhancing treatment programs for offenders thus requires careful articulation of relevant juvenile justice policies and how they can influence programming.

This chapter explores the range of policies and how they vary among different juvenile justice systems. As we point out, there is rarely one juvenile justice system in any jurisdiction. Further, juvenile justice systems frequently undergo changes in policies in response to public opinion and political will. Treatment programs (and the perceived value of particular programs) can wax and wane according to policy shifts. To illustrate the challenges faced by policy makers and how they can influence treatment options, we use the example of recent state-level reform efforts in California.

In an ideal world, policymakers focused on enhancing treatment of juvenile offenders would implement reforms based on the following critical steps. They would (1) lay out the scope of their reforms; (2) bring in subject matter experts to develop a treatment model based on the target population and identified treatment needs; (3) identify and secure the resources needed for the new model; (4) revise and/or draft policies to put the model into place; (5) establish the appropriate mechanisms for research and evaluation; (6) hire and/or train staff accordingly; (7) implement quality assurance and evaluation measures to ensure that the model is applied appropriately and accurately, and that the desired outcomes are being achieved; and (8) adjust the model and retrain, as necessary.

In the real world, the opportunity or mandate for reform does not always allow policymakers to follow the ideal model described above. Often, as in California—where recent juvenile justice reform efforts were driven by a court lawsuit—an organization may not have the luxury of time to finish planning and developing the new model before pressure sets in to begin implementation and demonstrate results. Being forced into early implementation does not automatically lead to failure, but it can make the path to reform and implementation of high-quality treatment programs exceedingly (and perhaps unnecessarily) difficult. This is particularly problematic if, as in California, an agency is forced to begin the implementation of a new model not only before it is fully developed, but also while the scope of reform (the first step in the sequence above) is still being debated!

Reforming any system or organization requires fixing many (sometimes hundreds of) policies. Most of the policies that have to be changed or developed are what we refer to as "small-p" policies. Small-p policies are the programs, procedures, and regulations that inform staff members of their responsibilities and determine the operations of any facility or organization. Revising these policies can be a very tedious and often complicated process. In California, as in many states, different administrations have taken different approaches to policy development. As a result, policies (where they exist in writing) exist in different manuals, but many accepted (and even expected) practices are not captured in any of these manuals.

Even though small-p policies can make or break reform efforts, they are usually not the focus of reform discussions. In California, for example, most of the public discussions about juvenile justice reform (through the media or legislative hearings) have been focused on broad-sweeping or big-*P* policy issues. For more than 2 years, legislators and others have continued to argue that the state should rethink the way youth are committed to secure facilities. Many have even argued that the state's facilities should be shut down entirely and all youth should be kept under the jurisdiction of local county probation departments (Garcia, 2005). This debate has continued even after the department filed its reform plans in court and received legislative authorization to begin implementation.

Essentially, in cases such as these, there is tension between big-*P* and small-*p* policies. Such a debate may end up being a fatal distraction to successful reform. Although it is very interesting, from a big-*P* policy perspective, to consider restructuring a state's juvenile justice continuum, it is not clear that any one structure is better or more effective than another. Clearly, as discussed throughout this volume, it is important to provide treatment programs in a big-*P* policy environment that supports rehabilitation and endorses evidence-based practices. Yet the reality is that implementing evidence-based practices requires far more small-*p* policy changes than big-*P* changes, and these changes are most likely to impact quality of implementation. For instance, if an agency is unable to focus its time and resources on implementing evidence-based programming with the proper staffing, training, and evaluation measures, they will never be able to provide the necessary treatment approaches and demonstrate the desired outcomes. Choosing to move toward an evidence-based model is a big-*P* policy decision, but doing it effectively is a small-*p* challenge.

There Is No Such Thing as a Unified Juvenile Justice System

It is impossible to talk about juvenile justice reform without first recognizing that there is no such thing as a unified juvenile justice system. Some might argue that every state has its own system, but it would probably be more accurate to say that every jurisdiction—whether a state, county, region, city, or even a school district—has its own set of policies and politics that determine how youthful offenders are handled. To add to this complexity, juvenile offenders rarely are confined to only one jurisdiction. Not only do they cross county lines, but at any point in time they may traverse several jurisdictions (state, local, school) simultaneously. When we talk about juvenile justice reform, it is important to keep in mind that there are many layers to this system, and very few, if any, efforts have succeeded in reforming them all.

The National Center for Juvenile Justice (NCJJ) tracks and documents variations among state juvenile justice policies and practices (National Center for Juvenile Justice, 2006). Nine distinctions are relevant for treatment programming: (1) differences in how juvenile detention is organized and administered from state to state; (2) how juvenile probation is organized and administered; (3) how states organize and administer aftercare services; (4) how states define the purposes of their juvenile courts; (5) the youngest and oldest age for original juvenile court jurisdiction in delinquency matters; (6) the extended age over which the juvenile court may retain jurisdiction; (7) which states prosecute juveniles as adults in criminal court; (8) each state's minimum age for transfer to a criminal court; and (9) which states have blended sentencing laws.

Looking at how juvenile delinquency services are organized, NCJJ divides states into three basic models (Griffin & King, 2006). Certain states (12) are characterized as centralized, meaning that a state executive agency has across-the-board control, including state-run juvenile probation services, institutional commitments, and aftercare. These may be the only states where it is actually accurate to refer to *one* state juvenile justice system. Other states (18) are characterized as decentralized, meaning, at a minimum, local control of probation services. The remaining 21 states are described as combination states, with a mix of state-controlled and locally operated delinquency services (the numbers total 51 because NCJJ includes the 50 states plus the District of Columbia in its analysis).

Even in decentralized states, however, there is at least one state-run (and/or state-operated through a contract) institution. The state facilities tend to house the most serious and/or the most difficult juvenile offenders. Of course, in centralized states where all of the facilities are state operated, this may be less true because there is nowhere other than a state facility to house the less serious offenders who need residential services. As NCJJ points out, the states differ considerably in how they determine where a youth will be placed, how long the youth will stay in a placement, and who will decide when he or she is ready to be released (Griffin & King, 2006).

NCJJ breaks placement options into three basic categories. The most common practice, used by 27 states, is one in which the agency that runs the state's juvenile corrections facilities makes the placement decision without significant participation from the committing court. This decision, of course, occurs only after the committing court has determined that the youth is delinquent and meets the minimum commitment standards, which also vary from state to state. In 23 other states, the court plays a significant role in determining placement specifics, in some cases by actually selecting the facility where the youth will be placed. In at least three states, the juvenile courts use dispositional guidelines or a placement matrix (Griffin & King, 2006).

An entire book could be devoted to the differences in how length of stay and release decisions are determined in various jurisdictions. From a policy perspective, this may be one of the most fascinating areas to explore in juvenile justice because the discussion inevitably approaches the purpose of confinement. If we agree that the reason to have a juvenile court is to provide a system of rehabilitation for juveniles (as discussed throughout this volume) that is separate and different from the adult criminal justice system, then the reasons for confinement, length of confinement, and release practices are critical to this philosophical difference from the adult system. In this chapter, however, we assume that juvenile practices are distinct from adult practices and acknowledge that they vary from jurisdiction to jurisdiction.

In most jurisdictions, juvenile commitments are indeterminate (unlike the adult criminal court system in which adults are sentenced, juvenile offenders are adjudicated and committed), but there is still a great deal of variation among states. According to NCJJ, in 20 states (making it the most common practice), all commitments are indeterminate, regardless of the offense for which a juvenile is adjudicated. Five states use indeterminate commitments with a minimum period specified by the court or statute. Six states have indeterminate commitments with a maximum. One state (Pennsylvania) has indeterminate commitments with a specified minimum and maximum commitment. Thirteen states either allow or require the court to use determinate or indeterminate commitments depending upon the circumstances. And, only six states use determinate commitments in which the period of time is determined in advance by the court or statute (Griffin & King, 2006). Not surprisingly perhaps, states also vary in terms of who makes the final decision about whether or not a youth is ready to leave confinement. This decision is made either by the agency to which the youth has been committed (24 states), by the court (10 states), by a parole board (7 states), or shared among all or some of the previous three (10 states) (Griffin & King, 2006).

Does It Matter How a State's Juvenile Justice System Is Structured?

California's reforms have gotten tangled in this question. Because of the wide range of variability in state juvenile justice structures (including a few that were discussed in the previous section) and the inherent difficulty in accurately measuring juvenile justice outcomes, it is essentially impossible to know whether one structure or process is more effective than another. Using the most basic outcome measure available for criminal justice statistics—recidivism—we immediately run into problems with comparing one state to another because states use different definitions and methods of tracking recidivism. Even if we were able to devise comparable recidivism rates, which would not be impossible to do, it *would be impossible* to isolate each of the variables that contribute to differences across jurisdictions: the many elements of structure, the size of the system, the age of the youth, the types of offenses handled at each level, and the practice of prosecuting as adults. And none of these variables even begins to touch upon whether or not evidence-based programs and principles are being implemented.

Perhaps the structure of the jurisdiction does not matter if the treatment model is evidence-based. This was the gamble that state administrators decided to take when they set out to reform California's troubled juvenile corrections facilities in 2004. The challenge, as these state administrators learned, is that external stakeholders interested in reform tend to be far more interested in the big-P policy issues such as organizational structure, age of jurisdiction, and sentencing options, than in the small-p policy questions regarding how to implement evidence-based programs (i.e., how case management is defined, which staff members develop the treatment plan, how criminogenic needs are addressed, what specific programs are used). However, internally, just the opposite tends to be true. Administrators find themselves facing the challenge of gaining staff "buy-in" and creating an internal environment that is supportive of change. In order to do so, staff members at the line level want to know the new expectations, and they must be provided with the skills and structural alterations necessary to support the change.

Understanding the Role of State and Local Agencies in California

California is one of 18 states in which juvenile justice is decentralized. Juvenile delinquency services in California are organized at both the state and local level. County probation departments are responsible for juvenile detention, predisposition investigation, and probation supervision, including placements in juvenile halls, county camps, and/or group homes or other nonsecure placements. The state-operated California Department of Corrections and Rehabilitation's Division of

Juvenile Justice (DJJ)—formerly the California Youth Authority—is responsible for operating the state's secure juvenile corrections facilities, as well as parole supervision and services for youthful offenders after their release from DJJ.[1] According to NCJJ, California's DJJ is the largest juvenile offender agency in the United States (National Center for Juvenile Justice, 2006).

However, the size of DJJ is much more a result of the size of California than it is the result of overcommitment to the state's facilities. The vast majority of juvenile offenders in California are never committed to DJJ. Instead, they are kept under the jurisdiction of county probation departments. According to the California Department of Justice, there were more than 222,000 juvenile arrests in 2005 and more than 190,000 juvenile probation department dispositions (Juvenile Justice in California, 2005). (Because juvenile arrest data are reported by law enforcement agencies and the disposition data are reported by probation departments, the two data sets should not be compared to each other.) Unlike the adult probation system in California, referrals to juvenile probation do not always come from the court. A referral to juvenile probation can come from law enforcement, parents, schools, or other community agencies (Probation Services Task Force, 2003, p. 52).

Of the 194,670 probation department dispositions, fewer than half (44%, or 98,919) resulted in a petition filed in juvenile court. About 64% of the petitions filed (62,824) resulted in an adjudication of formal wardship. Less than 1% of these adjudications (636) resulted in a commitment to the state's DJJ. By far, most juvenile offenders (approximately 99% of the youth who come into contact with the system each year) in California are handled at the local level. A relative few are committed to the state's jurisdiction. As these data suggest, selection of effective treatment programs and the resources for implementation largely are linked to local decision making rather than state mandated, or big-*P*, policies.

Once a youth is committed to the state's jurisdiction, he or she receives an indeterminate commitment with a maximum confinement time set by the committing judge. This can be no more than the maximum sentence an adult would receive for a similar offense (California Welfare and Institutions Code). California is one of only seven states in which the decision to release a youth from the state's correctional facilities is made by an independent parole board. Another significant and relatively unique factor of juvenile justice in California is the age of jurisdiction. California is one of only four states in which the extended age over which the juvenile court may retain jurisdiction is 24 (King & Szymanski, 2006). (Montana, Oregon, and Wisconsin are the other three.) As a result, the average age of a youth in one of DJJ's facilities is

19.5 years old (California Department of Juvenile Justice, 2007), presenting unique challenges for the treatment of juvenile offenders who are, in some sense, actually adult offenders or will be adults when released or transferred.

The Pressure for Reform in California

In order to understand the pressures around juvenile justice reform in California, it is important to understand the history and tensions between state and local jurisdictions. As previously discussed, most juvenile offenders are kept at the local level and handled under the jurisdiction of county probation departments. Over the years, there has been a great deal of tension between the state government and local probation departments, particularly related to fiscal issues.

In all but one of California's 58 counties, a single chief probation officer has responsibility for adult and juvenile probation.[2] According to a Probation Services Task Force that was formed in 2000 to undertake a comprehensive examination of probation, "California is the only state in the nation to follow a combination local and executive governance model" (Krauth & Linke, 1999, p. 4). In addition to a unique governance structure, probation in California also has a relatively unique funding structure. California is one of only two states in which the probation department receives primary funding exclusively from local government (and offender fees). Although limited-term federal and state grant funding is available, the state does not provide a stable or continuous revenue stream for local probation services (Probation Services Task Force, 2003, p. 2).

Perhaps not surprisingly, the first recommendation of the Probation Services Task Force in June 2003 was to provide probation departments with stable and adequate funding to protect the public and ensure offender accountability and rehabilitation (Probation Services Task Force, 2003, p. 105). It should be noted that in 2000, the legislature enacted the Juvenile Justice Crime Prevention Act, which established funding for local juvenile crime prevention and intervention. Through this funding, county probation departments have received funding on a per capita basis, approximately $100 million statewide annually, to implement multi-agency juvenile justice plans, but this funding must be reauthorized annually, and it has been proposed for reduction more than once since its inception (Statutes, 2000).

Therefore, when calls for reforming California's juvenile justice system began gaining momentum through legislative and media attention in 2003 and 2004, it was not clear whether the demand was to fix the state's correctional facilities or to overhaul the state's entire juvenile justice continuum. There were proponents and opponents of both approaches. Clearly, the focus was on the state's facilities, which were targeted by a state taxpayer lawsuit known as the *Farrell* lawsuit, after the plaintiff Margaret Farrell, a state taxpayer and mother of a youth committed to the California Youth Authority (2004). But many advocates saw this lawsuit and the attention it was garnering as an opportunity for broader juvenile justice reforms.

The state vacillated a little at the beginning—raising expectations that reform might include changes to some of the broader jurisdictional issues, such as age of jurisdiction and criteria for commitment. By the end of 2005 and throughout 2006, state leaders focused specifically on the state's correctional facilities and not on the other parts of the juvenile justice continuum, because technically these were neither under their direct control nor under the purview of the *Farrell* lawsuit.

The *Farrell* Lawsuit

In November 2004, the State of California entered into a momentous consent decree in the *Farrell v. Allen* lawsuit.[3] Unlike other lawsuits against departments within the Youth and Adult Corrections Agency (later to become the California Department of Corrections and Rehabilitation), the *Farrell* lawsuit was filed in state court, not in federal court. The state probably could have used the venue of the case as an excuse to treat it less seriously. Technically, state courts do not tend to have the power of federal courts, particularly with respect to demanding that state resources be spent on remedies. For many, the state's willingness to enter into the consent decree and to address the deficiencies identified in the lawsuit were positive signs that state leaders acknowledged the need for reform. There can be no doubt that the state's willingness to address these issues was at least in part a result of the heightened attention given the lawsuit and the problems the California Youth Authority was facing in early 2004.

Prior to the consent decree, the California Youth Authority (CYA) and the plaintiff's attorneys had agreed to an expert review of certain conditions at the CYA in the following areas: general corrections, mental health and substance abuse treatment services, health care services, education, sex offender programs, and disability access (*Farrell v. Tilton*). The experts were jointly selected by the parties. In January and February of 2004 the reports prepared by these experts were released to the plaintiff and the general public. The findings of the reports were very scathing and cited the following inadequacies:

- Excessive violence and a failure to ensure youth and staff safety
- Due process violations in segregation determinations and illegal conditions of confinement in segregation
- Inadequate medical and mental health care
- Lack of training, treatment, and rehabilitation
- Inadequate access to education, substance abuse, and sex offender treatment programs
- Denial of religious rights
- Improper and illegal conditions of confinement with respect to exercise opportunities, physical facilities, visiting and telephone calls, and access to courts
- Lack of access and accommodations for youth with disabilities

The release of these reports in early 2004 was followed by a series of legislative hearings and extensive media coverage on the problems at CYA.

The Approach to Reform in California

It goes without saying that the road to reform has been difficult. In January 2005, just a few months after the consent decree was signed, the parties filed a joint stipulated agreement acknowledging that it would take longer to draft the remedial plans than originally intended. In exchange for an extension of the deadlines, the state agreed to approach the remedial plans from a broader perspective by "reforming California's juvenile system to a rehabilitative model based on a therapeutic environment" (*Farrell v. Tilton*, 2005, p. 1). Nineteen months later, in August 2006, the state filed the last of six remedial plans. The final two plans involved several drafts and review by a panel of national experts. In the meantime, however, the state legislature demonstrated its support by authorizing more than $33 million in fiscal year 2005–2006 and more than $100 million in fiscal year 2006–2007 to implement the *Farrell* remedial plans. According to the California Budget Act of 2005–2006, by the end of the 4-year implementation schedule outlined by DJJ, the cost of the *Farrell* reforms was estimated to be more than $138 million (California Budget Act, 2005–2006).

A March 2006 report by a panel of experts (retained to review part of the state's *Farrell* remedial plans) posed the following question: "Can it be fixed?" The answer was, "Yes. But it will take great effort, money and lots of time. We know of no other state that has undertaken such major reform that has finished in as short a time (4 years) as DJJ proposes" (Murray, Baird, Loughran, Mills, & Platt, 2006, p. 1). The experts were conflicted about whether or not the state should take on the broader juvenile justice continuum issues or focus more specifically on its own house(s) first, as required by the *Farrell* lawsuit. Specifically, the report stated: "A comprehensive juvenile justice reform plan would look at all parts of the system—including probation, juvenile detention, and the relationship between the state and local government. Those issues are beyond the scope of *Farrell* and of this report" (Murray et al., 2006, p. 41).

Ultimately, the state's reform agenda was outlined in six remedial plans that were filed in court. Each plan addressed a particular area of DJJ, including education, health care, mental health care, services for youth with disabilities, sex behavior treatment, and general safety and welfare. None addressed the broader jurisdictional issues affecting the larger juvenile justice continuum in California.[4]

The remedial plans, which represent commitments to the court, include reducing living unit sizes from more than 60–80 youth in some cases to no more than 38 in any one living unit (depending on the type of program, some units would be no larger than 24); providing gender-specific services, including the possibility of placing female offenders in secure placements outside DJJ's facilities; enhancing staffing coverage to improve staff-to-youth ratios (previously close to 1:20 for direct-care staff); separating high- and low-risk (for institutional violence) offenders using objective classification criteria; implementing a validated risk needs assessment to target interventions aimed at reducing each youth's risk to re-offend; improving family involvement in the treatment process; revising the use-of-force policy; ensuring that health and mental health services conform to national standards; and improving access to, and quality of, educational services (among many other commitments).[5]

Implementing an Evidence-Based Treatment Model

A review of the research on "what works" in corrections led California administrators to the principles of effective intervention (Andrews et al., 1990). The basis of these principles is that to best reduce recidivism, objective assessments must be conducted to determine risk of re-offense; criminogenic needs must be targeted to reduce recidivism; resources must be prioritized, placing a greater emphasis on those most likely to re-offend; interventions must be provided in a manner that best meets the needs of the individual youth; staff must be appropriately trained; and quality assurance measures must be in place.

The decision was made to base the treatment/rehabilitative model on those principles, which helped lay the framework for interventions specifically targeting the reduction of criminal behavior and recidivism; however, because California also is responsible for providing medical, educational, mental health, and other services related to a residential population (whether or not the services are related to reduction in recidivism), the agency was required to develop a reform model that facilitated all services and provided necessary guidelines for staff to ensure appropriate and comprehensive services for youth.

The challenge, however, was to develop a model that facilitated multidisciplinary interventions with youth, including staff members from different disciplines working together to develop an overall plan for a youth's success and to create outcome measures that would provide a meaningful picture of the youth's accomplishments. These outcomes not only must be focused on the "usual" negative measures (violations, arrests, convictions), but also must include the positive outcomes, such as ability to obtain and maintain a job, stability on prescribed medications, and involvement in prosocial activities, as also discussed by Guerra and Leaf in Chapter 5.

The Challenges and Scope of Reform

It is far too early to know California's degree of success in reforming its state correctional facilities. Throughout the almost 24 months that the state spent preparing its remedial plans, a number of internal and external policy factors continued to challenge the department. From an internal perspective, one of the most significant challenges was the departmental reorganization that the Youth and Adult Correctional Agency (YACA) underwent with Senate Bill 737 in July 2005. Prior to the reorganization, YACA, like many of the governor's cabinet agencies, was weak. Most of the power rested with the directors of the departments instead of the agency secretary, who had very few staff and little to no direct authority. In the case of YACA, the directors of the California Department of Corrections (the adult prisons and parole) and CYA (the juvenile corrections facilities and parole) had direct authority over their agencies, which were separate and distinct departments.

The reorganization merged many of the administrative functions between these two previously distinct departments, including resources for budget, personnel, accounting, information technology, labor, legal, and communications. Although there has been a great deal of attention from inside and outside the department to ensure the integrity of juvenile justice separate from adult operations, it is difficult to ensure parity between an organization that has more than 170,000 adult inmates and more than 50,000 employees dedicated to adult services with one that houses fewer than 3,000 youth offenders and has fewer than 5,000 employees dedicated to juvenile services.[6]

There is no doubt that implementing reforms at the same time as a major reorganization occurs is going to pose additional challenges to the state's ability to execute its juvenile reform plans in a timely manner. Issues such as recruiting to fill vacant positions and processing contracts for services are bureaucratic challenges that threaten even functioning, stable state agencies.

From an external perspective, the state has had little chance to "catch its breath" since it committed to a new model in January 2005. In December 2005, a few days after the state filed one of its long-awaited plans in court, the plaintiff's attorney stated at a legislative hearing that he "had considered filing a motion to ask that the administration be held in contempt." He cited examples of commitments that had been made earlier that had yet to be implemented (Martin, 2005, p. B-1).

Perhaps more importantly, it is not clear that all of the key stakeholders were ever "on the same page" with respect to their expectations for reform. About midway through the planning process, in May 2005, the state filed a preliminary program description in court, outlining its vision for the new rehabilitative model. An article in the *Los Angeles Times* that same month reported, "Some critics applauded the new direction but said the specifics fall well short of their expectations." One advocate was quoted as saying, "I'd love to be able to say, 'Hurrah, go team!' . . . But we need an extreme makeover, and this isn't it" (Warren, 2005, p. A-1).

As suggested earlier, the State of California purposefully chose to seize the *Farrell* lawsuit as an opportunity for reform. The state could have instead (as others have done) continued to fight the lawsuit and spent taxpayer dollars trying to defend policies and practices that many knew needed to change. The question that may never be answered is: What should have been the focus of the reforms? California had several options. It could have focused specifically on the facilities and services under the state's jurisdiction (the focus of the *Farrell* lawsuit). It could have focused more broadly on the structure of the juvenile justice continuum in California and changed jurisdictional policies, such as who is sent to the state's facilities and how to provide state funding for local services. The most extreme version of this option was illustrated by one state senator's suggestion to shut down the state's facilities altogether and presumably transfer the functions to the county governments. Finally, it could have fought the *Farrell* lawsuit and resisted reforms altogether.

In the early days of the lawsuit, the state was extremely public about its intention to implement sweeping reforms. Governor Schwarzenegger was front and center when the state announced its plan to settle the lawsuit. *The New York Times* quoted, "California is wrong," Mr. Schwarzenegger said. "We make mistakes and therefore we should settle it. . . . We will continue until we repair a system that has been broken for many years" (Murphy, 2004, p. 18). This statement led many to believe that the focus would be on the broader structural issues of the juvenile justice continuum. Over the next 24 months, however, as discussed earlier, the state's planning efforts were focused far more specifically on implementing evidence-based programs in the state's correctional facilities. This is not to suggest that the direction the state took was the wrong one, only to point out that it never quite met external expectations.

Will California's Reforms Be Successful?

To be fair to the administrators of California's juvenile corrections system, the effectiveness of their reforms should be measured only against those policies and practices they sought to reform. These alone, however, are daunting. The six remedial plans filed in court require recruiting hundreds of staff into often difficult-to-fill positions and revising hundreds of small-*p* policies and procedures. The plans promise many long-term changes and many more short-term commitments—some of which the department has already failed to implement on time.

Unfortunately for these administrators, most critics are not going to limit their commentary to the objectives targeted by DJJ. Many of these critics do not want to see youthful offenders locked up in one of the state-run facilities. They will not be satisfied until the facilities themselves are shut down (Anderson, Macallair, & Ramirez, 2005). By the state's own admission, all eight of its facilities need to be replaced. As stated in one of the court's remedial plans, "None of DJJ's existing facilities meets the long-term programmatic needs set forth in this plan" (*Farrell v. Tilton*, 2006). But that, of course, does not mean that the state was committing to shutting down those facilities in the near future.

Should California have taken the leap to shut down its state-run facilities and transfer jurisdiction to county governments? It is difficult to imagine how a state the size of California, with more than 36 million residents, including more than 9 million youth under the age of 18, could not retain some responsibility for youthful offenders—particularly since, as was mentioned before, the state does not provide a stable revenue stream for local probation departments. Still, the idea may not be impossible.

The governor's proposed budget for fiscal year 2007–2008, which was released to the public in January 2007, may be the first indication that state leaders are still considering bolder juvenile justice reforms. If the governor's budget were adopted by the legislature as proposed, the DJJ would stop accepting nonviolent offenders, and county probation departments would receive a certain amount of funding to keep this population under their jurisdiction (Warren, 2007).[7]

Given the political tensions in California around state–local fiscal negotiations and the unknown capacity of county governments to serve this high-risk population at a local level (one might ask why they were sent to the state's facilities in the first place), it is impossible to predict the ultimate outcome. In the meantime, however, those working on the ground (both in headquarters and in the field) to implement the changes to which the state has already committed are going to struggle with how to focus time and resources on small-p policy revisions while the big-P policy issues are still being debated. For example, the state has committed to increasing the amount of time a youth receives direct-treatment services. However, given the current configuration of DJJ's facilities, most living units do not have enough treatment space to provide adequate one-on-one or small-group counseling. Unfortunately, it is going to be very difficult to plan for facility renovations when there is a possibility that DJJ's population may be significantly reduced within the next 12–24 months (a reduction that would most likely result in DJJ having to close some of its existing facilities). Similarly, because the latest proposed policy change could significantly alter the number and demographic of youth housed in the state's secure facilities, DJJ is going to face significant challenges in determining which programs to implement, where to place them, and how many staff members are needed.

There are hundreds of other examples like this one—examples that demonstrate how difficult it is to implement the critical small-p changes when the policy debate continues to focus on the big-P policy debates. Unfortunately, although these big-P policy issues may be "sexier" (much more interesting to discuss) than the narrower policies and procedures that govern a department, the details inherent in the small-p policies are what will make or break an evidence-based model.

Notes

1. Effective July 1, 2005, the Youth and Adult Correctional Agency was reorganized and became the California Department of Corrections and Rehabilitation, pursuant to Statutes 2005, c. 10, Senate Bill 737. As a result of this reorganization, the entity previously known as the California Youth Authority is now the Division of Juvenile Justice.
2. San Francisco County is the only county in California with separate adult and juvenile probation departments.
3. The lawsuit was originally filed as *Farrell v. Harper,* naming Jerry Harper, the director of the California Youth Authority at the time the suit was originally filed, as the defendant. When Harper was replaced by Walter Allen III, the defendant's name was changed. As a result of the state's reorganization in July 2005, the defendant was again changed to Roderick Hickman, the secretary of the California Department of Corrections and Rehabilitation. The current secretary is James E. Tilton, and the defendant's name is expected to change again. Throughout the remainder of the chapter, it will be referred to as the *Farrell* lawsuit.
4. Although, the Safety and Welfare Remedial Plan committed DJJ to develop a statewide juvenile justice operational master plan that would take into account statewide juvenile justice issues. Safety and Welfare Remedial Plan, filed on July 10, 2006, *Farrell v. Tilton,* Superior Court of Alameda County, RG 0379344.
5. All six remedial plans were filed in court and, as such, are part of public record. They can be found at DJJ's website (*www.cdcr.ca.gov/DivisionsBoards/ DJJ/remedial/remedialplans.html*).
6. Retrieved February 2007 from CDCR's website (*www.cdcr.ca.gov/Divisions-Boards/AOAP/FactsFigures.html*) and from DJJ's website (*www.cdcr.ca.gov/ ReportsResearch/summarys.html*).
7. As of July 31, 2007, the California legislature had yet to pass a final budget for fiscal year 2007–2008. However, based on language approved by the Conference Committee on Budget and Fiscal Review, which included three members of the State Senate and three members of the State Assembly, it appears that the legislature may only slightly modify the governor's juvenile justice proposal. Assuming that a two-thirds majority of both houses votes to approve this language and that the governor signs it, courts will no longer be able to commit nonviolent juvenile offenders to the state's Division of Juvenile Justice, effective September 1, 2007. Instead, these youth will remain under the jurisdiction of local probation departments. There are provisions in the bill for counties to receive funding as part of this process (Senate Bill 81, California State Legislature, 2007). We are not sure how to cite a bill that has not yet been chaptered, but here is the internet reference. The final budget act will be available at *www.dof.ca.gov/Budget/Historical_Documents.asp/*.

References

Administrative Office of the Courts and California State Association of Counties.(2005). Probation services task force final report. San Francisco: Author.

Anderson, C., Macallair, D., & Ramirez, C. (2005). California Youth Authority warehouses: Failing kids, families and public safety: Closing the warehouses and creating rehabilitation centers is the solution to the CYA crisis. An issue briefing from *Books Not Bars* and *The Center on Juvenile and Criminal Justice*. Retrieved January 2007 from *www.booksnotbars.org*

Andrews, D. A., Zinger, I., Hoge, R., Bonta, J., Gendreau, P., & Cullen, C. (1990). Does correctional treatment work? A clinically relevant and psychologically informed meta-analysis. *Criminology, 28*(3), 369–404.

California Budget Act of Fiscal Year 2005–2006. Retrieved August 1, 2007, from *www.dof.ca.gov/Budget/Budget_2005-06/Budget_2005-06.asp*

California Department of Justice, Criminal Justice Statistics Center. (2005). *Juvenile justice in California*. Sacramento: Author.

California Statutes 2000, ch. 353, Assembly Bill 1913. Retrieved August 1, 2007 from *info.sen.ca.gov/pub/99-00/bill/asm/ab_1901-1950/ab_1913_bill_20000908_ chaptered. pdf*

California Welfare Code, Section 731(b).

California Youth Authority (2004). Weeklong series of problems, covered by: Brandon Bailey and Karen de Sa, *San Jose Mercury News,* October 17–22, 2004: Scott Smith, Report critical of CYA: System called broken but useful, *Stockton Record,* December 23, 2004; Don Thompson, Close troubled Stockton youth facility, lawmakers urge, *San Francisco Chronicle,* June 20, 2005.

California Department of Juvenile Justice. (2007). Retrieved August 2, 2007, from *www.cdcr.ca.gov/ReportsResearch/summarys.html*

Farrell v. Tilton, *Consent Decree*, Superior Court of Alameda County, RG 03079344.

Farrell v. Tilton, *Safety and Welfare Remedial Plan,* filed on July 10, 2006, Superior Court of Alameda County, RG 03079344.

Farrell v. Tilton, *Stipulated Agreement*, filed on January 31, 2005, Superior Court of Alameda County, RG 03079344.

Garcia, E. (2005, December 6). Senator threatens prison budget: Critic of juvenile system rips reform plan. *San Jose Mercury News,* p. A-1.

Griffin, P., & King, M. (2006). National overviews. *State juvenile justice profiles.* Pittsburgh, PA: National Center for Juvenile Justice. Retrieved February 10, 2007, from *www.ncjj.org/stateprofiles*

King, M., & Szymanski, L. (2006). National overviews. *State juvenile justice profiles.* Pittsburgh, PA: National Center for Juvenile Justice. Retrieved February 10, 2007, from *www.ncjj.org/stateprofiles*

Krauth, B., & Linke, L. (1999). State organizational structures for the delivery of probation services (June 1999). Cited in *Probation Services Task Force Final Report,* June 2003, Administrative Office of the Courts and California State

Association of Counties, p. 61. Complete copy of Final Report available at *www2.courtinfo.ca.gov/probation*

Martin, M. (2005, December 6). Juvenile justice back in spotlight: State senator says governor's inaction part of the problem. *San Francisco Chronicle*, p. B-1.

Murphy, D. E. (2004, November 17). California settles lawsuit on juvenile prisons. *New York Times*, p. A-18.

Murray, C., Baird C., Loughran, N., Mills F., & Platt, J. (2006, March 31). Safety and welfare plan: Implementing reform in California. pp. 1, 41. Retrieved January 2007 from *www.prisonlaw.com/pdfs/DJJSafetyPlan.pdf*

National Center for Juvenile Justice. (2006). California: State juvenile justice profiles. Pittsburgh, PA: Author. Retrieved August 1, 2007, from *ncjj.org/stateprofiles*

Warren, J. (2005, May 16). State to detail reform of CYA: Intensive therapy and education would replace a punitive culture in California's youth penal system under the terms of a lawsuit settlement. *Los Angeles Times*, p. xxx.

Warren, J. (2007, January 15). Governor seeks to transfer juvenile offenders: His plan, now before the legislature, would ship about half the state's young inmates to county lockups by mid-2008. *Los Angeles Times*, p. B-1.

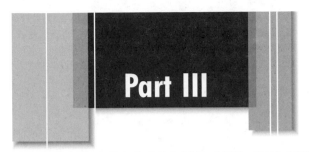

Part III

TREATMENT PROGRAMS AND POLICIES
FOR SPECIFIC OFFENDING GROUPS

Chapter 7

Treatment of Violent Offenders

Paul Boxer
Paul J. Frick

Although juvenile offenders are incarcerated for a variety of violent and nonviolent offenses, violent offenders represent a sizeable proportion of the adjudicated youth population. According to the 2006 report from the U.S. Office of Juvenile Justice and Delinquency Prevention (OJJDP) on juvenile offenders and victims, about 34% of youth remanded to secure custody are adjudicated for crimes against persons (Snyder & Sickmund, 2006). Approximately two-thirds of this interpersonally aggressive subgroup perpetrated at least one offense categorized as violent by the U.S. Federal Bureau of Investigation. The 2006 report of the OJJDP also confirms that, on average, youth incarcerated for crimes against persons spend more time in secure custody than do youth incarcerated for property, drug, public order, technical violation, or status offenses. Thus there is a clear need for guidelines for the management and treatment of aggressive and violent behavior in juvenile offenders.

In this chapter we review the current state of knowledge on youth violence, with attention to the theoretically specified internal processes thought to maintain violent behavior. We then consider contemporary views on effective interventions for this problem. Finally, we place this discussion in the broader framework of aggression and violence prevention and treatment to consider how practitioners and researchers might best work with violent youth. In line with contemporary views on the development and dissemination of validated "best practice" treatment approaches in clinical child and adolescent psychology (Boxer & Frick, in press; Silverman, 2006), we focus on the theoretical and empirical underpinnings of effective strategies to derive guidelines and suggestions for specific tactics in addressing violent behavior.

Definitional and Theoretical Issues

It is important to clarify a few terms used in this chapter. First, we note that we are considering specifically the treatment or modification of violent behavior, not antisocial or delinquent behavior construed more broadly. Second, although the terms "aggression" and "violence" have been applied interchangeably in the past, when considered more precisely they are not interchangeable, and we deal here principally with *violence.* As elaborated elegantly by Anderson and colleagues (2003), *aggression* may be viewed as an umbrella construct subsuming a variety of acts that share only the fact that they are committed with the intent to harm (i.e., injure or irritate) another person. Thus aggression is indicated by physical acts, such as slapping and kicking, as well as verbal acts, such as teasing or threatening, and relational acts, such as gossip and ostracism. *Violence* involves only aggressive acts that are physical in nature and that result in, or potentially result in, serious physical injury. As a hallmark example, the FBI defines "violent crime" as homicide, forcible rape, robbery, or aggravated assault. These crimes involve an unambiguous use of intentional injury or physical force.

Aggression and violence might be viewed along a continuum of severity ranging from relatively mild acts, such as teasing and pushing, to violent acts, such as beatings and weapon use. Indeed, some research supports the notion that violent youth offenders progress through a pathway of escalation that begins with mild aggression in childhood and continues to violence in adolescence (Loeber & Stouthamer-Loeber, 1998). Some degree of physical aggression appears to be normative. For example, the U.S. Centers for Disease Control and Prevention (CDC) typically find, in their biennial Youth Risk Behavior Surveillance Studies, that about one-third of high schoolers are involved in physical fights during a calendar year (see *www.cdc.gov/ yrbs*).

Given these findings, it can be tempting to view the escalation to violent behavior as a fairly linear process whereby youth offenders represent the extreme end of a continuum in the population of youth who engage in antisocial behavior. However, there is evidence to suggest that some youth commit a significant proportion of the most violent and aggressive acts and appear to differ from the general population and other youth with conduct problems on a number of risk factors (Frick, 2006; Moffitt, 2006). These youth have been referred to as the "early-starter" or "childhood-onset" subgroup, due to the finding that their pattern of highly aggressive behavior begins early in childhood and often persists into adolescence (Hinshaw, Lahey, & Hart, 1993; Patterson, Capaldi, & Bank, 1991). Moffitt (1993; 2006) labeled these individuals as the "life-course persistent" subgroup, based on longitudinal data demonstrating the tendency for early-starting aggression to continue beyond adolescence. Loeber, Farrington, and colleagues, in concert with official categorizations by OJJDP, refer to youth in this category as "serious, violent, and chronic" or "persistent serious" delinquents (Loeber & Farrington, 1998; Stouthamer-Loeber, Loeber, Wei, Farrington, & Wikström, 2002).

As noted above, youth categorized as demonstrating "childhood-onset," "life-course," or "persistent" antisocial behavior possess a large number of risk factors differentiating them from other youth who show conduct problems (for reviews, see Frick, 2006; Moffitt, 2006; Raine, 2002). These risk factors are remarkable not only for their sheer number but also for the great diversity in type. These risk factors include neurochemical (e.g., low serotonin) and autonomic (e.g., low resting heart rate) irregularities, neurocognitive deficits (e.g., in executive functioning), deficits in the processing of social information (e.g., hostile attributional bias), temperamental vulnerabilities (e.g., poor emotion regulation), and personality predispositions (e.g., impulsivity). In addition to these dispositional factors, at least as many contextual factors have been associated with early-onset violence. These include factors in the prenatal (e.g., exposure to toxins), early child care (e.g., poor quality), family (e.g., ineffective discipline), peer (e.g., association with deviant peers), neighborhood (e.g., high exposure to violence in the community), and media (e.g., heavy consumption of violent television and video games) contexts.

Callous–Unemotional Traits

There is general agreement on the importance of designating children with childhood-onset conduct problems as a group at particular risk for severe aggression and violence. However, there also is emerging evidence that a further distinction may be important as well (Frick,

2006). That is, one subgroup of children who begin showing conduct problems prior to adolescence also show callous–unemotional (CU) traits. Youth who rate high on measures of CU traits are those who tend to lack guilt and remorse and who show a lack of empathy (Frick, Bodin, & Barry, 2000; Essau, Sasagawa, & Frick, 2006).

Antisocial youth who also exhibit high levels of CU traits engage in more serious violence, show more pervasive patterns of violence, and have lengthier and more persistent histories of aggression and violence (e.g., Caputo, Frick, & Brodsky, 1999; Kruh, Frick, & Clements, 2005; Lynam, 1997; Salekin, Leistico, Neumann, DiCicco, & Duros, 2004). Importantly, their violence tends to include both reactive (i.e., in response to real or perceived provocations) and instrumental (i.e., in order to obtain some perceived reward) varieties (Frick et al., 2003; Kruh et al., 2005). Further, treatment studies have produced results suggesting that incarcerated youth displaying CU traits can be disruptive and even physically aggressive during treatment, and make less progress overall during treatment, compared to youth without those characteristics (e.g., Rogers, Johansen, Chang, & Salekin, 1997; Spain, Douglas, Poythress, & Epstein, 2004). However, recent findings also underscore the fact that high scores on measures of CU traits are not always associated with poor treatment effects (e.g., Caldwell, Skeem, Salekin, & Van Rybroek, 2006).

Thus the presence of CU traits seems to designate a particularly severe and difficult—yet not impossible to treat—group of violent youth. These traits also may be a marker for a group of children who have different causal processes leading to their behavioral problems, and these differences could contribute to the difficulties in finding the most effective interventions for them (see Frick, 2006; Frick & Morris, 2004, for reviews). For example, antisocial behavior seems to have a stronger genetic influence when the child also shows high levels of CU traits (Viding, Blair, Moffitt, & Plomin, 2005; Viding, Jones, Frick, Moffitt, & Plomin, in press). Further, other studies have shown that CU traits are associated with fearlessness (Pardini, 2006), thrill and adventure seeking (Frick et al., 2003; Frick, Lilienfeld, Ellis, Loney, & Silverthorn, 1999), lower levels of anxiety (Frick et al., 1999; Frick et al., 2003; Lynam et al., 2005), reduced sensitivity to cues of punishment (Fisher & Blair, 1998; Frick et al., 2003; O'Brien & Frick, 1996; Pardini, Lochman, & Frick, 2003), and reduced reactivity to threatening and emotionally distressing stimuli (Blair, 1999; Frick et al., 2003; Kimonis, Frick, Fazekas, & Loney, 2006; Loney, Frick, Clements, Ellis, & Kerlin, 2003).

The findings described in the preceding paragraph have been interpreted to suggest that youth with CU traits appear to have a temperamental style associated with reduced levels of emotional reactivity that could place them, as children, at risk for missing some of the early precursors to empathic concern, which involve emotional arousal evoked by the misfortune and distress of others (Blair, 1999; Frick & Morris, 2004). Also, this temperament style could lead these children to be relatively insensitive to the prohibitions and sanctions of parents and other socializing agents (Frick & Morris, 2004; Kochanska, 1993). Finally, it could create an interpersonal style in which these children become so focused on the potential rewards and gains of aggression that they ignore the potentially harmful effects of this behavior on themselves and others. For example, antisocial and delinquent youth who show CU traits are less distressed by the negative effects of their behavior on others (Pardini et al., 2003), are more impaired in their moral reasoning and empathic concern toward others (Blair, 1999; Pardini et al., 2003), and more predatory in their violence than antisocial youth without these traits (Caputo et al., 1999; Kruh et al., 2005).

Importantly, CU traits are typically found in only a minority of youth with childhood-onset antisocial behavior (e.g., Christian, Frick, Hill, Tyler, & Frazer, 1997) or adolescent violence (Kruh et al., 2005). Further, children with childhood-onset conduct problems who do not have these traits also can be at risk for aggression and violence (Frick et al., 2003; Kruh et al., 2005), but to a less severe degree and confined to reactive forms of aggression. Further, youths with childhood-onset conduct problems but without CU traits are more highly reactive to emotional and threatening stimuli (Kimonis et al., 2006; Loney et al., 2003) and are more distressed by the negative effects of their behavior on themselves and others (Frick et al., 1999; Pardini et al., 2003). Also, their aggressive behavior is associated more strongly with dysfunctional parenting practices (Oxford, Cavell, & Hughes, 2003; Wootton, Frick, Shelton, & Silverthorn, 1997) and with deficits in intelligence (Loney, Frick, Ellis, & McCoy, 1998).

These findings suggest that aggressive and violent youth who do not show high rates of CU traits may have difficulties with behavioral and emotional regulation related to high levels of emotional reactivity. Such poor emotional regulation can result from a number of interacting causal factors, such as inadequate socialization in their rearing environments, deficits in intelligence that make it difficult for them to delay gratification and anticipate consequences, or temperamental problems in response inhibition (Frick & Morris, 2004). The problems in emotional regulation can lead to impulsive aggressive acts for which the child may be remorseful afterward, but which he or she still has difficulty controlling. They can also lead to a higher susceptibility to anger due to perceived provocations from peers, catalyzing violent and aggressive acts within the context of high emotional arousal (Kruh et al., 2005).

General Approach to Treatment

Taken together, the findings discussed above suggest that there is a subgroup of antisocial youth who show a childhood-onset to their antisocial behavior and who seem to show the highest rates of violence and aggression. Further, even within this group, there seem to be distinct subgroups based on the presence or absence of CU traits. Both groups have multiple risk factors associated with their violent behavior. However, the types of risk factors seem to be different across groups, and this difference is consistent with different causal processes leading to their violent behavior. This general model leads to two general but important implications for interventions for violent youth (Boxer & Frick, in press; Frick, 2006). First, it suggests that interventions need to be comprehensive, addressing multiple risk factors to be effective. Second, the interventions need to be individualized to address the unique causal and maintenance factors across groups.

Such a model of intervention is exemplified by the multicomponent, community-based interventions delivered simultaneously through programs such as the well-validated multisystemic therapy (MST; Henggeler, Schoenwald, Borduin, Rowland, & Cunningham, 1998) or similar comprehensive treatment plans, such as the plans outlined by Borum and Verhaagen (2006). Recent research on MST, for example, has shown that the effects of this approach on preventing recidivism on violent youth offenders can be sustained, on average, about 14 years beyond treatment (Schaefer & Borduin, 2005). However, with violent youth offenders this sort of multimodal, community-based strategy might not always be practicable. Because MST and similar approaches generally require involvement of parents, schools, and other community agents, implementation during incarceration often is difficult.

Furthermore, MST and similar approaches involve the intensive application of parenting strategies to enhance monitoring and appropriate discipline. As noted previously, violent offenders who exhibit CU traits and who tend to the show the longest and most serious history of offending, might be less likely to respond to this style of intervention because their behaviors are less strongly linked to dysfunctional parenting practices. Although not with a violent youth offender sample, Hawes and Dadds (2005) recently explored the moderating effects of CU traits on treatment response in parenting skills intervention. Their sample was comprised of boys ages 4 to 9 referred to a mental health clinic for conduct problems. These authors reported that children with CU traits showed a less overall positive response to this treatment than other children with conduct problems. However, this differential effectiveness was not consistently found across all phases of the treatment. That is, children with and without these traits seemed to respond equally well to the first part of the intervention that focused on teaching parents methods of using positive reinforcement to encourage prosocial behavior. In contrast, only the group without CU traits showed added improvement with the second part of the intervention that focused on teaching parents more effective discipline strategies.

Person-Level Mediation of Violence: The Social–Cognitive Information-Processing View

As noted, MST and similar best-practice approaches involve multiple components, but routinely include some form of treatment that targets individual factors and most often via a fairly standard cognitive-behavioral approach (Borum & Verhaagen, 2006; Boxer & Frick, in press). Although family therapy, school monitoring, and probation monitoring are designed to promote internal changes through the modification of external conditions, they are indirect methods. We now turn our discussion to the issue of the individual- or person-level mediating mechanisms that are thought to maintain aggressive and violent patterns of behavior.

As mentioned earlier and discussed in other sections of this volume, within the social–ecological model of antisocial behavior development, a number of environmental conditions and dispositional characteristics are theorized to augment risk for engagement in antisocial behavior. Community conditions such as violence, crime, and poverty are linked positively to antisocial responding, as are family conditions such as interparental conflict and child physical abuse. Low IQ or related intellectual problems, sensation-seeking, impulsivity, and CU traits are fairly stable dispositional tendencies also associated with antisocial responding. These contextual and individual risk factors set the foundation for the development of aggressive and violent behavior by providing models and opportunities for observational and direct learning of aggressive responses, and increasing the risk that a youth will be exposed to those models and opportunities.

Theoretically, however, these risk factors lead to habitual patterns of aggressive and violent behavior, particularly from later childhood and into adolescence, through their influence on the development of a social–cognitive information-processing (SCIP) style (Crick & Dodge, 1994; Dodge, 2006; Huesmann, 1988, 1998). The SCIP style is an internal mediating system that links dispositional and contextual inputs to aggressive behavioral outputs (Boxer & Dubow, 2002). The SCIP framework has been the dominant theoretical framework, for many years, used to explain habitually aggressive and violent behavior, and it asserts broadly that the way youth process social information is central in the persistence of aggression. According to this theory, over time and across situations the process by which a youth initially attends to and interprets environmental cues, searches for and evaluates potential behavioral responses, and then evaluates the consequences of the chosen responses determines whether the specific behavior enacted will become an enduring style of behavioral response. In social-conflict situations, SCIP processes will account for chosen responses to conflict or provocation (e.g., reactive forms of aggressive responding); in nonconflictual or nonsocial situations, SCIP processes will provide the repertoire and rationale for chosen behaviors (e.g., proactively aggressive responding).

Within the SCIP framework, specific behavioral response patterns are represented as mental "scripts," which are cognitive structures "laying out the sequence of events that one believes are likely to happen and the behaviors that one believes are possible or appropriate for a particular situation" (Huesmann, 1998, p. 80). Developmental research has shown that aggression-supporting SCIP styles—for example, believing that it is "okay" to behave aggressively—become crystallized and begin to predict behavior reliably during the middle childhood years (e.g., ages 6–9; Huesmann & Guerra, 1997). SCIP styles subsume moral reasoning structures, which—for antisocial adolescents and adjudicated offenders, in particular—permit the use of aggression in a variety of situations (Tisak, Tisak, & Goldstein, 2006).

Both Huesmann (1988, 1998) and Crick and Dodge (1994) have offered detailed stepwise schematics for explaining the process through which situational cues (both internal, e.g., arousal, and external, e.g., provocation) lead to aggressive or violent behaviors. SCIP processes may be classed within three categories (Boxer, Goldstein, Musher-Eizenman, Dubow, & Heretick, 2005): (1) interpreting the causes of situational events; (2) generating and selecting appropriate behaviors to enact; and (3) interpreting and evaluating the consequences of the chosen behaviors.

Interpreting the Causes of Situational Events

According to Dodge (2006), how an individual attributes the causes of an event is a fundamental first step in determining whether the individual ultimately will behave violently. Research by Dodge and others (see Orobio de Castro, Veerman, Koops, Bosch, & Monshouwer, 2002, for a meta-analytic review) has demonstrated quite conclusively that aggressive youth are predisposed to interpret others' intentions in a hostile manner. Laboratory and field-based research studies have shown that when presented with some form of ambiguous social provocation (e.g., being bumped in a school corridor by a peer), aggressive youth tend to attribute the cause of the event to hostile intent on the part of the actor. That is, they tend to display a hostile attributional bias. Dodge (2006) asserts that the propensity to react aggressively to any form of provocation, intentional or otherwise, is fairly universal and evident early in life. Through the course of normal development and typical socialization, which includes acquiring the capacity to infer correctly the intentions, beliefs, and desires of others, children eventually assume benign attributional biases—in the face of ambiguity, they tend to give others the benefit of the doubt. Hostile biases that persist beyond early childhood are viewed as the product not only of preexisting tendencies toward impulsive responding but also of a socialization failure born from experiences with, for example, physical abuse and intensive exposure to aggressive models (Dodge, Bates, & Pettit, 1990).

The link between hostile attributional styles and aggressive behavior is supported by research showing that in comparison to non-aggressive peers, aggressive youth attend selectively to aggressive environmental cues (Gouze, 1987) and to fewer cues overall (Dodge & Newman, 1981). Importantly, there also is research to suggest that this hostile attributional style is largely correlated only with reactive, and not proactive or instrumental, forms of aggressive responding (Nas, Orobio de Castro, & Koops, 2005; Schwartz et al., 1998). Similarly, this response style has been observed only in youth with childhood-onset problems who do not show CU traits and who seem to show problems regulating their emotions (Frick et al., 2003). This finding is consistent with Dodge and Somberg's (1987) observation that hostile biases are more likely to be engaged under conditions of elevated emotional arousal. Arousal is a critically important cue during social situations; negative arousal (e.g., anger) is a key determinant of an aggressive response (Berkowitz, 1998). Thus, although hostile biases might not be relevant for all violence by youth offenders, they represent internal processes that augment violence risk in social interactions.

Generating and Selecting Appropriate Behaviors to Enact

As many have observed (see Tremblay, 2000), aggressive behavior begins early in life but only persists in a small subgroup of the population. With respect to the learning and internalization of aggressive scripts, this observation implies the following for youth who go on to become violent offenders: (1) through observational and direct learning, they have been reinforced over and over for employing aggression and violence as social problem-solving strategies (i.e., for accessing and implementing aggressive scripts); and/or (2) they have experienced a failure to learn, and therefore be reinforced for, nonaggressive and prosocial social problem-solving strategies (i.e., lack or relative lack of nonaggressive scripts). Studies have demonstrated that relative to nonaggressive youth, aggressive youth are more likely to offer aggressive strategies in response to hypothetical conflict situations (Dubow & Reid, 1994; Tisak & Tisak, 1996); mental rehearsal or fantasizing about engaging in aggressive behavior also is associated with a greater likelihood of aggressive responding (Eron, 2001). These findings suggest that aggressive youth, relative to nonaggressive youth, possess a mental–behavioral repertoire dominated by aggressive solutions to social problems, which is reinforced through actual as well as imagined engagement.

Following SCIP theory, however, a problem-solving style consisting primarily of aggressive responses is not sufficient for producing aggressive responses. Once a youth identifies a potential response to enact, it must be evaluated as acceptable to the situation. Three broad criteria have been shown to define this process: (1) is it appropriate? (i.e., normative beliefs; e.g., Huesmann & Guerra, 1997); (2) will it achieve the desired outcome? (i.e., outcome expectancies; e.g., Egan, Monson, & Perry, 1998); and (3) can it be done? (i.e., self-efficacy; Erdley & Asher, 1996). For all of these criteria, researchers have documented that aggressive youth, in comparison to nonaggressive peers, maintain evaluative styles supportive of aggressive responding. Aggressive youth tend to approve of aggression and violence as a response to provocation and as a general behavioral strategy (Crane-Ross, Tisak, & Tisak, 1998; Huesmann & Guerra, 1997); they tend to expect positive outcomes from aggressive actions (Egan et al., 1998; Smithmyer, Hubbard, & Simons, 2000); and they tend to see themselves as capable of successfully enacting aggressive actions (Erdley & Asher, 1996; Perry, Kusel, & Perry, 1988).

Interestingly, in contrast to what has been observed with respect to hostile biases, evaluative aspects of aggressive cognitive processing have been shown to correlate primarily with proactive, and not reactive, forms of aggressive responding (Crick & Dodge, 1996; Smithmyer et al., 2000). This finding is consistent with the more planful and reward-oriented nature of proactively aggressive behavior. In a sample of adolescent offenders, it was only youth high on CU traits who tended to emphasize the positive aspects of aggressive responses and minimize potential consequences to these behaviors (Pardini et al., 2003). Thus, as was the case with hostile attributions, problems at the evaluative stage of SCIP only seem to characterize certain violent youth, albeit a different group from those who tend to exhibit hostile attributions.

Interpreting and Evaluating the Consequences of the Chosen Behaviors

Following Huesmann (1998), this aspect of SCIP is critical to explaining how aggressive and violent behavior is maintained even in the context of strong sanctions (e.g., school expulsion, incarceration). The research reviewed earlier on developmental trends in youth violence suggests that this aspect of SCIP processing is central in considering violent responding among severe and persistent violent youth offenders. As discussed previously, the presence of CU traits in some violent youth suggests that they are predisposed to feel emotionally detached and uncaring with respect to the inter- and intrapersonal consequences of their aggressive actions (see Pardini et al., 2003). Aggressive youth also have been shown to value the rewards of violence (e.g., controlling their victims) and to devalue the punishing consequences of violence (e.g., the suffering of victims) more than do nonaggressive youth (Boldizar, Perry, & Perry, 1989). Musher-Eizenman et al. (2004) observed a positive association between aggression and a disregard for the consequences of hypothetical aggressive actions.

This step of SCIP deals with how youth consider the impact and consequences of their behaviors. For example, just with respect to observable outcomes of behavior, the youth who physically assaults a peer will experience a variety of consequences. He or she may see the victim struggling with pain or injury; he or she may see shock, horror, awe, or approval on the facial expressions of bystanders; he or she may ultimately be punished by parents, school officials, or law enforcement officials. Internally, the youth might experience pain or injury, physiological arousal, fear, or even satisfaction. The issue here is the extent to which the youth interprets these experiences as punishing or rewarding. Although an underlying element of callousness and unemotionality sets the stage for a cognitive reaction to violence as less punishing (e.g., violent youth with CU traits will be less likely to experience guilt over their own actions or compassion for their victims; Frick & Morris, 2004), the SCIP framework provides evidence to explain how aggressive and violent behavior can be interpreted as rewarding.

Treatment Implications of the SCIP Framework

As Boxer and colleagues have highlighted (Boxer & Butkus, 2005; Boxer & Dubow, 2002; Guerra, Boxer, & Kim, 2005), targeting individual process-level aspects of violent behavior ideally should occur in the context of broader modifications to a youth's social ecology. Following Guerra and colleagues in Chapter 4, and as mentioned briefly above, this is consistent with a general best-practice approach that attempts to address multiple risk factors when working with youth offenders. Still, highly controlled and research-based multicomponent approaches, similar to those comprising MST and other validated programs, are uncommon for a variety of reasons—for example, adopting and appropriately implementing such programs over time can be costly with respect to human and financial resources (Boxer & Dubow, 2002). As pointed out by Henggeler and Lee (2003), despite a wealth of efficacy and effectiveness evidence supporting its use, MST reaches only about 1% of youth at risk for incarceration.

At the same time, it seems quite reasonable to assume that regardless of the broader program or strategy being applied (e.g., employment training, academic remediation, group counseling), violent youth offenders who engage in some form of rehabilitative treatment during incarceration, under postrelease supervision, or in the context of diversion services are going to come into contact with therapeutic activities designed to modify individual-level processes. In this section, we consider how contemporary research on SCIP can be applied to address those processes. In so doing, we describe intervention activities derived from the SCIP approach and include examples from extant effective programs that incorporate those or similar tactics.

Modifying Attributional Tendencies and Improving Arousal Control

As described, an aggressive SCIP style involves attention to and interpretation of internal and external cues that support aggressive responding. This aspect of SCIP appears to be most relevant for reactively aggressive behavior displayed by youth without CU traits who have problems regulating their emotional responses, in comparison to the proactively aggressive behavior found in youth who are high on CU traits. Thus, intervention activities targeting this component of the SCIP model should have two goals: (1) reduce tendencies to attribute hostile intent in situations where intent is otherwise ambiguous, or promoting benign attributional biases; and (2) improve behavioral control over cognitive and emotional reactions to provocations.

Some of the best-researched and efficacious work on reducing youths' tendencies to engage in hostile bias has been conducted by Hudley and colleagues (Hudley et al., 1998; Hudley & Graham, 1993). Their "BrainPower Program," developed primarily as a selected prevention program for aggressive students in late elementary school grades, consists of several activities designed to modify the ways in which youth interpret social situations. Program activities are organized around three components: improving the interpretation of intentions (i.e., properly "reading" and categorizing different physical and verbal cues), increasing the linking of negative outcomes to accidental causes, and increasing the likelihood of responding to ambiguous provocations with nonaggressive behaviors. Most activities revolve around the presentation of different provocation situations, "brainstorming" about all reasons potentially underlying the provocations, and role-playing methods of handling those provocations.

Hudley's program emphasizes the reprocessing of external, environmental cues that might provoke aggressive responses. Of course, as noted earlier, internal cues—that is, negative forms of emotional arousal—also are critical. Reducing the effect of negative arousal on aggressive responding is subsumed by two interlocking components: reducing the impact of aggressive external cues on negative arousal (i.e., counterconditioning) and improving arousal management skills (e.g., anger control). The Coping Power Program (also, in some iterations, referred to as the Anger Coping Program), developed by Lochman and colleagues (e.g., Lochman & Wells, 2002; Lochman, Lampron, Gemmer, & Harris, 1987), also includes activities designed to help youth prevent the negative emotional responses associated with provocation. In one part of a "taunting game," treatment participants practice skills of ignoring to maintain calm while they are taunted verbally by others in the treatment group. The recipients of the taunts must attempt to remember a set of 10 numbers and stack a set of dominoes one-handed during 5-second blocks of provocation. Although careful supervision is warranted during this activity with aggressive youth (Boxer & Dubow, 2002), it can be an excellent counterconditioning strategy for uncoupling arousal-inducing situations from intense negative emotional reactions.

Preventing negative arousal in the face of provocation is ideal but certainly not always tenable. Thus it is critical for violent youth to have skills for managing negative arousal (e.g., anger) when it occurs. A "gold standard" for many years in the field for this task has been the general anger management approach exemplified in programs such as aggression replacement training (ART; Goldstein, Glick, & Gibbs, 1998), which includes Feindler's anger control training (e.g., Feindler,

1995). A major focus of anger control training is assisting youth to enact behaviors that will help them reduce the anger and associated negative arousal they might feel as the result of encountering external (e.g., verbal provocation) or internal (e.g., anger-promoting self-talk) "triggers" to anger. For example, treatment participants are taught three specific tactics for reducing anger: deep breathing, backward counting, and pleasant imagery. Participants are further challenged to generate self-talk statements also designed to help them reduce arousal (e.g., "Stay cool"; Boxer & Butkus, 2005).

Learning and Accepting Nonaggressive and Prosocial Behavioral Alternatives

The goal of Goldstein et al.'s (1998) ART approach is literally to "replace" aggressive responding with nonaggressive or prosocial responding. This task can be accomplished in part through the anger-control training described above, whereby youth learn to replace violent responses to anger with nonaggressive arousal control strategies. However, as described, angry, emotional aggression (i.e., reactive aggression) is only one type of aggression common in violent youth offenders, and negative arousal is neither necessary nor sufficient for producing an aggressive response.

As noted previously, youth who engage in proactive, instrumental forms of aggression are more likely to show CU traits and, thus, their aggressive behavior does not appear to be due to emotional undercontrol but rather more related to emotional detachment. However, this group views aggression as a means of goal attainment and social problem solving. ART includes a component implemented as a behavioral skills training module emphasizing role play, frequent practice, and overcorrection for developing new behaviors. Still, part of what is necessary to shape nonaggressive, prosocial behavioral styles for violent youth is increasing the cognitive accessibility of newly learned and nonviolent scripts. It is one thing to engage in intensive practice through role playing in the relative safety of an individual or group therapy session, but quite another to implement nonviolent behaviors in everyday situations. Many programs derived from the general SCIP model include "brainstorming" sessions designed to encourage participants to engage in alternative thinking in the context of potentially problematic situations (e.g., Guerra & Slaby, 1990; Lochman et al., 1987). Youth repeatedly are encouraged to generate as many nonaggressive solutions as possible in response to provocative scenarios, with the aim of promoting easier mental acquisition of those scripts.

A critical aspect of training new behavioral responses is convincing violent offenders to "buy in" to the idea of behaving in non-aggressive and prosocial ways. Despite the fact that offenders have experienced significant negative outcomes as the result of violence (e.g., incarceration; physical injury to self or others), offenders may still net a good deal of gain from a violent behavioral style. For example, developmental research has demonstrated that some aggressive youth are popular among their agemates (e.g., Rodkin, Farmer, Pearl, & Van Acker, 2000). Aggressive youth who also are popular have been shown to benefit less from targeted prevention programs than aggressive youth who are unpopular (Boxer, Huesmann, & Hanish, 2004). Violent youth also tend to have entrenched beliefs supporting aggression as a strategy for maintaining respect in their peer group (Slaby & Guerra, 1988). Further, Frick (2006) has proposed that one of the most difficult aspects of treating youth with CU traits is the difficulty in motivating them to employ new skills and use different behaviors.

Given those observations, it is important for intervention programs to include activities designed to modify directly the attitudes and beliefs that support aggressive responding. This goal can be accomplished, in part, by fostering consequential thinking skills that can aid youth in mentally anticipating and evaluating potential behavioral responses, and in considering both the short- and long-term outcomes of their behaviors (Guerra & Slaby, 1990). "Attitude-change" activities derived from social psychological research also can work in the service of this goal (Huesmann, Eron, Klein, Brice, & Fisher, 1983). For example, youth can be challenged to role-play "counselors" and convince actual counselors, role-playing as "students," that violent responding is wrong or ineffectual (Boxer, 2001). Goldstein et al.'s (1998) ART program includes a moral reasoning education component, based on moral development theory, in which youth debate pros and cons of various behavioral responses in different "problem situations."

Another difficult target for clinicians working with incarcerated youth is helping them to attend to the long-term, rather than short-term, consequences of their actions. Program activities targeting consequential thinking skills aim to enhance youths' abilities to anticipate the outcomes of provocative or problematic situations (e.g., Guerra & Slaby, 1990), but often these sorts of activities focus only on potential immediate or short-term outcomes. For example, in ART's moral reasoning education component, one scenario presented to participants involves a youth cajoling his friend to steal a car with him and take a joyride. The questions intended for participants to review with the facilitator emphasize the potential for short-term detrimental consequences (e.g., the perpetrator might have a family who would suffer if he were caught), but do not consider the longer view. It is important for violent youth to engage in consequential thinking activities designed to highlight the potential for long-term negative outcomes of violent responding, even in the face of short-term benefits.

In Boxer's STOP and GO Program (Boxer, 2001; Boxer & Butkus, 2005; Boxer, Dubow, Fiedler, & Fiedler, 2000),[1] participants are challenged to expand the "timelines" of their behavior to anticipate longer-term outcomes. For example, participants begin with a hypothetical scenario of angry provocation and are guided from short-term gains of aggression (e.g., "feeling tough") to long-term negative consequences (e.g., "self-harm" or "jail"). Going along with this type of activity, participants are required to develop longer-term positive goals for themselves, such as completing high school, finding stable employment, or establishing a family. They then are encouraged to discuss how aggressive and violent behavior, even though it might yield short-term benefits, can interfere with progress toward desired goals.

Modifying Individual–Ecological Transactions

The ideal violence prevention or intervention program based on contemporary SCIP and developmental–ecological theory would be able to implement and maintain changes at all levels of a youth's everyday ecology (Boxer & Dubow, 2002; Guerra et al., 2005), partially with the aim of making ecological responses to aggression consistent across contexts. This notion is a central premise of multilevel, multicomponent approaches to reducing and preventing violence, such as MST. Following SCIP, however, even in a multilevel approach, some effort must be devoted to modifying the ways a youth responds to the environmental contingencies of his or her aggressive behaviors. As discussed earlier, in comparison to nonaggressive youth, some aggressive youth (i.e., those high on CU traits) tend to value more the potential rewards of violence (e.g., dominance), devalue the potential punishers of violence (e.g., victim suffering), and be less concerned about the potential negative consequences of aggression.

Multilevel approaches are important for dealing with this aspect of SCIP because in order to promote the development of nonaggressive or even prosocial environmental interpretation, it is necessary to foster more prosocial behavioral norms in families, peer groups, and communities. It is also imperative that youth care about the impact that his or her behavior has on others in his or her ecology. Thus an important component of altering youths' evaluations of the consequences of their behavior is to improve the quality of their relationships with primary caregivers and other important people in their lives (e.g., siblings, teachers). The MST design includes a variety of opportunities for this sort of work, given that it requires involvement from caretakers and other family members in addition to school personnel involved with the target youth. Of course, for incarcerated violent offenders, it might only be possible to improve relationships with salient others indirectly, during individual therapy discourse about relationships or during family visits. Functional Family Therapy (FFT; Alexander et al., 1998), another best-practice approach for offenders discussed in Chapter 4, also affords opportunities for enhancing family relationships, but again might not be tenable for incarcerated youth.

SCIP and Best Practices for Treating Violent Youth Offenders

Many if not all of the best-practice recommendations outlined by Guerra and colleagues in Chapter 4 of this volume can be applied to treating violent youth offenders: for example, programs should be comprehensive (i.e., reducing risk and enhancing protection across multiple social–ecological levels), intensive (e.g., high dosage, close supervision), and delivered by well-trained professionals. These practice recommendations are consistent with research and policy summaries on reducing youth violence by public health directorates such as the U.S. National Institutes of Health (NIH; 2004) and the CDC (Thornton, Craft, Dahlberg, Lynch, & Baer, 2000).

With specific regard to dealing with violent youth offenders, we propose an infusion of the principles and practices implied by the SCIP framework into extant effective treatment models. As we and others have discussed (e.g., Boxer & Dubow, 2002; Boxer & Frick, in press; Frick, 2006; Hunter, Elias, & Norris, 2001; Silverman, 2006), theory and related empirical research are essential to psychotherapeutic programs because they can inform the design of therapeutic activities, the assessments necessary for gauging success, and ultimately the dissemination and broader implementation of programs.

From the research reviewed in this chapter, it is clear that habitual violent behavior arises from a complex array of risk factors that can differ for subgroups of antisocial youth. We have presented SCIP factors as core person-level components in the maintenance of aggression and violence over time and across situations. It is critical that interventions include a focus on these social–cognitive processes. However, research also has suggested that specific SCIP deficits may differ across groups of violent youth. As a result, interventions also need to be linked to careful assessments so that they can be individualized to reflect this variability in the maintenance factors for violent behavior (McMahon & Frick, 2005).

Note

1. The STOP and GO Program is not an empirically validated treatment program but is based on the SCIP framework and incorporates activities from several empirically supported programs. More information about this program can be obtained directly from the first author.

References

Alexander, J., Barton, C., Gordon, D., Grotpeter, J., Hansson, K., Harrison, R., et al. (1998). *Blueprints for violence prevention, book three: Functional family therapy.* Boulder, CO: Center for the Study and Prevention of Violence.

Anderson, C. A., Berkowitz, L., Donnerstein, E., Huesmann, R. L., Johnson, J., Linz, D., et al. (2003). The influence of media violence on youth. *Psychological Science in the Public Interest, 4,* 81–110.

Berkowitz, L. (1998). Affective aggression: The role of stress, pain, and negative affect. In R. G. Geen & E. Donnerstein (Eds.), *Human aggression: Theories, research, and implications for social policy* (pp. 49–72). San Diego: Academic Press.

Blair, R. J. R. (1999). Responsiveness to distress cues in the child with psychopathic tendencies. *Personality and Individual Differences, 27* 135–145.

Boldizar, J. R, Perry, D. G., & Perry, L. C. (1989). Outcome values and aggression. *Child Development, 60,*571–579.

Borum, R., & Verhaagen, D. (2006). *Assessing and managing violence risk in juveniles.* New York: Guilford Press.

Boxer, P. (2001). *The STOP and GO Program: Aggression reduction and anger control for adolescents.* Unpublished treatment manual, Northville, MI.

Boxer, P., & Butkus, M. (2005). Individual social–cognitive intervention for aggressive behavior in early adolescence: An application of the cognitive–ecological framework. *Clinical Case Studies, 4,* 277–294.

Boxer, P., & Dubow, E. F. (2002). A social–cognitive information-processing model for school-based aggression reduction and prevention programs: Issues for research and practice. *Applied and Preventive Psychology, 10,* 177–192.

Boxer, P., Dubow, E. F., Fiedler, J., & Fiedler, H. (2000, November). *Integrating social–cognitive research into adolescent anger management treatment: The STOP Angry Aggression Program.* Poster presented at the annual meeting of the Association for the Advancement of Behavior Therapy, New Orleans, LA.

Boxer, P., & Frick, P. J. (in press). Treating conduct problems, aggression, and antisocial behavior in children and adolescents: An integrated view. In R. Steele, M. Roberts, & T. D. Elkin (Eds.), *Handbook of evidence-based therapies for children and adolescents.* Newbury Park, CA: Sage.

Boxer, P., Goldstein, S. E., Musher-Eizenman, D., Dubow, E. F., & Heretick, D. (2005). Developmental issues in the prevention of school aggression from the social–cognitive perspective. *Journal of Primary Prevention, 26,* 383–400.

Boxer, P., Huesmann, L. R., & Hanish, L. (2004, March). *Peer popularity and program effectiveness: Findings from a randomized prevention trial.* Paper presented at the biennial meeting of the Society for Research on Adolescence, Baltimore, MD.

Caldwell, M., Skeem, J., Salekin, R., & Van Rybroek, G. (2006). Treatment response of adolescent offenders with psychopathy features: A 2-year follow up. *Criminal Justice and Behavior, 33,* 571–596.

Caputo, A. A., Frick, P. J., & Brodsky, S. L. (1999). Family violence and juvenile sex offending: The potential mediating role of psychopathic traits and negative attitudes toward women. *Criminal Justice and Behavior, 26,* 338–356.

Christian, R. E., Frick, P. J., Hill, N. L., Tyler, L., & Frazer, D. R. (1997). Psychopathy and conduct problems in children: II. Implications for subtyping children with conduct problems. *Journal of the American Academy of Child and Adolescent Psychiatry, 36* 233–241.

Crane-Ross, D., Tisak, M. S., & Tisak, J. (1998). Aggression and conventional rule violation among adolescents: Social-reasoning predictors of social behavior. *Aggressive Behavior, 24,* 347–365.

Crick, N. R., & Dodge, K. A. (1994). A review and reformulation of social information-processing mechanisms in children's social adjustment. *Psychological Bulletin, 115,* 74–101.

Crick, N. R., & Dodge, K. A. (1996). Social information-processing mechanisms in reactive and proactive aggression. *Child Development, 67* 993–1002.

Dodge, K. A. (2006). Translational science in action: Hostile attributional style and the development of aggressive behavior problems. *Development and Psychopathology, 18,* 791–814.

Dodge, K. A., Bates, J. E., & Pettit, G. S. (1990). Mechanisms in the cycle of violence. *Science, 250,* 1678–1683.

Dodge, K. A., & Newman, R. J. (1981). Biased decision-making processes in aggressive boys. *Journal of Abnormal Psychology, 90,* 375–379.

Dodge, K. A., & Somberg, D. A. (1987). Hostile attributional biases are exacerbated under conditions of threats to the self. *Child Development, 58,* 213–224.

Dubow, E. F., & Reid, G. J. (1994). Risk and resource variables in children's aggressive behavior: A two-year longitudinal study. In L. R. Huesmann (Ed.), *Aggressive behavior: Current perspectives* (pp. 187–214). New York: Plenum Press.

Egan, S. K., Monson, T. C., & Perry, D. G. (1998). Social–cognitive influences on change in aggression over time. *Developmental Psychology, 34,* 996–1006.

Erdley, C. A., & Asher, S. R., (1996). Children's social goals and self-efficacy perceptions as influences on their responses to ambiguous provocations. *Child Development, 67,* 1329–1344.

Eron, L. D. (2001). Seeing is believing: How viewing violence alters attitudes and behavior. In A. C. Bohart & D. J. Stipek (Eds.), *Constructive and destructive behavior: Implications for family, school, and society* (pp. 49–60). Washington, DC: American Psychological Association.

Essau, C. A., Sasagawa, S., & Frick, P. J. (2006). Callous-unemotional traits in a community sample of adolescents. *Assessment, 13*, 454–469.

Feindler, E. L. (1995). Ideal treatment package for children and adolescents with anger disorders. In H. Kassinove (Ed.), *Anger disorders: Definition, diagnosis, and treatment* (pp. 173–196). Washington, DC: Taylor & Francis.

Fisher, L., & Blair, R. J. R. (1998). Cognitive impairment and its relationship to psychopathic tendencies in children with emotional and behavioral difficulties. *Journal of Abnormal Child Psychology, 26*, 511–519.

Frick, P. J. (2006). Developmental pathways to conduct disorder. *Child and Adolescent Psychiatric Clinics of North America, 15*, 311–332.

Frick, P. J., Bodin, S. D., & Barry, C. T. (2000). Psychopathic traits and conduct problems in community and clinic-referred samples of children: Further development of the Psychopathy Screening Device. *Psychological Assessment, 12*, 382–393.

Frick, P. J., Cornell, A. H., Bodin, S. D., Dane, H. A., Barry, C. T., & Loney, B. R. (2003). Callous-unemotional traits and developmental pathways to severe conduct problems. *Developmental Psychology, 39*, 246–260.

Frick, P. J., Lilienfeld, S. O., Ellis, M. L., Loney, B. R., & Silverthorn, P. (1999). The association between anxiety and psychopathy dimensions in children. *Journal of Abnormal Child Psychology, 27* 381–390.

Frick, P., & Morris, A. S. (2004). Temperament and developmental pathways to severe conduct problems. *Journal of Clinical Child and Adolescent Psychology, 33*, 54–68.

Goldstein, A. P., Glick, B., & Gibbs, J. C. (1998). *Aggression replacement training.* Champaign, IL: Research Press.

Gouze, K. R. (1987). Attention and social problem solving as correlates of aggression in preschool males. *Journal of Abnormal Child Psychology, 15*, 181–197.

Guerra, N. G., Boxer, P., & Kim, T. (2005). A cognitive–ecological approach to serving students with emotional and behavioral disorders: Application to aggressive behavior. *Behavioral Disorders, 30*, 277–288.

Guerra, N. G., & Slaby, R. G. (1990). Cognitive mediators of aggression in adolescent offenders: 2. Intervention. *Developmental Psychology, 26*, 269–277.

Hawes, D. J., & Dadds, M. R. (2005). The treatment of conduct problems in children with callous-unemotional traits. *Journal of Consulting and Clinical Psychology, 73*, 737–741.

Henggeler, S. W., & Lee, T. (2003). Multisystemic treatment of serious clinical problems. In A. E. Kazdin & J. R. Weisz (Eds.), *Evidence-based psychotherapies for children and adolescents* (pp. 301–322). New York: Guilford Press.

Henggeler, S. W., Schoenwald, S. K., Borduin, C. M., Rowland, M. D., & Cunningham, P. B. (1998). *Multisystemic treatment of antisocial behavior in children and adolescents.* New York: Guilford Press.

Hinshaw, S. P., Lahey, B. B., & Hart, E. L. (1993). Issues of taxonomy and comorbidity in the development of conduct disorder. *Development and Psychopathology, 5*, 31–49.

Hudley, C., Britsch, B., Wakefield, W. D., Smith, T., Demorat, M., & Cho, S.

(1998). An attribution retraining program to reduce aggression in elementary school students. *Psychology in the Schools, 35,* 271–282.

Hudley, C., & Graham, S. (1993). An attributional intervention to reduce peer-directed aggression among African-American boys. *Child Development, 64,* 124–138.

Huesmann, L. R. (1988). An information processing model for the development of aggression. *Aggressive Behavior, 14,* 13–24.

Huesmann, L. R. (1998). The role of social information processing and cognitive schema in the acquisition and maintenance of habitual aggressive behavior. In R. G. Geen & E. Donnerstein (Eds.), *Human aggression: Theories, research, and implications for social policy* (pp. 73–109). San Diego: Academic Press.

Huesmann, L. R., Eron, L. D., Klein, R., Brice, R., & Fischer, R. (1983). Mitigating the imitation of aggressive behaviors by changing children's attitudes about media violence. *Journal of Personality and Social Psychology, 44,* 899–910.

Huesmann, L. R., & Guerra, N. G. (1997). Children's normative beliefs about aggression and aggressive behavior. *Journal of Personality and Social Psychology, 72,* 408–419.

Hunter, L., Elias, M. J., & Norris, J. (2001). School-based violence prevention: Challenges and lessons learned from an action research project. *Journal of School Psychology, 39,*161–175.

Kimonis, E. R., Frick, P. J., Fazekas, H., & Loney, B. R. (2006). Psychopathic traits, aggression, and the processing of emotional stimuli in non-referred children. *Behavioral Sciences and the Law, 24* 21–37.

Kochanska, G. (1993). Toward a synthesis of parental socialization and child temperament in early development of conscience. *Child Development, 64,* 325–347.

Kruh, I. P., Frick, P. J., Clements, C. B. (2005). Historical and personality correlates to the violence patterns of juveniles tried as adults. *Criminal Justice and Behavior, 32,*69–96.

Lochman, J. E., Lampron, L. B., Gemmer, T. C., & Harris, S. R. (1987). Anger coping intervention with aggressive children: A guide to implementation in school settings. In R. A. Keller & S. R. Heyman (Eds.), *Innovations in clinical practice: A source book* (Vol. 6, pp. 339–356). Sarasota, FL: Professional Resource Exchange.

Lochman, J. E., & Wells, K. C. (2002). The Coping Power Program for preadolescent aggressive boys and their parents: Outcome effects at the one-year follow-up. *Journal of Consulting and Clinical Psychology, 72,* 571–578.

Loeber, R., & Farrington, D. P. (Eds.). (1998). *Serious and violent juvenile offenders: Risk factors and successful interventions.* Thousand Oaks, CA: Sage.

Loeber, R., & Stouthamer-Loeber, M. (1998). Development of juvenile aggression and violence: Some common misconceptions and controversies. *American Psychologist, 53* 242–259.

Loney, B. R., Frick, P. J., Clements, C. B., Ellis, M. L., & Kerlin, K. (2003). Callous-unemotional traits, impulsivity, and emotional processing in antisocial adolescents. *Journal of Clinical Child and Adolescent Psychology, 32,* 66–80.

Loney, B. R., Frick, P. J., Ellis, M., & McCoy, M. G. (1998). Intelligence, psychopathy, and antisocial behavior. *Journal of Psychopathology and Behavioral Assessment, 20,* 231–247.

Lynam, D. R. (1997). Pursuing the psychopath: Capturing the fledgling psychopath in a nomological net. *Journal of Abnormal Psychology, 106,* 425–438.

Lynam, D. R., Caspi, A., Moffitt, T. E., Raine, A., Loeber, R., & Stouthamer-Loeber, M. (2005). Adolescent psychopathy and the Big Five: Results from two samples. *Journal of Abnormal Child Psychology, 33*(4), 431–443.

McMahon, R. J., & Frick, P. J. (2005). Evidence-based assessment of conduct problems in children and adolescents. *Journal of Clinical Child and Adolescent Psychology, 34,* 477–505.

Moffitt, T. E. (1993). Adolescent-limited and life-course-persistent antisocial behavior: A developmental taxonomy. *Psychological Review, 100,* 674–701.

Moffitt, T. E. (2006). Life-course-persistent versus adolescence-limited antisocial behavior. In D. Cicchetti & D. J. Cohen (Eds.), *Developmental psychopathology. Vol. 3: Risk, disorder, and adaptation* (2nd ed., pp. 570–598). Hoboken, NJ: Wiley.

Musher-Eizenman, D., Boxer, P., Danner, S., Dubow, E. F., Goldstein, S. E., & Heretick, D. M. L. (2004). Social–cognitive mediators of the relation of environmental and emotion regulation factors to children's's aggression. *Aggressive Behavior, 30,* 389–408.

Nas, C. N., Orobio de Castro, B., & Koops, W. (2005). Social information processing in delinquent adolescents. *Psychology, Crime, and Law, 11,* 363–375.

National Institutes of Health. (2004). *State of the science conference statement: Preventing violence and related health-risking social behaviors in adolescents.* Available at *www.consensus.nih.gov/ta/023/YouthViolenceFinalStatement011805. htm*

O'Brien, B. S., & Frick, P. J. (1996). Reward dominance: Associations with anxiety, conduct problems, and psychopathy in children. *Journal of Abnormal Child Psychology, 24,* 223–240.

Orobio de Castro, B., Veerman, J. W., Koops, W., Bosch, J. D., & Monshouwer, H. J. (2002). Hostile attribution of intent and aggressive behavior: A meta-analysis. *Child Development, 73,* 916–934.

Oxford, M., Cavell, T.A., & Hughes, J.N. (2003). Callous/unemotional traits moderate the relation between ineffective parenting and child externalizing problems: A partial replication and extension. *Journal of Clinical Child and Adolescent Psychology, 32,* 577–585.

Pardini, D. A. (2006). The callousness pathway to severe violent delinquency. *Aggressive Behavior, 32,* 590–598.

Pardini, D. A., Lochman, J. E., & Frick, P. J. (2003). Callous-unemotional traits and social–cognitive processes in adjudicated youth: Exploring the schema of juveniles with psychopathic traits. *Journal of the American Academy of Child and Adolescent Psychiatry, 42,* 364–371.

Patterson, G. R., Capaldi, D., & Bank, L. (1991). An early starter model for predicting delinquency. In D. Pepler & K. H. Rubin (Eds.), *The development and treatment of childhood aggression* (pp. 139–168). Hillsdale, NJ: Erlbaum.

Perry, D. G., Kusel, S. J., & Perry, L. C. (1988). Victims of peer aggression. *Developmental Psychology, 24,* 807–814.

Raine, A. (2002). Biosocial studies of antisocial and violent behavior in children and adults: A review. *Journal of Abnormal Child Psychology, 30,* 311–326.

Rodkin, P. C., Farmer, T. W., Pearl, R., & Van Acker, R. (2000). Heterogeneity of popular boys: Antisocial and prosocial configurations. *Developmental Psychology, 36,* 14–24.

Rogers, R., Johansen, J., Chang, J. J., & Salekin, R. (1997). Predictors of adolescent psychopathy: Oppositional and conduct-disordered symptoms. *Journal of the American Academy of Psychiatry and Law, 25,* 261–271.

Salekin, R. T., Leistico, A. R., Neumann, C. S., DiCicco, T. M., & Duros, R. L. (2004). Psychopathy and co-morbidity in a young offender sample: Taking a closer look at psychopathy's potential importance over disruptive behavior disorders. *Journal of Abnormal Psychology, 113,* 416–22.

Schaefer, C. M., & Borduin, C. M. (2005). Long-term follow-up to a randomized clinical trial of multisystemic therapy with serious and violent juvenile offenders. *Journal of Consulting and Clinical Psychology, 73,* 445–453.

Schwartz, D., Dodge, K. A., Coie, J. D., Hubbard, J. A., Cillessen, A. N., Lemerise, E. A., et al. (1998). Social-cognitive and behavioral correlates of aggression and victimization in boys' play groups. *Journal of Abnormal Child Psychology, 26,* 431–440.

Silverman, W. K. (2006). Shifting our thinking and training from evidence-based treatments to evidence-based explanations of treatments. *In Balance—Society of Clinical Child and Adolescent Psychology Newsletter, 21,* 1.

Slaby, R. G., & Guerra, N. G. (1988). Cognitive mediators of aggression in adolescent offenders: I. Assessment. *Developmental Psychology, 24,* 580–588.

Smithmyer, C. M., Hubbard, J. A., & Simons, R. F. (2000). Proactive and reactive aggression in delinquent adolescents: Relations to aggression outcome expectancies. *Journal of Clinical Child Psychology, 29,* 86–93.

Snyder, H. N., & Sickmund, M. (2006). *Juvenile offenders and victims: 2006 national report.* Washington, DC: U.S. Department of Justice, Office of Justice Programs, Office of Juvenile Justice and Delinquency Prevention.

Spain, S. E., Douglas, K. S., Poythress, N. G., & Epstein, M. (2004). The relationship between psychopathic features, violence and treatment outcome: The comparison of three youth measures of psychopathic features. *Behavioral Sciences and the Law, 22,* 85–102.

Stouthamer-Loeber, M., Loeber, R., Wei, E., Farrington, D. P., & Wikström, P. O. (2002). Risk and promotive effects in the explanation of persistent serious delinquency in boys. *Journal of Consulting and Clinical Psychology, 70,* 111–123.

Thornton, T. N., Craft, C. A., Dahlberg, L. L., Lynch, B. S., & Baer, K. (2000). *Best practices of youth violence prevention: A sourcebook for community action.* Atlanta, GA: Centers for Disease Control and Prevention.

Tisak, M. S., & Tisak, J. (1996). My sibling's but not my friend's keeper: Reasoning about responses of aggressive acts. *Journal of Early Adolescence, 16,* 324–338.

Tisak, M. S., Tisak, J., & Goldstein, S. E. (2006). Aggression, delinquency, and morality: A social–cognitive perspective. In M. Killen & J. G. Smetana (Eds.), *Handbook of moral development* (pp. 611–629). Mahwah, NJ: Erlbaum.

Tremblay, R. E. (2000). The development of aggressive behaviour during childhood: What have we learned in the past century? *International Journal of Behavioral Development, 24,* 129–141.

Viding, E., Blair, R. J. R., Moffitt, T. E., & Plomin, R. (2005). Evidence for substantial genetic risk for psychopathy in 7-year-olds. *Journal of Child Psychology and Psychiatry, 46,* 592–597.

Viding, E., Jones, A. P., Frick, P. J., Moffitt, T. E., & Plomin, R. (in press). Heritability of antisocial behaviour at age 9: Do callous-unemotional traits matter? *Developmental Science.*

Wootton, J. M., Frick, P. J., Shelton, K. K., & Silverthorn, P. (1997). Ineffective parenting and childhood conduct problems: The moderating role of callous-unemotional traits. *Journal of Consulting and Clinical Psychology, 65,* 301–330.

Chapter 8

Treating Gang-Involved Offenders

Robert Nash Parker
Todd Negola
Rudy Haapanen
Larry Miranda
Emily Asencio

Youth gangs in the United States (and elsewhere) have been considered a major problem and contributing factor to youth crime since at least the 1950s. Any serious effort to provide treatment programs for juvenile offenders must therefore consider the reality of gangs, gang activities, and whether they can be addressed successfully in a treatment context. This chapter provides an overview of what we know about juvenile offenders and gangs, gang membership, and gang activities. We focus particularly on the role of gangs in juvenile correctional facilities and how they can impact treatment efforts. Toward this end, we examine data from California and elsewhere to highlight the role that gangs play inside juvenile institutions, their impact on institutional life, institutional violence, and the institutional climate.

We begin with a brief historical discussion of the history of gangs, highlighting their emergence and development in the United States. We then emphasize how gangs and delinquency are intertwined, and we suggest that understanding gang involvement requires understanding both delinquency and the unique feature of gangs.

A Brief History of Gangs

Gangs have been in existence since early groups of humankind formed for protection, survival, and solidarity. Some have argued that gangs are nothing more than an extension of human social groupings (Venkatesh, 2000). Indeed, by nature, we are tribal. From the Native Americans to the early American colonists to the Eskimos of the North Pole, human beings divide along sophisticated and often unspoken alliances, boundaries, and lines.

The existence of gangs dates as far back as the 14th and 15th centuries. Although this is speculation, we can even make a case that gangs can be traced to prehistoric humans. Imagine the outcast Neanderthal man—perhaps one with only mediocre hunting skills. He and other outcasts or rejects form a union, merely for companionship and protection. Their internal sense of rejection or social displacement yields frustration and anger, taken out on their unsuspecting victims. Initially these victims may be anyone or anything (an extension of their frustration); eventually this frustration turns toward the group or society that rejected them and even among themselves. Now, imagine if the weapons were AK-47s rather than clubs and sticks.

Early researchers have documented the existence of gangs in Colonial America during the 17th and 18th centuries. There was substantial evidence of group or gang delinquency in New England around this period (Covey, Menard, & Franzese, 1992). In *The Dunlap's American Daily Advertiser* there were complaints about groups of delinquent males creating problems in Philadelphia, and in 1791 the citizens of Philadelphia met to address these concerns. Specifically, drinking, fighting, reading of sexually oriented materials, sexual experimentation, and theft were of chief concern among all the delinquent boys' behaviors. These groups were considered transitory, lacking in cohesion, and shared other characteristics of many contemporary gangs.

Asbury (1927) traced gangs in the United States to the early 1800s in Chicago and New York. The first gang may have been known as the Forty Thieves, hailing from New York. Later, gangs such as the Pug Uglies, known because of their pub hats; the Shirt Tails, because they let their shirt tails hang out of their pants; the Bowery Boys, Kerryonians, Roach Guards, and Dead Rabbits—were all recorded, reported, and observed. All of these groups operated out of the Five Points, Hell's Kitchen, and Bowery sections of New York City. These gangs were known for inter- and intra-gang conflicts. Burt (1925) even mentioned that Charles Dickens's book, *Oliver Twist*, describes what gangs during 19th-century England, in the Victorian age, may have been like. They were described as loosely structured groups of youths who committed various street crimes to support their gang. It was assumed that joining a gang was a way of survival in Victorian society. It was during the 1870s that New York gangs such as the 19th Street Gang, the Sort Boys, and others were often linked to saloons and/or political parties. They were known to drive out competition, ensure election outcomes, and accept payment for providing protection for government officials, including police.

The main conceptualization lies in understanding the social dynamics of gangs. A gang is like a group of neighborhood friends who desire only friendship, companionship, and excitement. If any member is attacked, the group members feel such a dedication to the group that they retaliate. This retaliation is likely to be followed by a counterstrike. The cycle of violence escalates to the point of a formation of large sets or "nations" to protect themselves. Membership in a nation is dictated by race but often subject to further splits within races (e.g., Mexican gangs in California were originally united until they divided into north and south). The unwritten rule is "You kill one of mine, I kill one of yours," and on it goes. After years of violence, fear, and hypervigilance, the "survivors" gain respect. This respect equates to power, and the more power, the more respect. A gang member is jailed, killed or crippled, grows rich and powerful, and/or retires. The pressure of always being "186" on the alert causes most to tire, and/or they are kicked out by younger members. If the gang stays together, it will become big and strong enough to survive or join forces with other gangs. The longer the gang survival, the more members it possesses and the stronger it becomes. The gang will often include family members—sometimes several generations.

As this overview suggests, gangs are both deviant and adaptive. Their historical endurance suggests they serve an important social function of providing both social connectedness and protection from harm. In one of the first comprehensive research efforts to explore gang membership, "The Gang: A Study of 131 Gangs in Chicago," Thrasher (1927, 1936) postulated that gangs spontaneously evolve from social/play groups characterized by juvenile behavior that can become delinquent. This behavior, which was seen as generally learned from older peers, becomes part of the group's normal behavior, wherein the group helps establish the youth's sense of personal and social identity. Thrasher speculated that the lack of controls, a permissive environment, and the presence of criminals who have a high status in the community are contributing factors to why youth are attracted to, and ultimately engage in, criminal activities.

Still, not all youth growing up in neighborhoods with high levels of gang activity become involved in gangs. This fact begs the question of how best to understand the causes and correlates of gang involvement, and how to develop corresponding prevention and intervention programs. Of course, gang involvement is inherently tied to criminality. Otherwise put, in order to understand gang behavior, we must understand how it is intertwined with crime. Let us now turn to a discussion of the links between delinquency and gang involvement.

Links Between Delinquency and Gang Activity

More recent studies have demonstrated a clear connection between delinquency and gang membership (Walker, Watt, & White, 1994). For example, Knox and Tromanhauser (1991) found that approximately two-thirds of gang members had engaged in four or more fights involving the use of potentially deadly weapons during their lifetime, as compared with approximately one-third of nongang respondents. Other studies have found that in contrast to nongang members, gang members were more often convicted of at least one violent offense, had their first offense at a younger age, and had higher evidence of conviction rates (e.g., Santman, Myner, Cappeletty, & Perimutter, 1997). Interestingly, there appear to be some gender differences in types of delinquency associated with gang involvement. In one study of male and female gang members in a Midwestern city, Rhodes and Fischer (1993) found that males were more likely to have violated laws, been arrested, engaged in aggressive offenses, and sold drugs. On the other hand, females were more likely to have committed status offenses such as running away and truancy.

In many cases, delinquency has become an accepted part of the gang lifestyle, with violence (or willingness to use violence) deemed one the key features for membership. The range of violence that typifies any particular gang depends most on the type and nature of the gang itself; however, it becomes apparent that within most, if not all, gangs, violence is inevitable. Whether it is protection from rivals, protection of turf, or simply for excitement and camaraderie, violence in the gang community is highly prevalent (Harris, 1994).

This alignment with violence is supported by evidence that gang members have higher rates of violent criminal activity than do nongang members (Lyon, Henggeler, & Hall, 1992). Although fighting is the most prototypical type of violence, gang violence also includes homicide. In many cities, increases in homicide rates are almost completely due to increases in gang-related homicides. For example, Roger (1993) studied homicide rates in Los Angeles, California, reporting that in 1990, 18.5% of all homicides were gang-related, in contrast to 1995 when 35.1% were determined to be gang-related. Further, gang violence is not limited to street activity but also extends to correctional institutions. For example, Knox et al. (1997) found that among incarcerated youths, gang members exhibit higher rates of poor adjustment including fights, weapons, and disciplinary reports.

Given these clear linkages between gang involvement and serious youth crime, it is critical that treatment services for juvenile offenders address the issue of gang involvement. As we shall see later in this chapter, the issue becomes even more acute within youth correctional facilities, where gangs yield considerable influence and power. Unfortunately, there is a dearth of evidence-based programming aimed at preventing gang involvement or redirecting gang members toward more conventional, noncriminal lifestyles. Before turning to a review of the treatment literature, we examine some of the more prominently featured individual and contextual correlates and causes of gang involvement. We highlight characteristics that predict criminal behavior more generally, consistent with what has been discussed in other chapters throughout this volume. However, we also point out unique contributions of specific risk factors to adolescent involvement with gangs.

Why Youth Join Gangs

In some neighborhoods, the lure of gangs looms large, and it is relatively easy for youth to become ensnared in the gang lifestyle. As one youth commented:

> Without a doubt, I was engaged in criminality. But my activity gravitated around a survival instinct: kill or be killed. Conditions dictated that I evolve or perish. I was engaged in a war with an equal opponent. I did not start this cycle, nor did I conspire to create conditions so that this type of self-murder would take place. My participation came as second nature. To be in a gang in South Central, when I joined—and it still is the case today—is the equivalent of growing up in Grosse Point, Michigan, and going to college; everyone does it. Those who don't aren't part of the fraternity. And as with everything from a union to a tennis club, it's better to be in than out. (in Shakur & Scott, 1994, p. 137)

This statement illustrates the extent to which gang involvement becomes more of a "lifestyle" that is adaptive under certain conditions, and not simply a group to which one belongs or actions one may take. This perspective is also consistent with the developmental life-course

(DLC) theories discussed in Chapter 2 of this volume. However, not all youth growing up in neighborhoods like South Central join gangs, leading us to ask what factors best predict gang involvement. Similarly, for treatment purposes with youth who are already gang-involved, we must ask what factors best predict desistance from involvement with the gang lifestyle. However, most studies simply examine gang involvement and its correlates and do not provide clear directives for prevention versus treatment. We are thus limited to an examination of general predictors of criminality and gang involvement among youth.

Individual Correlates of Gang Involvement

Most efforts to identify individual predictors of gang involvement have noted factors examined more broadly in the delinquency literature. Presumably, these factors contribute to individual delinquency, and when combined with social factors such as the presence and status of gangs in a specific neighborhood, can also predict gang involvement. For example, in recent years biological theories of delinquency have regained prominence in the field. These theories do not explain gangs per se, but they may provide insights into why some individuals are prone to crime and, hence, more likely to join gangs.

For example, one of the most well-tested and detailed biological theories to date has been proposed by Mednick and colleagues (Mednick & Christiansen, 1977; Mednick & Shoham, 1979; Mednick, Mednick, & Griffith, 1981; Mednick, Moffitt, Gabrielli & Hutchings, 1985; Mednick, Moffit, & Stack, 1987). This theory asserts that parents provide their offspring with a set of genetic factors that influence later criminal activity. Mednick's work suggests that a genetic susceptibility to a slower or reduced autonomic nervous system when reacting to stimuli may lead to difficulty, as could a slower learning curve in managing aggressive or antisocial tendencies. Therefore, individuals with this trait may be at greater risk of becoming law violators. Indeed, the criminal history of parents is a strong predictor of children's later criminal behavior, with some support for a genetic link. Similarly, gang-involved youth often have gang-involved parents and even gang-involved grandparents, although less has been done to "unpack" the potential genetic contribution (Belitz & Valdez, 1994; Santman et al., 1997) than the socioenvironmental factors leading to gang membership. A focus on biological determinants could shed light on why specific individuals may be attracted to a criminal and gang lifestyle, but there are still a host of other individual and contextual factors that contribute to this selection process.

As a group, gang members have been shown to present with a greater variety of related disorders, including clinical diagnoses, than their non-gang-involved counterparts. In one study by Santman et al. (1997), gang members received more diagnoses associated with conduct disorder and depressive disorders, such as posttraumatic stress disorder, than nongang members. They have also been found to be more likely to receive more diagnoses associated with antisocial personality disorder (Belitz & Valdez, 1994) than nongang members. Their tendency to become aggressive or violent may be considered a coping mechanism to deal with the possible comorbid depression or posttraumatic stress disorder diagnoses (Belitz & Valdez, 1994).

Family and School Correlates of Gang Involvement

In addition to individual factors, many specific family factors have been associated with gang membership. Gang members tend to come from dysfunctional families, such as those with a history of familial substance abuse (Belitz & Valdez, 1994). A great deal of research has been focused upon factors such as poor familial relations as contributing to gang membership. Another factor is the notion that many gang members are likely to come from homes in which the parents are involved in criminal activities themselves (Belitz & Valdez, 1994; Klein, 1968). Broken homes are another factor associated with gang membership (Belitz & Valdez, 1994; Klein, 1968). Many gang members are reared in "single-parent, female-centered homes, with inadequate parenting or supervision of the children, domestic violence, family members with a history of alcoholism and drug addiction, poverty and inadequate housing, pressures of acculturation and discrimination" (Vigil, 1988, p. 76).

Examining the research provides guidance for identifying those adolescents who are at risk for gang membership. Vigil (1988) described how the gang becomes a *surrogate family* that formulates its own norms, rituals, and means for identifying other members, providing structure, support, and regularity to daily life. For example, gang members adopt certain norms involving dress, linguistic patterns, gait, and gestures. In addition, many gang members may begin to formulate an identity based on certain symbols related to the gang. Examples include nicknames or a moniker, brands, and tattoos commonly associated with the gang. It is easy to see how gangs can be particularly attractive for the most disenfranchised and marginalized youth, who lack strong families and futures to sustain them.

Gang membership has also been linked to difficulties in school, including poor attendance and achievement (Hardman, 1967; Huff,

1989; Johnstone, 1981) more so than nongang members. Knox et al. (1999) noted that gang members were more likely to be "bullies" in the academic arena, and Harris (1994) found that gang members had weaker school bonds. Once again the issue of lower intelligence is cited by Campbell (1987) as well as the notion that "machismo" (an exaggerated sense of power or toughness for males) and "marianismo" (similar for females) attitudes may be another contributing factor to both poor academic performance and the attraction to gangs to gain status and power.

Extent of the Gang Problem in Communities and Institutions

We have provided a context for understanding the emergence of gangs throughout history, with particular reference to developments within the United States. We have highlighted both their adaptive and criminal functions, suggesting that gang involvement reflects a coalescing of multiple sources of risk at the level of communities, families, schools, and individuals. The connection between gang involvement and adolescent offending provides a strong rationale for focusing treatment programs for offenders specifically on gang-involved youth. In order to assess the scope of this mandate, we must also examine the distribution and severity of the gang problem both in communities and in juvenile correctional facilities.

Distribution and Severity of Gang Problems at the Community Level

A major source of controversy in the gang literature is the degree to which gangs have spread or are spreading from very large urban centers (e.g., Los Angeles, New York, Chicago) to other parts of the country and into smaller and medium-size cities. New information on this topic comes from the National Youth Gang Survey (NYGS), an effort funded by the U.S. Office of Juvenile Justice and Delinquency Prevention (OJJDP) to conduct surveys of law enforcement agencies in order to assess the degree, prevalence, and changes in the distribution of gangs in communities across the United States and to track changes over time in these aspects of gang problems from a law enforcement perspective. The strengths of the NYGS are that it captures data from a representative sample of U.S. communities, has response rates of 85% and higher, and has consistently used many of the same survey questions over the nine annual surveys conducted since 1996, allowing for trend analysis.

From these data, it seems that gangs, or at least gang-like groups (including wannabe gang-like groups), have become more wide-spread. For example, 769 cities reported gang activity in 1992 (Klein, 1995) compared with more than 1,400 cities reporting gang activity between 1999 and 2001 (Egley, Howell, & Major, 2004). This increase may be due, in part, to changing law enforcement practices and legal structures, such as field identification cards and gang charging and sentencing enhancements. Gang activity is still markedly higher in urban areas. For example, overall in 2004, 29% of the jurisdictions reporting had a gang problem, defined in the NYGS as the presence of an active youth gang in the jurisdiction (National Youth Gang Center, 2006). Of larger cities with a population greater than 100,000, 99% reported a gang problem; in rural communities, only 11% reported a gang problem in 2004. Considering the number and size of gangs, in 2004 most smaller cities and rural areas had fewer than 6 gangs and fewer than 200 gang members. Large suburban counties and large cities reported more gangs and more gang members. For example, a majority of large cities reported having 7 or more gangs and 50 or more gang members (more than 40% of these cities reported having 200 or more gang members). Suburban counties were in the middle, with most reporting the existence of 15 or fewer gangs and between 0 and 500 gang members (National Youth Gang Center, 2006).

The picture of the national gang problem that emerges from the NYGS is one of significance but not unilaterally bad and getting worse. There are regional variations as well as city-size class variations. For example, in the South and Midwest, about half the jurisdictions report gang problems, whereas in the West, the same estimate is 74%, and in the Northeast, the figure is 31%. The period between 1996 and 2001 showed a significant decline in most jurisdictions, and there have only been slight increases through the most recent survey, 2004. This is not to say that gangs and gang members are not dangerous and violent; the NYGS also collects data from jurisdictions on gang murders. Once again, city size accounts for major differences in gang homicides: 99.6% of cities with fewer than 50,000 in the NYGS sample reported 10 or fewer gang murders, and 70% reported none (Maxson, Curry, & Howell, 2002). In contrast, half the cities with more than 200,000 people reported 11 or more gang murders, and only 7% reported none (Maxson et al., 2002).

Data from the sources considered thus far suggest a serious but not universal gang problem in many, but by no means all, places in the

United States. Gang members are violent, outside and within institutions, but most places have relatively low levels of serious gang violence. In fact, two cities in the NYGS sample, Chicago and Los Angeles, account for more than 50% of the gang murders reported annually (Klein & Maxson, 2006; Egley & Major, 2004).

Gangs in Institutions

It is likely that gang membership (based on percentages of the total population) is significantly higher within juvenile correctional facilities, in part because gang involvement (or presumed gang involvement) will lead to criminal activity and an increased likelihood of being incarcerated. Indeed, given the gang enhancement laws that California (a leader in gang activity) and other states have on their books, any presumed gang member convicted or adjudicated for an offense is likely to receive a harsher sentence than a non-gang-involved youth for the same offense. Further, California's effort at limiting the juvenile justice population to only very serious offenders means that gang membership is fast becoming a criterion for institutionalization.

One study of incarcerated individuals in 17 states, conducted by the National Gang Crime Research Center (NGCRC; National Gang Crime Research Center, 1999), found that out of more than 10,000 incarcerated youth surveyed, almost 41% reported they were active gang members. Although the sampling involved in this study was not random or representative, the opportunity to examine survey responses from such a large number of juveniles, both gang and nongang members, was significant. Because these respondents were asked to self-identify, the gang involvement and attitudes reported were likely to be more reliable and more valid than reports based on law enforcement identifications or institutional classifications of gang membership and activities. However, the estimate of 41% gang involvement is higher than what has been reported in most studies of incarcerated populations.

One exception is a study by LeBlanc and Lanctot (1998) that provided a definition of gang involvement for respondents that encompassed both gang and nongang forms of group delinquency. In this study, 62% of respondents indicated they had participated in organized groups that engaged in delinquency. An important point related to self-reporting of gang membership raised by Klein and Maxson (2006) is that typically a very small core group of members engages in most of the gang's activities, but a much larger group of individuals identify as members, although they do not really participate in gang activities.

On the other hand, the NGCRC (1999) study included juveniles and adults—in fact, half of the respondents were under 18, 72.5% were under 25, and 90% were under 35. Some of the incarcerated samples discussed in other studies also included adults, but the proportion of self-identified gang members is substantially lower in these studies, ranging from 4% to 15% (Bennett & Holloway, 2004). However, the studies reported by Klein and Maxson (2006) do show higher rates of gang involvement among juveniles than adults, a finding replicated by the NGCRC study (National Gang Crime Research Center, 1999), who reported that the overall mean age for all their respondents was 22.2, and the mean age of gang members was 18.6. Thus the prevalence of gang members in the Knox study is not out of the realm of possibility, given the variability reported by Klein and Maxson (2006).

How do the gang members in the NGCRC (National Gang Crime Research Center, 1999) differ from nongang members? Findings revealed that gang members were significantly more likely than nongang members to use force in everyday interaction to get what they wanted and were less likely to avoid risky situations. Gang members were also significantly more likely to report a lack of parental supervision and to report that their own parents had served time in prison. Although the majority of gang members reported that they bullied others in school, both gang and nongang respondents were equally likely to have been exposed to violence in the home and to have been victims of sexual violence in childhood. Gang members were more likely to report having sold crack cocaine and to having been actively involved in the drug trade, although 87.9% of active drug sales among gang members were described as done for the respondent personally rather than in the service of the gang as an organized entity. As reported in a number of other studies, gang members are much more likely to have friends in gangs than to have friends who are nongang members. Indeed, 77.4% of gang respondents reported having five or more friends in gangs, whereas only 18.7% of nongang respondents reported the same level of gang-involved peers.

With regard to the impact of gang membership on behavior outside and inside the institution, gang members were much more likely to be involved in serious violence and problematic behavior. For example, 31.4% of gang members reported having fired a gun at a police officer, whereas only 9.3% of nongang members reported this seriously violent act. Inside the institution, gang members were more likely to have been cited for disciplinary problems. Looking at involvement in physical altercations within the institution, gang members were significantly more likely to report such involvement than nongang members. Gang members also reported significantly higher rates of "carry[ing] a homemade weapon in the institution" than nongang members and were more likely to have threatened institutional staff.

The portrait of the institutionalized gang member that emerges from this and other studies is one of a violent offender, both in the institution and in the community, with personal and social traits and orientations suggesting that he (most frequently) or she is particularly difficult to manage and to rehabilitate. Indeed, several findings from the NGCRC (National Gang Crime Research Center, 1999) study have significant implications for programs seeking to encourage desistance or quitting the gang. For instance, although the NGCRC (National Gang Crime Research Center, 1999) reported that 79% of gang members stated that they would quit the gang if they were given a second chance in life, and more than 50% of gang members hid their gang membership from parents and thought they could quit the gang if they wanted to, gang members were also very attached to their gangs. For example, 54% felt loved and protected by their gang, and more than 70% felt the gang had kept its promises to them. Although gang members reported some ambivalence toward the gang, in truth, they were personally, emotionally, and behaviorally attached to the gang and its associated criminal behaviors.

We have provided a general description of gang involvement in juvenile correctional facilities, including some of the associated characteristics. Let us now turn to a more specific example based on research conducted in the California Division of Juvenile Justice.

A Detailed Analysis of Gang Involvement, Disciplinary Problems, and Violence in an Institutionalized Population: The Case of the California Division of Juvenile Justice

The data in Tables 8.1, 8.2, and 8.3 represent the population institutionalized in the juvenile facilities of the Division of Juvenile Justice (DJJ), a unit of the California Department of Corrections and Rehabilitation, as of March 1, 2007. Overall, Table 8.1 shows that the vast majority of youth committed in these institutions are indeed gang members, as determined by both what the inmates say and by staff investigations and assessments upon intake. Almost 77% of all juveniles incarcerated in DJJ facilities are gang members, and the problem is most pronounced among male inmates. There is a clear relationship between ethnicity and gang membership in California, with gang membership being much more likely among Latinos, African Americans, and Asian Americans, as shown in Table 8.1. The national survey of institutionalized gang members by the NGCRC (National Gang Crime Research

TABLE 8.1. Characteristics of Institutionalized Juvenile Population, California Division of Juvenile Justice, March 1, 2007: Gender, Ethnicity, Geographic Area, and Institutional Location

| | Gang member | | | |
| | No | | Yes | |
	N	%	N	%
Sex				
Male	553	22.6	1,899	77.4
Female	51	39.5	78	60.5
Ethnicity				
White	173	50.7	168	49.3
Latino	197	15.0	1,116	85.0
African American	198	24.7	603	75.3
Asian American	12	17.6	56	82.4
Native American	9	34.6	17	65.4
Filipino	3	27.3	8	72.7
Pacific Islander	7	50.0	7	50.0
Other	5	71.4	2	28.6
Area of commitment				
San Francisco Bay Area	126	27.5	332	72.5
Other Northern California	196	24.4	606	75.6
Los Angeles County	102	16.1	530	83.9
Other Southern California	180	26.1	509	73.9
Type of commitment offense				
Homicide	42	32.1	89	67.9
Robbery	127	19.8	516	80.2
Rape	33	42.9	44	57.1
Assault	116	15.0	656	85.0
Extortion/kidnapping	8	25.0	24	75.0
Burglary	59	19.4	245	80.6
Theft (except auto theft)	11	20.4	43	79.6
Auto theft	11	14.3	66	85.7
Arson	11	57.9	8	42.1
Sex offenses (except rape)	162	60.4	106	39.6
Drug offenses	11	15.1	62	84.9
Other offenses	13	9.9	118	90.1
Youth correctional facility				
Southern Clinic (Norwalk)	100	54.9	82	45.1
N. A. Chaderjian (Stockton)	82	41.4	116	58.6
O. H. Close (Stockton)	47	20.6	181	79.4
El Paso de Robles (Paso Robles)	16	8.7	168	91.3
DeWitt Nelson (Stockton)	74	20.9	280	79.1
Preston (Lone)	93	24.1	293	75.9
H. G. Stark (Chino)	103	13.3	674	86.7
Ventura Female (Ventura)	51	39.8	77	60.2
Pine Grove Camp (Jackson)	18	24.3	56	75.7
Ventura Camp (Ventura)	20	28.6	50	71.4

TABLE 8.2. Characteristics of Institutionalized Juvenile Population, California Division of Juvenile Justice, March 1, 2007: Mental Health Status, Sexual Offenders, and Drug Problems

	Gang member			
	No		Yes	
	N	%	N	%
Mental health program				
No	448	74.2	1,616	81.7
Yes	156	25.8	361	18.3
Sex offender				
No	386	63.9	1,793	90.7
Yes	218	36.1	184	9.3
Drug problem				
No	235	38.9	387	19.6
Yes	369	61.1	1,590	80.4

TABLE 8.3. Characteristics of Institutionalized Juvenile Population, California Division of Juvenile Justice, March 1, 2007: Months Added to Length of Stay for Disciplinary Infractions

Year of first release	Gang member	
(parole or discharge)	No	Yes
1995	2.2	1.9
1996	2.4	2.6
1997	2.3	3.6
1998	2.4	4.8
1999	3.1	6.0
2000	3.4	7.1
2001	3.3	7.0
2002	4.0	8.4
2003	3.9	9.2
2004	3.7	9.6
2005	3.8	11.0
2006	3.0	11.0
2007	3.6	10.8

Note. These figures indicate that early on, gang membership was not related to violent or disruptive behavior in institutions. Over the last 12 years, disciplinary time added for nongang members has increased (but not doubled), whereas time added for gang members has increased by a factor of 5.

Center, 1999), discussed above, revealed a similar pattern by ethnicity, with Latinos and Asian Americans having significantly higher proportions of gang membership among the institutionalized population than European Americans. We return to this issue below in discussing the nature of an institutional-based antigang intervention.

Concerning the severity of offenses for which youth have been institutionalized, gang members present a very serious offense profile. More than 80% of those institutionalized for robbery, assault, auto theft, drug offenses, and burglary are gang members. In only two offenses do nongang members predominate: arson and sex offenses other than rape. In the case of murder, rape, kidnap, and theft, a significant majority of those committed for these offenses are gang members. Gang membership is strongly associated with serious violent offenses among those institutionalized in California, and strongly associated with involvement in drug crimes, a finding similar to that reported by the NGCRC (National Gang Crime Research Center, 1999) and discussed previously. Finally, Table 8.1 shows that among the 10 institutions in which juveniles are incarcerated in California, the vast majority are dominated by gang populations, with some variation in a few of the institutions.

Table 8.2 suggests that in some areas of concern, gang members are not worse off and may, in fact, show fewer symptoms than nongang members in these California institutions. For example, although 18% of gang members received services in a mental health intervention program, over 25% of nongang members received these services. Gang members in these institutions are much less likely to be sex offenders, but they have a higher rate of drug involvement.

Table 8.3 demonstrates that gang members constitute a higher-risk population within the California institutionalized settings than do nongang members, especially in the last 5 years of these data, 2003–2007. Almost a year of extra time is added to the sentence served for gang members in these institutions. This summary measure is similar in its implications to those presented earlier from the NGCRC (National Gang Crime Research Center, 1999) study, in which gang members had significantly higher levels of involvement in disciplinary problems and physical aggression in the institutions.

Treatment of Institutionalized Juvenile Offenders

This chapter emphasizes the treatment of juvenile offenders who are gang members in general, with a specific focus on interventions for institutionalized youth. However, a major problem is that, to date, there is relatively little evidence of successful treatment programs for institutionalized gang members. As discussed by Guerra et al. in Chapter 4, most evidence-based programs for offenders have emphasized prevention or early intervention, with very few vetted programs for more serious and/or gang-involved youth, and even fewer targeting gang-involved youth. We find little evidence (one exception is a very recently established pilot program in California, which is discussed below) that institutions where juvenile offenders are incarcerated have established, let alone tested and evaluated, programs designed to address the problems that gang membership causes within these institutions and the contribution gang membership makes to recidivism after these youth have been released back into the community.

This is not to say that gangs and gang members have been ignored, in general. A great deal of attention, effort, and money has been devoted to addressing the gang problem in the United States. Most interventions that have been evaluated emphasize community responses, with a focus on suppression and intervention (although intervention is defined broadly and left up to communities to determine, and suppression often "wins the day"). However, as we argue, there is little in these programs that emphasizes treatment and/or how to provide treatment for offenders more broadly while simultaneously recognizing the lure of gang involvement.

TABLE 8.4. Characteristics of Institutionalized Juvenile Population, California Division of Juvenile Justice: Admissions of Gang Members

Year of first admission	Total	Nongang	%	Gang	%
1995	3,791	1647	43.4	2,144	56.6
1996	3,488	1368	39.2	2,120	60.8
1997	2,241	726	32.4	1,515	67.6
1998	2,153	623	28.9	1,530	71.1
1999	2,186	627	28.7	1,559	71.3
2000	1,902	645	33.9	1,257	66.1
2001	1,592	473	29.7	1,119	70.3
2002	1,402	351	25.0	1,051	75.0
2003	1,230	321	26.1	909	73.9
2004	1,056	270	25.6	786	74.4
2005	992	220	22.2	772	77.8
2006	836	147	17.6	689	82.4

Note. Gang membership has increased for new admissions since 1995. It jumped in 1997, when the fee structure for counties was enacted. It jumped again in 2001, when gang enhancements meant lower fees.

Indeed, conventional wisdom in the 1980s led to an emphasis on deterrence and law enforcement approaches to the gang problem that still dominates; what is surprising is that although these efforts have led to substantial increases in the incarceration of gang members in institutions (see Table 8.4; the proportion of gang members admitted to institutions in California increased from 56% in 1995 to more than 80% in 2006), the institutions have not taken up the challenge to design, implement, and test programs within their walls that address the gang problem directly.

We now turn to a review of both community (due to the lack of available institution-based programs) and institution-based treatment programs for gang members. We also describe the recently piloted California treatment program in DJJ institutions, and discuss a proposed antigang policy being reviewed by the State of California.

Community-Based Intervention/Prevention Programs

Despite the popularity of the distinction between *intervention* and *prevention* (Spergel, 1995; Klein & Maxson, 2006), we would argue that any prevention program is also an intervention program, and conceptually it might help those attempting such efforts to recognize this point. Gang prevention programs are usually defined as those attempting to prevent juveniles from joining gangs; the utility of this strategy seems to be based partly on the conventional wisdom that once kids have joined gangs, it is too late to do anything about it, and that inevitably gang membership is a one-way ticket to a life of crime, violence, and imprisonment. An assumption of this approach is that without the prevention effort, youth would be tempted to join gangs, and thus these efforts are really conceptually similar to intervention programs.

Conceiving these efforts as interventions might lead those who design such programs to be more explicit about such things as the target of the program, that is, what behavior or outcome the program is designed to change. This clarification might also lead to a more explicit notion of the appropriate outcomes to measure to see if the program is effective. As Klein and Maxson (2006) demonstrate in their review of six major community- and law-enforcement-based antigang programs, these and other problems—conceptual, methodological, measurement, and process—resulted in the fact that all six of the programs they reviewed were multimillion-dollar failures.

Two community-based intervention/prevention programs are worth additional discussion here. Gang Resistance, Education, and Training program (G.R.E.A.T.) was created by the Phoenix, Arizona Police Department and funded as a national program by the U.S.

Department of Alcohol, Tobacco and Firearms beginning in 1991; by the year 2000, 3,500 police officers were delivering the program in all 50 states. Despite the fact that the name of the program begins with *gang*, it was not really an antigang program; the content was not gang specific, but rather was devoted to enhancing life skills and positive attitudes. The assumption behind this content is the notion that such skills and attitudes undermine the attractiveness of gang membership to youth, and that this message, coming from police officers, would be effective. The major longitudinal outcome study of the impact of G.R.E.A.T showed that the program was largely ineffective (Esbensen, Osgood, Taylor, Peterson, & Freng, 2001; Klein & Maxson, 2006).

The second major prevention/intervention program is Spergel's comprehensive model (Klein & Maxson, 2006). This program was based on Spergel's earlier "Little Village" intervention and research, and was funded by the Office of Juvenile Justice and Delinquency Prevention (OJJDP) in 1995 to implement the comprehensive model in five sites around the country: Tucson, Arizona; Mesa, Arizona; San Antonio, Texas; Riverside, California; and Bloomington, Illinois. Unlike the G.R.E.A.T program, the Spergel model had an explicit focus on gang members, although there was some variation in this emphasis across the five sites (Klein & Maxson, 2006). One of the strengths of the Spergel model was that it was a comprehensive approach with the potential to address the multifaceted and multidimensional nature of the gang problem. The gang problem was thus understood as imbedded in the individuals, groups, and communities in which gangs emerge and thrive.

However, this strength was also a weakness, as the difficulty of implementing a comprehensive model involving, at a minimum, 11 different organizations led to failures to implement the Spergel model in several sites (Parker, 2002). If a program were difficult to implement, it would have little chance of succeeding—and indeed that was the case (Klein & Maxson, 2006).

Law Enforcement-Based Gang-Suppression Programs

Suppression programs, based almost entirely on law enforcement efforts, have also demonstrated little capacity for impacting gang members' behavior or gang formation and sustainability. Three such major programs are CRASH, or Community Resources Against Street Hoodlums, and the related Operation Hammer, both implemented by the Los Angeles Police Department (LAPD), and Operation Hardcore, an antigang prosecution unit in the Los Angeles County District Attorney's office.

CRASH was a special unit within the LAPD that was designed to target gang crime, gang members, and gangs themselves. The unit had subunits assigned to different divisions within the LAPD, and the notion was to have officers specialize in gathering intelligence about gangs in their division, conduct long-term investigations, and focus specifically on gang members. Operation Hammer was initiated by the CRASH units as a specific roundup of gang criminals in 1987; this effort resulted in massive sweeps during particular weekends involving more than 1,000 officers and resulting in more than 1,400 arrests. However, 1,350 of those arrested were released immediately, half of those arrested were not gang members, and fewer than 2% had felony charges (Klein & Maxson, 2006). The entire structure of CRASH and Operation Hammer broke down when the Rampart Division CRASH unit was found to be involved in some of the most spectacular police corruption in U. S. history, with thousands of convictions subject to review and four officers eventually convicted of corruption, abuse, and other criminal acts (Starr, 2004).

Operation Hardcore was a prosecutorial effort that focused on obtaining convictions of gang leaders and serious offenders within gangs (Klein & Maxson, 2006). Hardcore involved vertical prosecution (assigning one attorney to prosecute a case from beginning to end), resisting plea bargains, increased use of witness protection programs, special warrants, and enhanced training for prosecutors involved in gang cases. Although one evaluation suggested that the program was successful in increasing conviction rates in gang-related cases, the program seemed to have little or no impact on the gang members and gang formation and sustainability (Dahmann, 1982; Klein & Maxson, 2006).

California's Pilot Institutional-Based Gang Intervention Program: Project IMPACT

Given the relative failure of community-based prevention/intervention gang programs, the overall lack of impact of enforcement and suppression programs on gang behavior, and the potentially explosive consequences of gang activity within juvenile institutions, it seems prudent to look toward developing gang treatment programs for youth who are incarcerated. As we have shown, gang involvement is high, but motivation to change may also be greater. In this final section we briefly discuss one example of a recently established pilot program utilized by California's DJJ.

Project IMPACT, or Incarcerated Men Putting Away Childish Things, is a program developed by adult inmates at California's San

Quentin Prison. Although it is delivered in group sessions and conducted by the DJJ's Juvenile Operations Unit, the content is designed to address individual, family, and community contexts of gang involvement—something often lacking in many antigang programs. The DJJ initiated a pilot test of Project IMPACT at two of its facilities in January 2006, enrolling 70 gang members; on May 1, 2006, the first full-fledged implementation of Project IMPACT was initiated at a third facility with 50 youth. It is too early to reach any conclusions regarding program effectiveness, but this program represents at least a first step toward developing and evaluating intervention programs for incarcerated youth.

References

Akers, R. L. (1999). *Criminological theories.* Los Angeles: Roxbury.

Asbury, H. (1927). *The gangs of New York.* Garden City, NY: Garden City Publishing.

Belitz, J., & Valdez, D. (1994). Clinical issues in the treatment of Chicano male gang youth. *Hispanic Journal of Behavioral Sciences, 16*(1), 57–74.

Bennett, T., & Holloway, K. (2004). Gang membership, drugs and crime in the U.K. *British Journal of Criminology, 44,* 305–323.

Burt, C. L. (1925). *The young delinquent.* London: University of London Press.

Campbell, A. (1987). Self definition by rejection: The case of girl gangs. *Social Problems, 34* 451–466.

Covey, H. C., Menard, S., & Franzese, R. J. (1992). *Juvenile gangs.* Springfield, IL: Thomas.

Egley, A., Jr., Howell, J. C., & Major, A. K. (2004). Recent patterns of gang problems in the United States. In F. A. Esbensen, S. G. Tibbetts, & L. K. Gaines (Eds.), *American youth gangs at the millennium* (pp. 90–108). Long Grove, IL: Waveland.

Egley, A., Jr., & Major, A. K. (2004). *Highlights of the 2002 National Youth Gang Survey.* Washington, DC: Office of Juvenile Justice and Delinquency Prevention.

Esbensen, F. A., Osgood, D. W., Taylor, T. J., Peterson, D., & Freng, A. (2001). How great is G.R.E.A.T? Results from the longitudinal quasi-experimental design. *Criminology and Public Policy, 1,* 87–118.

Hardman, D. G. (1967). Historical perspectives of gang research. *Journal of Research in Crime and Delinquency, 4,* 5–27.

Harris, A. R. (1994). Race, class and crime. In J. F. Sheley (Ed.), *Criminology* (2nd ed., pp. 95–119). Belmont, CA: Wadsworth.

Huff, C. R. (1989). Youth gangs and public policy. *Crime and Delinquency, 35,* 524–537.

Johnstone, J. W. C. (1981). Youth gangs and black suburbs. *Pacific Sociological Review, 24,* 355–375.

Klein, M. W. (1968). *The Ladino Hills Project: Final report*. Los Angeles: Youth Studies Center, University of Southern California.

Klein, M. W. (1995). *The American street gang: Its nature, prevalence, and control*. New York: Oxford University Press.

Klein, M. W., & Maxson, C. J. (2006). *Street gang patterns and policies*. New York: Oxford University Press.

Knox, G. W., Harris, J. M., McCurrie, T. F., Elder, A. P., Tromanhauser, E. D., Laskey, J. A., et al. (1997). *The facts about gang life in America today: A national study of over 4,000 gang members*. Peotone, IL: National Gang Crime Research Center.

Knox, G. W., & Tromanhauser, E. D. (1991). Gangs and their control in adult correctional institutions. *Prison Journal, 71*, 15–22.

LeBlanc, M., & Lanctot, N. (1998). Social and psychological characteristics of gang members. *Journal of Gang Research, 5*, 15–28.

Lyon, J., Henggeler, S. W., & Hall, J. A. (1992). Family relations, peer relations, and criminal activity of Caucasian and Hispanic-American gang members. *Journal of Abnormal Child Psychology, 20*, 439–449.

Maxson, C. L., Curry, G. D., & Howell, J. C. (2002). Youth gang homicides in the U. S. in the 1990s. In W. L. Reed & S. H. Decker (Eds.), *Responding to gangs: Evaluation and research* (pp. 107–137). Washington, DC: National Institute of Justice.

Mednick, S. A., & Christiansen, K. O. (Eds.). (1977). *Biosocial bases of criminal behavior*. New York: Gardner Press.

Mednick, B., Mednick, S. A., & Griffith, J. (1981). Some recommendations for the design and conduct of longitudinal investigations. In F. Schulsinger, S. A. Mednick, & J. Knop (Eds.), *Longitudinal research: Methods and uses in behavioral science* (pp. 285–295). Hingham, MA: Martinus Nijhoff.

Mednick, S. A., Moffitt, T., Gabrielli, W., & Hutchings, B. (1985). Genetic factors in criminal behavior: A review. In J. Block, D. Olweus, & M. R. Yarrow (Eds.), *The development of antisocial and prosocial behavior* (pp. 33–50). New York: Academic Press.

Mednick, S. A., Moffitt, T. E., & Stack, S. A. (Eds.). (1987). *The causes of crime: New biological approaches*. New York: Cambridge University Press.

Mednick, S. A., & Shoham, S.G. (Eds.). (1979). *New paths in criminology: Interdisciplinary and intercultural explorations*. Lexington, MA: D.C. Heath.

Merton, R. K. (1938). Social structure and anomie. *American Sociological Review, 3*, 672–682.

Miller, W. B. (1982). *Crime by youth gangs and groups in the U.S.* Washington, DC: Office of Juvenile Justice and Delinquency Prevention.

Miller, W. B. (2001). *The growth of youth gang problems in the U.S.: 1970–98*. Washington, DC: Office of Juvenile Justice and Delinquency Prevention.

Moore, J. (1990). Mexican American women addicts: The influence of family background. In R. Glick & J. Moore (Eds.), *Drug use in Hispanic communities* (pp. 211–244). New Brunswick, NJ: Rutgers University Press.

National Gang Crime Research Center. (1999). *The facts about gang life in America today*. Peotone, IL: Author.

National Youth Gang Center. (2006). *National Youth Gang Survey Analysis.* Retrieved March 23, 2007, from *www.iir.com/nygc/nygsa*

Parker, R. N. (2002). *Project Bridge local evaluation, 1994–1999.* Riverside, CA: Presley Center for Crime and Justice Studies, University of California.

Raine, A. (1993) *The psychopathology of crime: Criminal behavior as a clinical disorder.* San Diego, CA: Academic Press.

Reckless, W. C. (1961). A new theory of delinquency and crime. *Federal Probation, 25,* 42–46.

Reiner, I., 1992. *Gangs, crime and violence in Los Angeles: Findings and proposals from the district attorney's office.* Arlington, VA: National Youth Gang Information Center.

Rhodes, J. E., & Fischer, K. (1993). Spanning the gender gap: Gender differences in delinquency among inner-city adolescents. *Adolescence, 28,* 879–889.

Rogers, C. (1993). Gang-related homicides in Los Angeles County. *Journal of Forensic Sciences, 38,* 831–834.

Santman, J., Myner, J., Cappeletty, G. C., & Perimutter, B. F. (1997). California juvenile gang members: An analysis of case records. *Journal of Gang Research, 5,*(1), 45–53.

Shakur, S., & Scott, K. (1994). *Monster: Autobiography of an L.A. gang member.* New York: Penguin.

Shaw, C. R., & McKay, H. D. (1942). *Juvenile delinquency and urban areas: A study of delinquents in relation to differential characteristics of local communities in American cities.* Chicago: University of Chicago Press.

Spergel, I. A. (1995). *The youth gang problem: A community approach.* New York: Oxford University Press.

Starr, K. (2004). *Coast of dreams: California on the edge, 1990–2003.* New York: Knopf.

Sutherland, E. (1939). *The principles of criminology.* Philadelphia: Lippincott.

Thornberry, T. P., Krohn, M. D., Lizotte, A. J., & Chard-Wierschem, D. (1993). The role of juvenile gangs in facilitating delinquency. *Journal of Research in Crime and Delinquency, 30,* 55–87.

Thrasher, F. A. (1927). *The gang: A study of 131 gangs in Chicago.* Chicago: University of Chicago Press.

Thrasher, F. A. (1936). The Boys' Club and juvenile delinquency. *American Journal of Sociology, 42,* 66–80.

Venkatesh, S. A. (2000). The social organization of street gang activity in an urban ghetto. *American Journal of Sociology, 103,* 82–111.

Vigil, J. D. (1988). *Barrio gangs: Street life and identity in Southern California.* Austin: University of Texas Press.

Walker, J. T., Watt, B., & White, E. A. (1994). Juvenile activities and gang involvement: The link between potentially delinquent activities and gang behavior. *Journal of Gang Research, 2,* 39–50.

Wang, A. Y. (1994). Pride and prejudice in high school gang members. *Adolescence, 29,*(114), 279–291.

Chapter 9

Juvenile Sexual Offending
An Evidence-Based Approach
to Assessment and Intervention

Gary O' Reilly
Clodagh Ann Dowling

This chapter focuses on the assessment and treatment of a subgroup of juvenile offenders who commit sexual offenses, labeled adolescent sex offenders. This is an important subgroup because research has shown that a significant proportion of sexual offenses are perpetrated not by adults but by those who are themselves children or adolescents. Further, research suggests that the causes of juvenile sexual offending are distinct from the causes of adult sexual offending. As we discuss throughout this chapter, adolescent sex offenders are a unique group who require specific and targeted assessment and treatment.

Prevalence of Juvenile Sexual Offending

Empirically identifying the extent to which children and adolescents are responsible for abusive sexual behavior is a difficult task. However, the research literature from the United States and European countries, including the United Kingdom and Ireland, estimates that between one-quarter to one-third of those who sexually assault others are under 18 years of age (Marshall & Barbaree, 1990; O' Reilly & Carr, 1999; Vizard, Monck, & Misch, 1995).

Rich (2003) summarized the international research literature in this area as follows. Young people between the ages of 7 and 17 years are responsible for 40% of sexual assaults against children under the age of 6; 34% of sexual assaults against children between the ages of 7 and 11; and 24% of sexual assaults against children between the ages of 12 and 17. This literature also indicates the following. Among juvenile offenders, 14-year-old boys perpetrate the greatest number of sexual offenses. Young people are most likely to use threats or violence when offending against older, rather than younger, children. In instances where the child victim is under 6 years of age, the juvenile offender is most likely to be a sibling or other close family member. Older children who are sexually victimized typically know the person responsible for their abuse, and in the case of a juvenile offender, it is statistically most likely to be a sibling, close relative, babysitter, neighbor, or some other person known to the victim.

Young people who sexually abuse others are not engaged in some form of "teenage experimentation." Indeed, their behavior has considerable potential for harm to others. For example, O' Reilly et al. (1998) reported the following concerning a sample of attendees at a community-based intervention program (who were, on average, 15.5 years old at the time they received the intervention and 14.2 years at the time of their first known offense): 56.5% had victimized a single child; 43.5%, more than one child; 26% had only one known offense, and 74% had between 3 and 50 known offenses. The extent of the problem and its effects on innocent victims underscore the need to understand the correlates of sexual offending in order to develop effective treatment.

Correlates of Juvenile Sexual Offending

Young people who sexually abuse differ in several important ways from adults who offend. Thakker, Ward, and Tidmarsh (2006) have summarized some key issues illustrated by empirical research on differences between juveniles and adults who commit sexual offenses. First, within the adult sexual offender literature there appear to be important differences in the psychological functioning of men who commit sexual crimes against adult women compared with those who perpetrate offenses against children. This distinction appears to have less utility within juvenile sexual offending populations. Second, the adult sexual offender literature demonstrates important associations between the type of sexual crime perpetrated within a category and that adult's sexual preferences. For example, an adult offender who sexually abuses a prepubescent boy is likely to be engaged in a behavior that reflects his underlying sexual orientation. Again, among juveniles these types of associations appear to be weaker. That is, the sexual preferences of adolescents are less well established and so may not be reflected in their offense histories. Third, for adult sexual offenders there are some characteristics that have a clear, empirically identified association with higher risk of recidivism, such as victim gender and degree of familiarity. Among juveniles, these associations appear to be weaker.

What emerges is a portrait of juvenile sexual offending that is fairly distinct from adult patterns, suggesting also that treatment programs for adults may be ill-suited to adolescent sex offenders. A logical follow-up question is: What are the primary characteristics of adolescent sex offenders that distinguish them from their nonoffending peers? The most recent, comprehensive review of these findings was conducted by Epps and Fisher (2004). They identified several differences within juvenile sexual offending and nonoffending groups that can be organized into the following four categories: abuse history, psychiatric disorder, education and academic attainment, and psychological functioning.

Abuse History

A history of physical abuse, witnessing family violence, emotional abuse, and sexual abuse was found more frequently among young people who sexually abuse than their nonoffending peers. Rates of prior sexual abuse among young people who offend varied between 4 and 60%, and physical abuse rates varied between 41 and 83%. Further, there is evidence that emotional and physical abuse were more frequently experienced by juvenile and adult offenders than sexual abuse (O' Reilly et al., 1998; O' Reilly, 2004).

Psychiatric Disorder

Higher levels of psychiatric disorder among adolescent sex offenders compared with their nonoffending peers have been reported in the empirical literature. Rates of psychiatric disorder among juvenile sexual abusers varied between 37 and 87%. For some young people, sexual offending appears to be part of a larger pattern of conduct disorder.

Education and Academic Attainment

Educational and academic attainment problems are found to be more likely among young people who engage in sexually abusive behavior compared with their nonoffending peers.

Psychological Functioning

Juvenile abusers have been found to display difficulties in self-image, distorted cognitions regarding sexuality and offending, victim- specific empathy deficits, social skills deficits, and problematic peer relationships.

However, these findings should be viewed cautiously. Indeed, much of the research in this area is confounded by serious methodological problems. First, it is difficult to access a sizable population of suitably homogeneous young people who sexually offend to allow for meaningful comparisons. Second, it is often difficult to motivate these young people to participate in assessments and interventions. Further, young abusers often present with denial and minimization concerning their psychological functioning. Finally, there is often reluctance among mental health professionals, teachers, and parents to allow access to suitable comparison groups of young people with other nonsexual offending difficulties or no difficulties, due to what often is perceived as a stigma associated with the research population. Still, empirical findings have been integrated into a number of important theoretical perspectives that can guide assessments and treatment.

Theoretical Perspectives on Adolescent Sexual Offending

A number of influential theories of adolescent sexual offending propose specific mechanisms or pathways to offending. We present brief outlines of the major positions of Marshall and Barbaree (see Barbaree & Marshall, 2006, for a complete review) and O' Reilly and Carr (see O' Reilly & Carr, 2004b, for a complete review).

The Marshall and Barbaree Model of Adolescent Sexual Offending

The Marshall and Barbaree model (Barbaree, Marshall, & McCormick, 1998; Marshall & Barbaree, 1990) traces the individual origins of sexual offending in adolescents and adults to key experiences throughout childhood and adolescence. According to this model, a developmental pathway that culminates in sexual offending begins in infancy and early childhood with attachment relationships with primary caregivers (usually parents) that are of a significantly poorer quality than those experienced by most children. These attachment difficulties usually reflect abusive, neglectful, or nonnurturing home environments. In such home settings, although parents may be physically present, they are frequently emotionally unavailable. This emotional unavailability can be due to a host of problems, including substance abuse, mental health, or other personal problems. As such, the earliest relationship environment of the child is one where (according to attachment theory) the child expresses his or her developmentally driven predisposition to establish a bond with parents who are, in turn, unable to reciprocate that bond.

Building on attachment theory, various attachment-style responses to such a relationship environment are possible. The child may learn that his or her needs are not responded to and so they must be suppressed or self-soothed. Or, the child may elicit an inconsistent but occasional response to relationship needs by engaging in disruptive and demanding behavior. When parents respond to this behavior with an aggressive, coercive, and manipulative parenting style, the child experiences a model of parental behavior that models aggression, coercion, and manipulation while it severely limits the positive relationship experiences that would lay the developmental foundations for healthy interpersonal skills. Within attachment theory these external behavioral relationship environments are believed to become internalized by developing children who uses them to set the cognitive–affective templates they will draw upon and develop over the course of their life to inform their self-concept (positive or negative), their view of others (positive or negative) and their view of relationships (reciprocal or one-sided).

The next significant step in the model occurs when a child with the disruptive/coercive relationship experience characterized above begins to attend school. Such a child is unlikely to successfully manage the many opportunities for prosocial development offered by the school environment. Instead of developing good relationships with peers and teachers, a child whose interpersonal style is predominantly aggressive, coercive, and manipulative is unlikely to form stable and satisfying relationships. Consequently, the developmental benefits offered by the successful formation of relationships outside the home are not enjoyed by the child. Instead, he or she further develops a negative self-image, a lack of self-confidence, and is additionally blocked in his or her potential for interpersonal development.

The intermediate childhood outcome of this developmental trajectory culminates in "a syndrome of social disability" that has five features: (1) an inability to establish and maintain intimate relationships;

(2) low self-esteem; (3) diverse antisocial, criminal attitudes and behaviors; (4) a lack of empathy; and (5) cognitive distortions that support and justify criminal and antisocial behavior. Although puberty heralds the emergence of new developmental challenges for all young people, it has an added significance for those whose life is characterized by the syndrome of social disability. During puberty normative developmental tasks include the emergence and sharing of personal identity and the establishment of sexual intimacy in some relationships. Consider this unfolding for males who must also come to terms with their own masculinity. Boys from nurturing families can establish successful and appropriate intimate relationships as a natural outgrowth of their history of healthy interpersonal interactions. In contrast, those from abusive family backgrounds are less well equipped and thus more likely to have experiences of repeated failure in establishing intimate relationships based on reciprocity and mutual sexual attraction. Consequently, they experience themselves as powerless, excluded, and emotionally isolated. This perception further undermines their self-concept, particularly their sense of masculinity, and may leave them with strong feelings of anger and resentment.

Being ill-equipped to achieve intimate relationships through healthy interpersonal means, the young male may utilize his default attachment style, laid down in early childhood by his interactions with primary caregivers, and apply his aggressive, manipulative, and coercive interpersonal strategy. Such a young person may seek sex either forcefully or with a younger, more vulnerable child. Such sexual experiences achieved through force, manipulation, or coercion establish memories of sexual contact that may be elaborated into inappropriate sexual fantasies that are subsequently reinforced through masturbation. Repeated recall of such fantasies may promote an urge to act them out in reality. Over time this process establishes and consolidates a conditioned interest in deviant sexuality. Once the adolescent begins to sexually offend, he becomes progressively more desensitized and distorted in thinking about the distress of his victims and the fear of being caught.

The Ward and Siegert Model of Sexual Offending

Ward and Siegert (2002) describe a model that draws on elements of the work presented by Marshall and Barbaree (1990), Finkelhor (1984), Hall (1996), and Hall and Hirschman (Hall & Hirschman, 1991, 1992). Ward and Siegert's integrative model outlines five distinct developmental pathways that may lead to sexual offending: (1) intimacy and social skills deficits; (2) deviant sexual scripts; (3) emotional dysregulation; (4) antisocial cognitions; and (5) multiple dysfunctional mechanisms. Each of the pathways reflects a distinct etiology and pattern of behavior discussed below. Some have more relevance for adults than for adolescents.

Pathway 1: Intimacy and Social Skills Deficits

The first pathway reflects the development of sexually abusive behavior as an outcome of a dysfunctional intimacy and social skills mechanism. It is very similar to the developmental trajectory described by Marshall and Barbaree (1990). However, according to this pathway, offenders typically begin their sexually abusive behavior in adulthood, replacing children for adults as relationship partners. Sexually abusive behaviors often follow an experience of rejection by adult partners (or potential partners) or periods of isolation. The offender treats the victimized child as a "pseudo-adult" or "surrogate partner" and develops distorted thinking that is supportive of this view, such as that the child accepts the adult offender's sexual needs.

Pathway 2: Deviant Sexual Scripts

On this pathway, the development of sexual offending is described as primarily an outcome of a deviant sexual script. Sexual scripts are mental representations acquired by an individual during life that reflect relevant past experience. These scripts organize and guide thoughts, feelings, and behavior related to sexuality. The major sexual script dysfunction concerns the context in which sexual behavior is seen as acceptable. In essence, sexual behavior is equated with the expression of interpersonal closeness. Interpersonal emotions such as loneliness are misinterpreted as signaling sexual needs. Given the confusion of interpersonal closeness with sexual acts, a pathway 2 offender may distort any behavior that a child displays. In other words, behavior that reflects the child's feelings of closeness to the abuser is distorted as a sexual expression. Similarly, any sexually abusive behavior by the abuser is internally misconstrued, according to a dysfunctional sexual script, as an expression of interpersonal closeness.

Accordingly, a person on pathway 2, with its associated sexual script dysfunction, is expected to experience four areas of difficulty: deviant patterns of sexual arousal, intimacy deficits, inappropriate emotional experiences, and inappropriate cognitive distortions. Pathway 2 sexual offending typically begins in adulthood, is more likely to be episodic rather than continuous, and will be associated with emotional loneliness and rejection; self-esteem among this group of offenders is likely to be low. Children become the targets of sexual behavior for this group of offenders as an outcome of opportunistic situational factors combined with the emotional and sexual demands of the offenders, rather than as an outcome of a dominant deviant sexual orientation.

Pathway 3: Emotional Dysregulation

The third pathway that leads to the development of sexually abusive behavior is characterized by emotional dysregulation. Emotional regulation is described as the ability of an individual to control affective states in order to meet personal goals. A range of emotional regulation difficulties is outlined as having the potential to significantly foster the development of sexually abusive behavior. These include problems recognizing emotions, an inability to adjust (i.e., regulate, modulate) emotional states when they are experienced, anger management problems, the experience of strong negative affective states such as low mood or high anxiety, and an inability to utilize appropriate social supports during times of emotional difficulty. Pathway 3 offenders respond in one of two ways to their emotional dysregulation. They either become overwhelmed and sexually uninhibited, or they use sexual behavior as an inappropriate soothing strategy. Pathway 3 offenders tend to prefer sexual activity with age-appropriate partners but shift to sexual activity with children at times of severe emotional dysregulation.

Difficulties with the regulation of emotions may be experienced in adolescence as well as adulthood. Consequently, those on pathway three may begin their offending behavior during their teenage years. When they are not experiencing high levels of stress, these individuals exhibit normal sexual interests and behaviors. Pathway 3 offenders are unlikely to attempt to groom a "close" relationship with a child prior to sexual assault. The self-esteem of individuals in this group may be low or high depending on the person concerned.

Pathway 4: Antisocial Cognitions

Pathway 4 is characterized by offending diversity. This is the pathway of a subgroup of offenders whose sexually abusive behavior is part of a wider pattern of more general criminal behavior. This subgroup holds a range of beliefs and cognitions that support antisocial behavior. The sexual abuse of children is one of many antisocial acts, including substance abuse, theft, and violence. Pathway 4 offenders are likely to have difficulties with impulsivity and often engage in behavior consistent with conduct disorder from childhood. More specifically, their sexual offending behavior is usually reflective of their general antisocial outlook on life combined with poorly controlled sexual impulses and opportunistic situational factors. Consequently, their offending behavior may not reflect a persistent deviant sexual preference directed toward children. Given that their abusive behavior is part of a broader pattern of long-standing criminal and anti-social behavior, they may begin to engage in sexually abusive behavior from a relatively early age.

Pathway 5: Multiple Dysfunctional Mechanisms

Although those on pathway 5 have multiple dysfunctional mechanisms, they are clearly described as having a particular sexual script dysfunction that promotes child–adult sexual activity in combination with pronounced difficulties in all of the other pathway mechanisms. Offenders in this category inappropriately prefer sexual relationships with children rather than adults. Compared to those on the other pathways, these individuals are considered the "pure" pedophiles. The development of a pedophilic sexual script in these individuals usually reflects childhood experiences of sexual victimization and/or exposure to sexual behavior or material at a young age. Pathway 5 offenders often begin to sexually abuse others before they reach adulthood. A feature of this group is that prior to committing their first offense, they fantasize about sexual contact with children, reflecting their underlying pedophilic sexual orientation. Pathway 5 offenders: (a) demonstrate an early onset of sexually abusive behavior; (b) have ingrained cognitive distortions regarding sexual activity with children; (c) undergo deviant patterns of sexual arousal in response to children; and (d) experience positive affect in response to their offending behavior. Given their underlying sexual orientation toward children, they are unlikely to develop intimate and mature relationships with other adults. They are also likely to hold themselves in high self-esteem because they believe their sexually offending behavior is justified.

Emerging Consensus in the Field Regarding Juvenile Sexual Offending: Toward a Common Ground for Management and Treatment

We have presented evidence regarding the prevalence of juvenile sexual offending and empirically validated correlates and causes. Further, we have reviewed two major theoretical perspectives that offer unique insights into the plausible developmental histories of this group of offenders. These positions are, indeed, further supported by an emerging consensus in the field, with particular relevance for the management and treatment of adolescent sex offenders.

This point is illustrated by Hackett, Masson, and Phillips (2006), who empirically identified the points of consensus and divergence of opinion among mental health professionals working with adolescents who engage in sexually abusive behavior. The researchers surveyed 78 professionals who were (at the time of the survey) working intensively with this population. Of the professionals who participated in this study, 57 were social workers, 8 were psychologists, 4 were psychiatrists, 4 were clinical nurse specialists, and the remaining 5 were from a family therapy, occupational, or play therapy background.

Among survey respondents, there was 99% agreement that those under 18 years of age who engage in sexually abusive behavior "are first and foremost children and should not be regarded as mini-adult sex offenders" (Hackett et al., 2006, p. 149). There was very high agreement among this group (82%) that young people who are sexually abusive are capable of serious and harmful behavior. There was also very high agreement (81%) that sexually abusive behavior by those under 18 is not simply a reflection of prior sexual victimization experienced by the child but may reflect one of a number of potential developmental pathways. Finally, this group strongly endorsed the view (90%) that among young people who sexually abuse, there is a subgroup of those who are at high risk for sexual recidivism; however, the vast majority do not go on to sexually offend in adulthood.

In summary, juvenile sexual offenders appear to be a diverse group with multiple pathways that distinguish them from adult sexual offenders and each other. This diversity raises the issue of the extent to which they need targeted assessment and treatment, can benefit from protocols used with the general offender population, or need some combination of services used with offenders in general but also tailored to their unique profiles and needs. We now turn to a discussion of assessment practices, followed by a review of treatment approaches.

Conducting Assessments with Adolescent Sexual Offenders

Assessing adolescent sex offenders is a requisite to treatment planning. However, it is a complex process requiring careful attention to the details of how to conduct assessments and what to include in the protocols. Specifically, the assessment phase of the process can be thought of as having structural and content components, with recommended strategies to optimize success.

The Structure of Assessments

Whom to Include in the Assessment

All appropriate participants should be invited to play a part, including the young person, his or her parents or guardians (if available), and other professionals such as teachers, case workers, social workers, and mental health professionals involved with the young person and his or her family.

Managing Denial and Minimization

The assessment team should accept that the young person and his or her family can be at various psychological points along a continuum from complete denial to full acknowledgment of the sexually abusive behavior. It is unrealistic to expect full acknowledgment prior to, or even during, the assessment process, although this may occur. To do so would exclude the vast majority of young people or their families from assessment. Instead it is more helpful to regard full acknowledgment of the sexually abusive behavior as a goal of intervention.

Adopting Therapist Features Associated with Positive Outcome

An important component in successful psychotherapy outcomes consists of specific therapist characteristics. Just like any young person and his or her family attending a therapeutic service for intervention, those who engage in sexually abusive behavior respond best to therapists who encourage active participation from the client, ask open-ended questions, and demonstrate respect, empathy, warmth, genuineness, clarity, appropriately rewarding and encouraging behavior, and directive or reflective intervention as needed (Marshall, Anderson, & Fernandez, 1999).

Confronting and aggressively challenging a young person about his or her abusive behavior in assessment is likely to be counterproductive and potentially harmful to the client, especially if this response echoes past experiences of coercively styled relationships. Consequently, during assessment the therapist strives to create a collaborative but noncollusive relationship with the young person and his or her family. This style of relationship breaks down denial and minimization in a respectful and effective manner. That is, if a young person feels respected and respects the therapist, then he or she can use assessment and intervention to face the difficult reality of prior sexually abusive behavior with appropriate remorse but without inappropriate shame.

Inclusion of Other Sources of Information

The assessment should complement the information gathered from clinical interviews with the young person and his or her family and other sources of information. These additional sources should include the results of psychometric assessment instruments to clarify aspects of the young person's functioning, such as his or her IQ level, general psychological health (e.g., the Achenbach System of Empirically Based Assessment [ACEBA] scales), and sexual-offense-specific aspects of his or her functioning. Accessing third-party reports, such as victim statements to police, court reports, and social services reports, also provides vital information.

Clear Formulation and Communication of Findings and Recommendations

At the conclusion of the assessment, all of the information should be integrated to reflect an understanding of how the young person's development led to sexually abusive behavior, the nature of the behavior engaged in, the offense-specific intervention needs (i.e., relapse prevention based on risk factors), and the more holistic intervention needs (i.e., relapse prevention based on the attainment of positive life goals). This formulation should be clearly articulated in a written report that is shared with the young person and his or her family and appropriately disseminated to the child's protection network and the judicial system. It should conclude with a clear expression of recommendations and treatment goals that form the basis of a written contract for intervention that supports the young person.

The Content of Assessments

The content areas covered during the assessment should be guided by theoretical models and empirical research such as those described above (see O' Reilly & Carr, 2004b). A useful source of information on what aspects of the young person's sexual-offense-specific functioning should be considered comes from an expert panel established by the American Psychiatric Association (American Psychiatric Association Task Force, 1999), as outlined in Table 9.1. However, in keeping with the continuous development of ideas regarding the clinical assessment

TABLE 9.1. American Psychiatric Association Recommended Content Areas for the Clinical Assessment of a Young Person with Sexually Abusive Behavior

- Victim statements to police, social services, mental health professionals, etc.
- Background information, including family history, educational history, medical history, psychosocial history and developmental history.
- Interpersonal relationship history.
- Sexual history, including deviant sexual interests and the emergence of sexually aggressive behavior over time.
- Reported use of deviant sexual fantasies and interests.
- Intensity of sexual arousal during the time surrounding each offense.
- Dynamics and process of victim selection.
- Use of coercion, force, violence, and weapons.
- Behavioral warning signs.
- Identifiable triggers leading to inappropriate sexual behaviors.
- Thinking errors such as cognitive distortions or irrational beliefs.
- Spectrum of injury to the victim, from the violation of trust, to instigation of fear, to physical injury.
- Sadistic elements to the sexually abusive behavior.
- Ritualistic and obsessive characteristics of the sexually abusive behavior.
- Deviant nonsexual interests.

- History of assaultive behavior.
- Issues related to separation and loss.
- Antisocial characteristics.
- Psychiatric diagnosis, including disruptive behavior disorders, affective disorders, developmental disorders, personality disorders, posttraumatic stress disorder, substance abuse disorder, and organic mental disorder.
- Ability to accept responsibility.
- Degree of denial or minimization.
- Understanding wrongfulness.
- Concern for injury to victim.
- Quality of social, assertive, and empathic skills.
- Family's response (from denial, minimization, support, to ability to intervene appropriately).
- Exposure to pornography.
- History of sexual, physical, and/or emotional victimization.
- Ability to control deviant sexual interest.
- Knowledge and expression of appropriate sexual interests.
- School performance and educational level.
- Mental status examination.

Note. Data from American Psychiatric Association Task Force (1999).

of young people who sexually abuse, this content needs to be complemented by the inclusion of an additional focus that inquires about the strengths and psychological resources that the young person and his or her family possess.

Standardized clinical assessment tools, such as the Estimate of Risk of Adolescent Sexual Offense Recidivism (ERASOR; Worling & Curwen, 2001) and the Juvenile Sex Offender Assessment Protocol–II (J-SOAP-II; Prentky & Righthand, 2003), are available to help guide the collection of relevant information. The general risk–need instruments described by Hoge in Chapter 3 of this volume may be useful in assessing the broader personal and psychological characteristics and needs of the young person.

Interventions for Adolescent Sex Offenders

As we mentioned at the outset of this chapter, juveniles are responsible for a significant portion of sexual offending. Further, rates of committing further sexual offenses are high, ranging from 10 to 37% in various surveys (Hanson et al., 2002; Rubenstein, Yeager, Goodstein, & Lewis, 1993; Sipe, Jensen, & Everett, 1998). Still, research on the effectiveness of therapeutic interventions with this group is sparse. To date, most efforts involve the application of empirically validated programs such as multisystemic therapy (MST; Henggeler, Schoenwald, Borduin, Rowland, & Cunningham, 1998), adaptation of programming based on cognitive-behavioral principles, and/or customized programs developed within juvenile treatment or correctional settings. Morrison (2004) outlined 10 organizational steps essential for the implementation of effective sex offender treatment programs. These are:

- Define and map service needs.
- Establish a clear mandate for service provision.
- Set service eligibility requirements.
- Establish a philosophy for the service.
- Establish policy for nontherapeutic aspects of service.
- Develop program.
- Prepare and manage staff.
- Engage in external networking.
- Continuously evaluate service.
- Avoid pitfalls.

To be effective, newly developed programs must incorporate "best bets" for specific areas to target. Toward this end, Hackett et al. (2006) asked professionals working with juvenile sexual offenders to identify the treatment intervention components they regarded as important to the therapeutic process. The results of this survey are presented in Table 9.2. As shown, leading candidates for inclusion are the development of emotional competence; anger management; changing cognitive distortions (specifically about sexuality and relationships); development of a range of prosocial emotional, cognitive, and behavioral skills; and, perhaps most specific to offenders, their understanding of the offense cycle and pathways to sexually abusive behavior.

TABLE 9.2. Recommended Components of Intervention Programs for Young People Who Sexually Abuse, as Endorsed by Professionals Working in the Area

Component	Percentage of professionals agreeing
Essential (80–100% agreement)	
1. Development of emotional competence skills, including the management of anger and distress	93%
2. Changing cognitive distortions about sexuality and relationships	90%
3. Development of prosocial emotional, cognitive, and behavioral skills	87%
4. The young person gaining an understanding of his or her offense cycle and/or pathways into sexually abusive behavior	85%
5. Sexuality education	85%
6. Life space work (understanding boundaries and social interaction and the development of social skills)	84%
7. Development of relapse prevention skills	84%
8. Family work	82%
9. Understanding the consequences of further abusive behavior	81%
10. Development of empathy	81%
Desirable (70–79% agreement)	
1. Dealing with deviant sexual urges	79%
2. Problem solving	71%
Additional (less than 69% agreement)	
1. Changing sexually abusive fantasies and promoting appropriate positive sexual fantasies	63%

Data from Hackett, Masson, and Phillips (2006).

A Final Word

Assessment and intervention with young people who engage in sexually abusive behavior is a complex task. However, there is an expanded theoretical and evidence base that provides a useful starting point for effective treatment with this population. Future research in this area should aim to further our understanding of young people who sexually offend and their families, refine the essential and supplemental ingredients of intervention that are effective, and identify young people who are at risk of committing a sexual crime. These goals are certainly achievable and will further contribute to a reduction in sexual crimes.

References

American Psychiatric Association Task Force. (1999). *Dangerous sex offenders: A task force report of the American Psychiatric Association.* Washington, DC: American Psychiatric Association.

Barbaree, H. E., & Marshall, W. L. (Eds.), (2006). *The juvenile sex offender* (2nd ed.). New York: Guilford Press.

Barbaree, H. E., Marshall, W. L., & McCormick, J. (1998). The development of sexually deviant behavior among adolescents and its implications for prevention and treatment. *Irish Journal of Psychology, 19,* 1–31.

Epps, K., & Fisher, D. (2004). A review of the research literature on young people who sexually abuse. In G. O' Reilly, W. Marshall, A. Carr, & R. Beckett (Eds.), *The handbook of clinical intervention with young people who sexually abuse* (pp. 62–102). London: Brunner-Routledge.

Finkelhor, D. (1984). *Child sexual abuse: New theory and research.* New York: Free Press.

Hackett, S., Masson, H., & Phillips, S. (2006). Exploring consensus in practice with youth who are sexually abusive: Findings from a Delphi study of practitioner views in the United Kingdom and the Republic of Ireland. *Child Maltreatment, 11,* 146–156.

Hall, G. C. N. (1996). *Theory based assessment, treatment and prevention of sexual aggression.* New York: Oxford University Press.

Hall, G. C. N., & Hirschman, R. (1991). Towards a theory of sexual aggression: A quadripartite model. *Journal of Consulting and Clinical Psychology, 59,* 662–669.

Hall, G. C. N., & Hirschman, R. (1992). Sexual aggression against children: A conceptual perspective on etiology. *Criminal Justice and Behavior, 19,* 8–23.

Hanson, R. K., Gordon, A., Harris, A. J. R., Marques, J. K., Murphy, W., et al. (2002). First report of the collaborative outcome data project on the effectiveness of psychological treatment for sex offenders. *Sexual Abuse: A Journal of Research and Treatment, 14,* 169–193.

Henggeler, S. W., Schoenwald, S. K., Borduin, C. M., Rowland, M. D., & Cunningham, P. B. (1998). *Multisystemic treatment of antisocial behavior in children and adolescents.* New York: Guilford Press.

Marshall, W. L., Anderson, D., & Fernandez, Y. (1999). *Cognitive behavioral treatment of sexual offenders.* Chichester, UK: Wiley.

Marshall, W. L., & Barbaree, H. E. (1990). An integrated theory of the etiology of sexual offending. In W. L. Marshall, D. R. Laws, & H. E. Barbaree (Eds.), *Handbook of sexual assault: Issues, theories and treatment of the offender* (pp. 257–275). New York: Plenum Press.

Morrison, T. (2004). Preparing services and staff to work with young people who sexually abuse: Context, mandate, pitfalls, and frameworks. In G. O' Reilly, W. Marshall, A. Carr, & R. Beckett (Eds.), *The handbook of clinical intervention with young people who sexually abuse* (pp. 385–418). London: Brunner-Routledge.

O' Reilly, G. (2004). *An independent evaluation of the Irish Prison Service sexual offender intervention program.* Unpublished doctoral dissertations, Department of Psychology, University College, Dublin.

O' Reilly, G., & Carr, A. (1999). Child sexual abuse in Ireland: A synthesis of two studies. *Irish Journal of Psychology, 20,* 1–14.

O' Reilly, G., & Carr, A. (2004). A review of theoretical models of sexual offending. In G. O' Reilly, W. Marshall, A. Carr, & R. Beckett (Eds.), *The handbook of clinical intervention with young people who sexually abuse* (pp. 163–190). London: Brunner-Routledge.

O' Reilly, G., Sheridan, A., Carr, A., Cherry, J., Donohoe, E., McGrath, K., et. al. (1998). A descriptive study of adolescent sexual offenders in an Irish community-based treatment programme. *Irish Journal of Psychology, 19,* 152–167.

Prentky, R. A., & Righthand, S. (2003). *Juvenile sex offender assessment protocol: Manual.* Bridgewater, MA: Justice Resource Institute.

Rich, P. (2003). *Understanding, assessing, and rehabilitating juvenile sexual offenders.* New York: Wiley.

Rubenstein, M., Yeager, C. A., Goodstein, C., & Lewis, D. O. (1993). Sexually assaultive male juveniles: A follow-up. *American Journal of Psychiatry, 150,* 262–265.

Sipe, R., Jensen, E. L., & Everett, R. S. (1998). Adolescent sexual offenders grown up. Recidivism in young adulthood. *Criminal Justice and Behavior, 25,* 109–124.

Thakker, J., Ward T., & Tidmarsh, P. (2006). A reevaluation of relapse prevention with adolescents who sexually offend: A good-lives model. In H. E. Barbaree & W. L. Marshall (Eds.), *The juvenile sex offender* (2nd ed., pp. 313–335). New York: Guilford Press.

Vizard, E., Monck, E., & Misch, P. (1995). Child and adolescent sex abuse perpetrators: A review of the research literature. *Journal of Child Psychology and Psychiatry, 5,* 731–756.

Ward, T., & Siegert, R. J. (2002). Towards a comprehensive theory of child sexual abuse: A theory knitting perspective. *Psychology, Crime and Law, 8,* 319–351.

Worling, J. R., & Curwen, T. (2001). *Estimate of Risk of Adolescent Sexual Offense Recidivism* (ERASOR). Toronto: Thistletown Regional Centre for Children and Adolescents.

Chapter 10

Mental Health, Substance Abuse, and Trauma

Bonita M. Veysey

Try to imagine what the world looks like to a 3-year-old child who is raped by her father at night. She thinks this is normal. She doesn't know any better. She has no adult perspective, no objective context in which to understand this experience; to know that this is not how children are supposed to grow and thrive. Her reality is full of pain and fear. The adult who is supposed to protect her betrays her while others stand silent witness. Try to imagine life to a 10-year-old who is afraid to go home after school because he doesn't know if tonight will be the night when he is beaten unconscious or, worse, have to witness his sister's terrible unmoving and silent body. He has begun to understand that not all the children he knows live like this. This child pretends to the outside world that everything is fine. He attributes his poor school performance to his own inherent laziness and stupidity, not to the constant worry and distraction of survival. He lives a double life. He has learned shame and secrecy.

Both of these children will grow up with their personalities formed by abuse. They grow and mature with violence and betrayal shaping their relationships, beliefs, and hopes. These children create emotional and physical strategies to survive. They are adept at these skills and yet, at the same time, feel wildly out of control. As they age, both their survival strategies and their rage and despair appear to the authorities with whom they have contact as mental health problems or, more commonly, as delinquency. There is no one set of behaviors that characterizes abuse. Children may lack empathy, chronically lie, or be abusive toward other children or animals. They may just as likely be lethargic, depressed, or suicidal. They may run away, be sexually active at a very young age, or drink or drug heavily. These behaviors are often understood as symptoms of psychopathology or bad behavior by the adults in their lives and not as the predictable coping skills that they are.

The role of abuse and neglect in delinquent and violent behavior has long been established, whereas the role of abuse and neglect in the emergence of psychiatric disorders and substance abuse and dependence is a more recent topic of investigation in mental health research. The most pressing challenge in this field is to integrate these bodies of research into a comprehensive whole to (1) understand the complex causal relationships among abuse and neglect, delinquency, and co-occurring mental health and substance use disorders, and (2) to apply this knowledge to the development of effective treatment interventions for justice-involved youth.

This chapter presents the prevalence of mental and substance use disorders and the co-occurrence of the two; the rates of abuse among justice-involved youth; and the nature of the relationship between childhood abuse and co-occurring disorders in this population. Principles of trauma[1]-informed treatment and promising integrated approaches to the treatment of co-occurring mental health and substance use disorders and trauma conclude the chapter.

The following sections make important distinctions between girls and boys and between points of contact in the juvenile justice system. Life experiences and exposure to abuse, psychosocial and physical developmental, psychiatric problems, use of alcohol and other drugs, socialization and delinquent behavior differ by gender. Therefore, when possible, information is presented by gender. The point of contact in the juvenile justice system has implications for youth characteristics and treatment interventions. The deeper into the system, the more severe or greater the delinquency and the more severe the presenting mental health and substance use problems and trauma experiences. Developmental stage (or age) and culture also are critical features. However, the research and treatment programs reviewed in this chapter do not present findings by age or cultural group.

Prevalence of Mental Health and Substance Use Disorders among Justice-Involved Youth

The prevalence of mental health disorders[2] among adolescents in the juvenile justice system is markedly high, especially among girls. In studies assessing a broad range of psychiatric disorders or general mental status (summarized in Table 10.1), girls have higher rates than boys. Timmons-Mitchell and colleagues (1997) estimated that 84% of girls compared to 27% of boys, had evidence of serious mental health symptoms. Similarly, Teplin, Abram, McClelland, Dulcan, & Mericle (2002), in the most rigorous epidemiological study of psychiatric illnesses among youth in detention to date, estimated that 74% of girls, compared to 66% of boys, met the criteria for a current disorder.

Both girls and boys are likely to be diagnosed with more than one disorder, particularly a mental disorder with a substance use disorder. Studies of psychiatric comorbidity consistently report higher prevalence rates among girls in detention than comparable boys. Ulzen and Hamilton (1998) found that 82% of girls, compared to 58% of boys, met the criteria for two or more disorders. Similarly, in a study of comorbidity of substance abuse/dependence with a second psychiatric diagnosis, virtually all girls (99%) met criteria for comorbidity, compared to 69% of boys (Randall, Henggeler, Pickrel, & Brondino, 1999).

Specific Diagnoses

The following sections provide rates of specific disorders. These diagnoses are organized into the five broad categories, as suggested by the Columbia University Guidelines for Child and Adolescent Mental Health Referral (Wasserman, Ko, & Jensen, 2001): (1) mood disorders, including major depression, dysthymia, and bipolar disorder; (2) anxiety disorders, including generalized anxiety, specific phobias, separation anxiety, social phobia, panic, agoraphobia, obsessive–compulsive, and posttraumatic stress; (3) disruptive disorders, including attention-deficit/hyperactivity, conduct and oppositional defiant; (4) substance use disorders, including alcohol, marijuana, and other drug abuse and dependence; and (5) schizophrenia. Nine studies assessed a broad range of diagnoses, whereas the remaining 14 studies focused on only one or two diagnoses or correlates.

Mood Disorders

Of the studies (Bickel & Campbell, 2002; Duclos et al., 1998; Myers, Burket, Lyles, Stone, & Kemph, 1990; Richards, 1996; Rhode, Mace, &

TABLE 10.1. Prevalence Rates of Mental Health Symptoms/Disorders among Youth in the Juvenile Justice System

Authors	Sample size	Location	Point in justice system	Age (years)	Prevalence (female)	Prevalence (male)	Measure
Teplin, Abram, McClelland, Dulcan, & Mericle (2002)	N = 657 females, 1,172 males	Chicago	Detention	Range = 10–18 Mean = 14.9	73.8% Any of the listed disorders 70.0% Any except CD 27.6% Any affective disorder 21.6% MDE 15.8% Dysthymia 1.8% Manic episode 1.0% Psychotic disorder 30.8% Any anxiety disorder 1.5% Panic 18.6% Separation anxiety 12.3% Overanxious 7.3% Generalized anxiety 10.6% OCD 21.4% ADHD 45.6% ADBD 17.5% ODD 40.6% CD 46.8% Any substance abuse disorder 26.5% Alcohol use 40.5% Marijuana use 6.9% Other substance use 20.9% Alcohol + other drug	66.3% Any of the listed disorders 60.9% Any except CD 18.7% Any affective disorder 13.0% MDE 12.2% Dysthymia 2.2% Manic episode 1.0% Psychotic disorder 21.3% Any anxiety disorder 0.3% Panic 12.9% Separation anxiety 6.7% Overanxious 7.1% Generalized anxiety 8.3% OC 16.6% ADHD 41.4% Any DBD 14.5% ODD 37.8% Conduct disorder 50.7% Any substance abuse disorder 25.9% Alcohol use 44.8% Marijuana use 2.4% Other substance use 20.7% Alcohol + other drug	Diagnostic Interview for Children (DISC-2.3; Shaffer et al., 1996)

(continued)

213

TABLE 10.1. (continued)

Authors	Sample size	Location	Point in justice system	Age (years)	Prevalence (female)	Prevalence (male)	Measure
Bickel & Campbell (2002)	N=7 females, 43 males	Tasmania, Australia	Detention	Range = 12–18 Mean = 15.7	100% CD 57.1% MDD 28.6% Dysthymia 85.7% Mood disorder 57.1% PTSD 71.4% Anxiety without PTSD 71.4% Anxiety with PTSD 0% Adjustment disorder 42.9% Somatization disorder 28.6% ADHD 100% Substance abuse disorder	97.7% CD 25.6% MDD 14.0% Dysthymia 39.5% Mood disorder 32.6% PTSD 25.6% Anxiety without PTSD 41.9% Anxiety with PTSD 25.6% Adjustment disorder 18.6% Somatization disorder 48.8% ADHD 58.1% Substance abuse disorder	Adolescent Psychopathology Scale (APS; Reynolds, 1998)
Randall, Henggeler, Pickrel, & Brondino (1999)	N = 25 females, 93 males	Charlston, SC	Detention	Range = 12–17 Mean = 15.2	99% Comorbid (mental health disorders with substance abuse/ dependence)	69% Comorbid (mental health disorders with substance abuse/ dependence)	DSM-III-R (Spitzer et al., 1998) Diagnostic Interview Schedule for Children—Child Report (DISC-2.3; Shaffer et al., 1992)
Ulzen & Hamilton (1998)	N = 11 females, 38 males	Toronto, Canada	Secure custody facility	Mean = 15.4	72.7% Present depression 36.4% Past depression 54.5% PTSD	18.4% Present depression 7.9% Past depression 15.8% PTSD	Diagnostic Interview for Children and Adolescents—

					54.5% Separation anxiety disorder 54.5% Overanxious disorder 18.2% CD 18.2% ADD/ADHD 63.6% ODD 63.6% Alcohol dependence 45.5% Dysthymia 18.2% Mania 81.8% Comorbidity	23.7% Separation anxiety disorder 18.4% Overanxious disorder 31.5% CD 28.9% ADD/ADHD 39.5% ODD 31.5% Alcohol dependence 21.1% Dysthymia 28.9% Mania 57.9% Comorbidity	Revised (DICA-R; Welner et al., 1987)
Duclos et al. (1998)	Northern Plains reservation (Native American only)	N = 86 females, 64 males	Detention	Range = 12–18 Median = 15	16% Mood disorder 13% Anxiety disorder 19% Disruptive disorder (CD, ODD, or ADHD) 39% Substance abuse	6% Mood disorder 13% Anxiety disorder 23% Disruptive disorder (CD, ODD, or ADHD) 37% Substance abuse	Diagnostic Interview Schedule for Children (DISC2.3; Shaffer et al., 1989)
Cauffman, Feldman, Waterman, & Steiner (1998)	California	N = 96 females, 93 males	California Youth Authority Ventura School; incarceration	Range = 13–22 Mean = 17.2	65.3% Lifetime PTSD 48.9% Current PTSD 11.7% Partial symptoms of PTSD at time of study	— 32.3% Current PTSD 9.4% Partial symptoms of PTSD at time of study	Revised Psychiatric Diagnostic Interview (Othmer et al., 1981)
Timmons-Mitchell et al. (1997)	Ohio	N = 52 females, 121 males	Juvenile institution	Mean = 15.7	84% Serious mental health symptoms	27% Mental health symptoms	Symptom Checklist-90—Revised (SCL-90-R; Derogatis, 1994)

(continued)

215

TABLE 10.1. (continued)

Authors	Sample size	Location	Point in justice system	Age (years)	Prevalence (female)	Prevalence (male)	Measure
Timmons-Mitchell et al. (1997)	*N* = 25 females, 25 males	Ohio	Juvenile institution	Mean = 15.7	88% Mood disorder 72% Anxiety disorder 56% Substance abuse disorder 96% CD 12% Psychotic disorder 68% ADHD 76% Sleep disorder 16% Eating disorder	72% Mood disorder 52% Anxiety disorder 88% Substance abuse disorder 100% CD 16% Psychotic disorder 76% ADHD 68% Sleep disorder 0% Eating disorder	Diagnostic Interview Schedule for Children (DISC; Costello et al, 1984)
Rohde, Mace, & Seeley, (1997)	*N* = 97 females, 457 males	N/A	Secure detention facility	Mean = 15.3	21.6% Current suicidal ideation 39.8% Lifetime history of attempt	12.7% Current suicidal ideation 15.1% Lifetime history of attempt	Current suicidal ideation assessed with questions previously used by Lewinsohn et al. (1996); researchers developed additional questions
Rohde, Mace, & Seeley (1997)	*N* = 16 females, 44 males	N/A	Secure detention facility	Mean = 14.9	62.5% Lifetime episode of major depression 43.8% Lifetime history of suicide attempt	31.8% Lifetime episode of major depression 34.1% Lifetime history of suicide attempt	Version of the Schedule for Affective Disorders and Schizophrenia for School Age Children (Orvaschel et al., 1982); researchers developed questions for lifetime history of attempt

Study	N	Location	Age	Findings	Instrument
Richards (1996)	$N = 20$ females, 80 males	New Zealand	Range = 12–20 Mean = 16.1	65% CD 80% Substance abuse disorder 15% Major depression dysthymia ASPD 0% Schizophrenia 0% ADHD 35% Personality disorder 20% Three diagnoses 65% Two diagnoses 15% One diagnosis	Semistructured interview with DSM-III-R criteria
				72.5% CD 70.1% Substance abuse 12.5% Major depression dysthymia 8.7% ASPD 5.0% Schizophrenia 5.0% ADHD 3.7% Personality disorder 26.2% Three diagnoses 60.0% Two diagnoses 13.8% One diagnosis	
Miller (1994)	$N = 45$ females, 39 males	Western state	Mean = 16.1	65% Thought about suicide ever 56% Attempted suicide	Student Questionnaire (Miller, 1990, 1993)
				26% Thought about suicide ever 26% Attempted suicide	
Eppright, Kashani, Robison, & Reid (1993)	$N = 21$ females, 79 males	Midwestern United States	Range = 11–17 Mean = 15.5	48% BPD 22% BPD	Diagnostic Interview for Children and Adolescents—Revised (DICA-R; Herjanic et al., 1977) Structured Clinical Interview for DSM-III Personality Disorders (SCID-II; Spitzer et al., 1989)

Note. ADD, attention-deficit dsorder; ADHD, attention-deficit/hyperactivity disorder; ASPD, antisocial personality disorder; BPD, borderline personality disorder; CD, conduct disorder; DBD, disruptive behavior disorder; MDD, major depressive disorder; MDE, major depressive episode; OCD, obsessive–compulsive disorder; ODD, oppositional defiant disorder; PTSD, posttraumatic stress disorder.

Seely, 1997; Teplin et al., 2002; Timmons-Mitchell et al., 1997; Ulzen & Hamilton, 1998) that estimated the prevalence of mood disorders (with or without further diagnostic refinement), the rate of disorders for girls ranged from 15 to 88%, whereas boys ranged from 6 to 72%. Major depression is the most common diagnosis among the mood disorders. Estimates of a current depressive episode range from 15 to 73% for girls and from 13 to 26% for boys. Dysthymia rates range from 16 to 46% for girls and from 12 to 21% for boys. Like the trend in general mood disorders, girls have higher rates of depression and dysthymia than boys. Only two studies investigated the prevalence of bipolar disorder or manic episodes. The studies varied significantly on the magnitude of the estimates, from below 5% for both boys and girls to 20–30% for boys and girls. However, in both studies the rates were higher for boys than girls.

Anxiety Disorders

Anxiety disorders are common among youth in the juvenile justice system. Rates range from 13 to 72% for girls and from 13 to 52% for boys in studies assessing anxiety generally (Bickel & Campbell, 2002; Cauffman, Feldman, Alterman, & Steiner, 2002; Duclos et al., 1998; Myers et al., 1990; Teplin et al., 2002; Timmons-Mitchell et al., 1997; Ulzen & Hamilton, 1998). The rates of specific anxiety disorders, like mood disorders, generally are more common among girls than boys. One quarter to one-half of all girls in the juvenile justice system have existing symptoms of at least one anxiety disorder.

Among the specific anxiety disorders, posttraumatic stress among girls ranged from 49 to 57% and from 16 to 33% among boys. Estimates of separation anxiety disorder ranged from 19 to 55% of girls and from 13 to 24% of boys. From 12 to 55% of girls had symptoms of overanxious disorder, whereas between 7 and 19% of boys had symptoms of this disorder.

Disruptive Disorders

Disruptive disorders, such as conduct and oppositional defiant, are common among juvenile justice populations of both girls and boys. This prevalence is at least partially due to the fact that delinquent behavior is symptomatic of these diagnoses. In addition, attention-deficit disorder (ADD) with or without hyperactivity (ADHD) is highly correlated with involvement in the juvenile justice system and is often included in this class of disorders. Studies assessing disruptive disorders as a class find that from 19 to 46% of girls and 23 to 41% of boys had symptoms of at least one of these disorders (Bickel & Campbell, 2002; Duclos et al., 1998; Richards, 1996; Teplin et al., 2002; Timmons-Mitchell et al., 1997; Ulzen & Hamilton, 1998).

Studies assessing specific disruptive disorders varied substantially on both the rate of disorder in the population as a whole (i.e., girls and boys together) and whether girls or boys have higher rates. Conduct disorder, in general, ranges from 15 to 100%, with higher rates found more commonly among boys. Not surprisingly, the detention samples have higher rates than the community samples. In the two studies that evaluated oppositional defiant disorder, girls had higher rates than boys. Girls' estimates ranged from 18 to 64%, whereas boys ranged from 15 to 40%. The prevalence of ADD/ADHD also varied widely, from a low of 0% to a high of 68% for girls and from 5 to 76% for boys. In all studies except one, boys were more likely than girls to have this diagnosis.

Substance Use Disorders

Substance use and consequent diagnoses of abuse and dependence are common for both girls and boys in the juvenile justice system. In most studies substance abuse is the norm (i.e., more than half; Bickel & Campbell, 2002; Duclos et al., 1998; Kataoka, 2001; Myers et al., 1990; Richards, 1996; Teplin et al., 2002; Ulzen & Hamilton, 1998). Substance use disorders range from 39 to 100% among girls and 37 to 88% among boys. Findings were inconsistent across studies in whether girls or boys have higher rates of substance use disorders.

Among specific substances, alcohol and marijuana are common drugs of choice. Alcohol abuse/dependence ranges from 27 to 64% among girls, compared to 26 to 32% among boys. In the two studies that contrast the sexes, girls are more likely to be diagnosed with an alcohol-related disorder than boys. In general, rates of marijuana abuse/dependence are higher than for alcohol. In the one comparative study assessing marijuana abuse/dependence, boys were more likely to abuse marijuana than girls (45 vs. 41%).

Psychotic Disorders

Psychotic disorders are rare in the general population and are rare in juvenile justice populations as well. However, although rare, they are more prevalent in justice settings than in the community. The rate of psychotic disorders ranges from 0 to 12% for girls and from 1 to 16% for boys. In the two studies contrasting the genders, boys had equal or higher rates than girls (Teplin et al., 2002; Timmons-Mitchell et al., 1997).

Summary

Clearly many, if not most, justice-involved youth exhibit mental health and substance use problems. More importantly, when one problem exists, there is a high probability that the other exists as well. The third critical aspect that commonly presents with co-occurring disorders—that is, the consequences of childhood traumatic events—is not often assessed. However, its importance is clear in the rates of posttraumatic stress disorder (PTSD) and other diagnostically related conditions, among justice-involved youth. For example, personality and somatization disorders commonly exceed 25% of the participants, particularly in girls, and suicide attempts are high, ranging from 15 to 56% of boys and girls.

Trauma and Co-Occurring Disorders

Children with histories of abuse and neglect may be diagnosed with borderline and antisocial personality disorder, conduct and oppositional disorders, psychotic and affective disorders, sleep and eating disorders, and somatization disorders. They may be diagnosed with PTSD or other anxiety disorders. Every one of these diagnoses may be caused by abuse or neglect. This is not to say that abuse/neglect is the sole cause; other genetic, physiological, or environmental factors may also function as significant risk factors. This is also not to say that every child who has experienced abuse or neglect will develop one or more of these disorders. However, it is clear that the more negative events a child experiences, the likelihood of having a mental, substance use, or medical problem increases geometrically.

It has long been known that justice-involved children have high rates of abuse, and that abuse is a consistent predictor of delinquency and status offenses, as well as adult violence and criminality. Estimates vary by study, but most exceed 50% for both boys and girls in the juvenile justice system. For example, 55% of status offenders and 55% of delinquents had documented histories of child abuse or neglect. Combining the two groups, 24% experienced physical abuse, 9% sexual abuse, 15% emotional abuse, and 15% neglect (Famularo, Kinscherff, Fenton, & Bolduc, 1990). Further, in a therapeutic community program, 66% of delinquents had histories of abuse, almost all had a parent perpetrator, and nearly a third had multiple forms of abuse (Sandberg,

1986). Childhood abuse and neglect are associated with an increased likelihood of delinquency (Stouthamer-Loeber, Loeber, & Hornish, 2001) and running away, which, in turn, is predictive of juvenile arrest (Kaufman & Widom, 1999; Widom & Ames, 1994). Further, sexual and physical abuse and neglect are associated with higher rates of sex offenses, and sexual abuse is predictive of arrest for prostitution, both male and female (Widom & Ames, 1994). Juveniles with a history of abuse are also more likely to recidivate (Ryan, 2006; Ryan & Testa, 2005).

In single-sex studies or studies that contrast boys and girls, similarities and differences between the sexes emerge. Delinquent girls are more likely to have experiences of physical and/or sexual abuse than boys (Brosky & Lally, 2004) and display higher rates of PTSD symptoms (Brosky & Lally, 2004). For girls exposed to multiple forms of abuse, sexual abuse is a strong predictor of both violent and nonviolent criminal behavior, and physical abuse is associated with assaults on parents (Herrera & McCloskey, 2003). Sexual abuse in girls is also associated with higher rates of delinquency (Wright, Friedrich, & Cinq-Mars, 2004; Kankar, Friedmann, & Peck, 2002), arrest in adulthood (Siegel & Williams, 2003), and self-injury and other self-destructive behaviors (Wright et al., 2004; Kankar et al., 2002)

Among adolescent boys and girls, abuse and exposure to violence in the home are related to anger, depression, and symptoms of post-traumatic stress. Girls are more likely to display internalizing and interpersonal coping strategies, whereas boys tend to rely on instrumental ones (Flannery, 1998). More disturbing, youth beliefs that "power" creates safety and the witnessing of violence are highly predictive of the escalation of violent offending for youth in a secure facility (Van Dorn & Williams, 2003).

Consistently, family members are most frequently the perpetrators in abuse cases (Stouthamer-Loeber et al., 2001). In a study of incarcerated adolescent males, 70% had been molested or sexually abused (Brannon, Larson, & Doggett, 1989). Among those molested (57%), the average age of first incident was 9.3 years old. Sixty-one percent of the perpetrators were well known (e.g., friends, neighbors, babysitters) and 26% were family members. In 58% of cases, the perpetrator was female. Among those abused (13%), the average age of first incident was 8 years old, 75% of the perpetrators were well known to the victim (38% family and 38% friends, neighbors, babysitters), and in all cases the perpetrator was male (Brannon et al., 1989). These youth also have higher rates of sexual offending, underscoring the need to address the issue of sexual abuse from both a victim and perpetrator perspective (Brannon et al., 1989).

As children age into adulthood, the effects of abuse persist. Retrospectively, 68% of adult male felons reported some form of childhood abuse or neglect (Weeks & Widom, 1998). In this same study, violent offenders reported more neglect, but not more physical abuse, than nonviolent offenders, and sex offenders reported more childhood sexual abuse that other offenders (Weeks & Widom, 1998). In another study, 59% of male inmates reported being sexually abused before the age of 13. In this sample, friends and family members were the most common perpetrators, and 10% were male (Johnson, Ross, & Taylor, 2006).

Abused and neglected children are more likely than those without such histories to behave violently (i.e., hit others, throw things at someone) in young adulthood (White & Widom, 2003). Men who were abused and neglected as children had higher rates of dysthymia and antisocial personality disorder than those without; women who were abused and neglected had higher rates of these same disorders and higher rates of alcohol problems than women without (Horwitz, Widom, McLaughlin, & White, 2001). For male offenders, child abuse is directly related to violence; for women, child abuse is indirectly related to violence through problem alcohol use (Widom, 1989; Widom, Schuck, & White, 2006; Widom & White, 1997).

The Relationship of Traumatic Events to Behavioral Health Problems

Childhood traumatic events, particularly abuse and neglect, are associated with many adolescent (and adult) emotional, health, and behavioral problems. Negative childhood events are related to poor mental health in general (Edwards, Holden, Anda, & Felitti, 2003), hallucinations (Whitfield, Dube, Felitti, & Anda, 2005), depression (Chapman et al., 2004), and suicide attempts (Dube et al., 2001). They are also related to early initiation into alcohol use in adolescence (Dube et al., 2006), illicit drug use (Dube et al., 2003), adolescent pregnancy and fetal death (Hillis et al., 2004), and sexual risk behaviors (Hillis, Anda, Felitti, & Marchbanks, 2001).

As the number of negative life experiences increases, the odds of displaying any number of problems under investigation increase. This dose–response effect is present for mental health disturbances, including panic reactions, depressed affect, anxiety, and hallucinations; somatic health disturbances, including sleep disturbance, severe obesity, and multiple somatic concerns; substance abuse, including smoking, alcoholism, illicit drug use, and injected drug use; and sexuality issues, including early intercourse, promiscuity, and sexual dissatisfaction (Anda et al., 2006). Compared to persons without negative childhood events, the odds increase typically by a factor of 2 to 10 times when four or more are present (Anda et al., 2006). Sexual abuse, in particular, is related to increased suicide attempts (Dube et al., 2005).

Physical and sexual abuse have long been thought to be more damaging to children than neglect or emotional abuse. Emerging research in human and animal studies is now showing that profound neglect, particularly in the earliest years of life, has severe and direct effects on brain development, and consequently on the ability to form attachments, as well as on intellectual functioning (see Perry, 2002, for a review). Furthermore, Perry (2002) suggests that the nature of harm (i.e., neglect vs. physical threat) and the timing, duration, and intensity of the harm is related to the specific neurological dysfunction. Early childhood lack of sensory stimulation (i.e., pervasive neglect) affects stages of neurodevelopment and is related to "failure to thrive" dwarfism, developmental delays, very low intelligence scores, and autism spectrum disorders. In fact, in a study of children removed from their homes due to abuse or neglect, 85% of the children evidenced significant developmental delays (Perry, 2002).

The physical threat associated with physical or sexual abuse tends to cause a persistent arousal of the physiological aspects of the stress response. Traumatic stress and this persistent arousal also have specific and profound effects on brain function, and the effects, in fact, appear very similar to the neurochemical and structural abnormalities found in patients with schizophrenia. Further, the earlier in life the abuse begins and the longer it lasts are directly related to the degree and permanency of the damage (Read, Perry, Moskowitz, & Connelly, 2001).

Emotional abuse has long been overlooked as an unfortunate, but unimportant, factor in troubled children's lives. Childhood negative events in general are related to increased risk of psychiatric problems. When comparing the relative damage of various types of abuse, recent research suggests that emotional abuse is a significant predictive factor of psychiatric problems. In fact, it has comparable effects to witnessing domestic violence and non-familial sexual abuse, and effects that are greater than those of familial physical abuse. When found in combination with witnessing family violence, emotional abuse exceeds the effects of familial sexual abuse on several of the psychiatric outcome measures (Teicher, Samson, Polcari, & McGreenery, 2006).

Increasingly, research demonstrates that various types of negative childhood events rarely occur in isolation. When one is present, typically others are as well. As the number of negative events increases, the number of health and behavioral problems, as well as the severity of the problems associated with them, increases *not* in an additive fashion but multiplicatively (Dong, Anda, Felitti, Dube, & Giles, 2004).

Principles for Trauma-Informed and Trauma-Specific Treatment

When a mental health and substance abuse treatment professional first encounters a troubled, justice-involved youth, the tendency is to understand how the clinician might best assist the child from within the clinician's expertise and training. That is to say, substance abuse clinicians will focus on the substance abuse problem. The same can be said for mental health clinicians. Similarly, over the past several decades, there has been an ongoing discussion among mental health and substance abuse practitioners regarding how to treat people with co-occurring problems. Much of this discussion has revolved around the need to disentangle the effects of alcohol and other drugs on mood and thinking from the use of substances to self-medicate. The general rule of thumb was that the individual had to be clean and sober to benefit from mental health treatment. On the other hand, to be engaged in recovery the individual had to be psychologically stable. Although there is some merit in these assumptions, silo philosophies and isolated treatment require the youth to fragment a problem that is very complex and dynamic. Although effective treatment models exist in the substance abuse and mental health arenas, few models exist that can accommodate the three interrelated problems of trauma, mental health problems, and substance abuse.

When treating justice-involved youth for co-occurring mental health and substance use problems, it is critical to (1) understand the prevalence of abuse in the lives of justice-involved youth; (2) understand how trauma, emotional distress and mental illnesses, and substance use are related and interact; and (3) supervise and treat youth in a manner that does not cause additional harm.

Many juvenile justice facilities and providers who treat justice-involved youth in the community may not have the capacity to offer integrated treatment. In these situations, ensuring that treatment is trauma-informed is critical. Principles of trauma-informed treatment are described below.

Assess (and Treat) Trauma-Related Symptoms, Not Events

Standardized assessment tools typically ask the respondent about either experiences or symptoms. There are many reasons why event-based assessments are less desirable than symptom-based assessments and treatment, including (1) refusal to disclose due to shame, lack of trust, fear of reprisal; (2) failure in memory and recall (i.e., the event may be repressed); (3) denial or minimalization; and (4) retraumatization and compromised emotional safety. Further, the degree of trauma reaction to any given event is individual. Some youth may have few or no reactions and, therefore, treatment would not be indicated. Distress comes not from the event per se, but from the persistent stress symptoms. *Symptoms,* therefore, should be the target of intervention. For youth with trauma reactions, assessors should anticipate disruptions in cognition, emotion, and behavior.

Empower Youth by Involving them in Treatment Decisions

Because the essential nature of trauma is powerlessness, coercion of any sort is damaging at worst and not helpful at best. Clinical staff are trained to be the experts in the therapeutic relationship. This expertise ("I know what's best for you") is often perceived by youth in treatment as coercive. Wherever possible, youth should be involved in decisions in substantive ways (i.e., not simply asking a youth to sign off on a treatment plan). This involvement may take the form of (1) informing youth about all procedures and possible outcomes, (2) explaining what the information will be used for and respecting youths' wishes not to disclose, (3) partnering with youth in treatment planning and goal setting, and (4) maximizing youths' control over crisis interventions through advance directives.

Identify Developmental Disruptions

The age at which the youth first experienced a traumatic event has direct implications for child development as well as treatment. Children who are abused at very young ages (i.e., preverbal) will have difficulty identifying when the abuse occurred and exactly what happened (because memory is largely language based). The later the abuse occurred, the more developmental stages a youth is likely to have successfully completed and, therefore, the more resources he or she will bring to treatment. Assessment and treatment should focus on age-related markers, such as grade level or important family events. This focus will give the clinician a better understanding of when the youth first began to have emotional problems, when he or she began to use substances and why, and how trauma may or may not be related to his or her behavioral health problems.

Assure Safety

Provision of emotional and physical safety are a first duty. Assessment of safety is critical. If the youth does not feel safe, treatment is irrelevant. It is important to know whether the youth is currently being abused at home by a primary caregiver or other household member, whether the abuser is a nonresident family member or friend, and whether the youth currently is being abused by staff or other residents (if in a facility). This information is necessary to understand the youth's current experience and perception of physical and emotional safety. Threats of reprisal for disclosure as well as the emotional costs of family betrayal should be taken seriously. Staff members also should be cognizant of the lack of real protection that they can offer.

Provide Treatment Continuity

Continuity of care is critical in this population. Developing and maintaining trust are essential. Keeping in mind that abused and neglected children have not had consistent adult support in their lives, treatment professionals have the opportunity to serve as surrogate parents and thereby enable a child to learn that adults can be safe. To the degree possible, the assessments and treatment should be provided by the same people and all services managed in an integrated fashion. In this way youth (1) can create trusting, stable relationships, and (2) do not have to recount their stories repeatedly.

Be Trauma-Informed

Given the high incidence of abuse among youth in juvenile corrections/detention, all services and staff members, including medical, psychological, substance abuse, social work, education, and security, should be trauma-informed. All personnel must be able to identify symptoms of trauma, interact with the youth appropriately, and refer, as needed. Because substance use, mental health issues and medical problems are intimately related to trauma and each other, treatment services, in particular, should be trauma-informed. In addition, trauma-specific services should be developed to address trauma-based reactions.

Provide Integrated Care

Because trauma reactions are intertwined with substance use and mental health problems, assessment and treatment for any one of these issues should address the interactions of all issues. Integrated mental health and substance abuse treatment for persons with histories of trauma is superior to both parallel and sequential treatment. To the degree possible, youth should have opportunities to explore the relationships among these problems to identify new, and more functional, adaptive strategies to trauma.

Involve Security Staff in Behavioral and Crisis Management

Depending on the point in the justice system, probation and juvenile corrections officers (as well as family and educators) spend many more hours of each day with youth than do treatment providers. Involvement of these staff members in behavioral and crisis management is critical. Like assessment and treatment staff, security staff members must be trained in trauma issues, standard operating procedures (SOPs) for physical management should be reviewed, and all staff should work together to identify and implement concrete behavioral management plans. At a minimum, corrections staff should refrain from the use of excessive force and shaming.

Provide Gender-, Culturally, and Developmentally Appropriate Care

Treatment must reflect the various gender, cultural, and developmental aspects of youth. To a large degree, symptom-based assessments and treatment avoid some of the gender and cultural pitfalls of pursuing the meaning of events. Assessment and treatment can be improved to the degree that staff personnel reflect the characteristics of the youth. Individuals are embedded in networks in which the meanings of events are socially constructed. Rapport, empathy, and understanding are increased to the degree that assessors/treatment personnel share those networks. Treatment should be tailored to age groups and gender and implemented within a culturally competent framework.

Treatment

Treatment for co-occurring mental health and substance use disorders in juvenile justice settings generally has not been implemented. Parallel or sequential services for mental health and substance abuse treatment are the most common service delivery methods in juvenile corrections. The problem for many justice-involved youth is that mental health and substance use problems are interrelated and entangled. Given the exceedingly high rates of trauma histories among justice-involved youth, particularly justice-involved youth with co-occurring problems, trauma treatment is a necessary third component of integrated services.

It is also important to understand the intended goals of the interventions as well as their by-products. Most mental health and substance abuse treatment programs are targeted toward reducing psychiatric symptoms and substance use. To the degree that the problem itself causes or increases the risk of delinquent or criminal behavior, treatment may have the effect of reducing crime. However, in many circumstances the illness is concomitant with, but not causally related to, criminality. Therefore, treatment is the right thing to do for the purpose of reducing distress, but should not be judged on its effect, or lack of effect, on recidivism.

This is a critical point for justice-involved youth and the agencies that supervise them. Custodial facilities must provide treatment to reduce harm; community agencies have no such mandate. Both community and facility-based corrections are committed to reducing recidivism. However, in facilities, the first priority is the emotional and physical safety of youth; reduced recidivism is secondary. In the community, reduced recidivism is primary, and health and well-being are the purview of other community-based agencies.

Evidence-based practice models, therefore, must be evaluated with a clear understanding of the specific agency's context and goals.

Treatment Goals

The primary presenting symptoms of trauma for youth with histories of sexual and other abuse fall into three categories: (1) physiological responses; (2) intrusive images, thoughts, and nightmares; and (2) constriction of action and behavior. These symptoms often are accompanied by the inability to effectively regulate bodily functions, particularly eating and sleeping, and emotions, particularly rage and despair.

In order to control or suppress distress associated with these symptoms, youth may dissociate; become emotionally numb or have flat affect; develop unusual thought processes or reality structures; use substances; and/or self-injure. Youth also may act in ways that concretely or figuratively reenact their abuse. For example, a youth who was molested at a young age may become sexually aggressive in an effort to reclaim control.

All persons suffering from trauma reactions will experience hyperarousal (i.e., physiological changes), intrusive thoughts, and constriction of action and behavior. It is important to understand that, depending on the intensity and duration of the abuse, these reactions may never go away, regardless of treatment. Treatment, therefore, should help the youth to:

- Understand that these reactions are normal responses to what has happened to them.
- Understand when and under what circumstances they are likely to emerge.

- Plan for these occurrences.
- Develop symptom management strategies to use when they do occur.

Also, treatment should focus on helping the youth understand:

- Typical and youth-specific adaptive survival strategies (i.e., dissociation, depression, substance use, self-injury).
- How the survival strategy helped.
- When survival strategies become ineffective or damaging.
- Replacement strategies of self-soothing.

In addition to concrete strategies for symptom management, the long-term goal of treatment is "recovery." Adults who have successfully negotiated a path to what they themselves call "living life well" often report a lifetime struggle with negative emotions, beliefs about themselves, and trauma symptoms (Higgins, 1994). The presence of symptoms, however, does not preclude a person's ability to live well. Recovery, in the broadest sense of the term (one can never recover the state of being prior to the abuse), involves several stages. Most clinicians and theorists who have proposed models of recovery agree on several important stages. First, physiological needs must be met; second, emotional and physical safety must be assured; third, a period of naming and claiming must occur; and finally, reinforcing relationships must be developed and skills to support a new reality and identity must be constructed.

Most abused youth believe that they are flawed and that they caused the events that happened to them. These beliefs are selectively reaffirmed by their role and behavior in existing social networks. Long-term treatment should focus on:

1. Developing empowering relationships.
2. Placing appropriate blame on the perpetrator.
3. Moving from a status of victim to survivor.
4. Gaining emotional and physical autonomy (apart from, or despite, the trauma).

Key Components of Effective Intervention Programs

Several elements are shared by effective interventions. These elements apply regardless of whether the intervention is group-based or individual.

Problem-Oriented, Symptom-Focused

Treatment is focused on adaptive strategies and, to some degree, trauma symptoms that cause distress or significant problems in completing normal tasks of daily living.

Nonintrusive

Treatment is respectful of individual differences in the willingness and desire to disclose abuse details. No one should be *required* to disclose information. At the same time, some individuals find that discussing details is cathartic and a way of uncovering patterns. When working with groups, the leader should develop guidelines and protections in anticipation of the likelihood that one individual's disclosure may trigger trauma reactions in other group members.

Strengths-Based

Treatment should focus on mobilizing youths' strengths and resiliencies and not on "fixing" deficits. The most notable feature of abused youth is the fact that they have survived in spite of overwhelming odds. Even adaptive strategies can be used as examples of their strength and creativity.

Relationship-Based

Treatment uses group and therapeutic relationships as a means of achieving change. Abuse occurs within the context of relationship. Children are hurt in relationship. It is in relationship that they heal. A typical professional therapeutic relationship is necessary, but not sufficient, for this healing. Group peer and therapist relationships serve several important purposes: They model "good" relationships, provide opportunities for relational skill development, reduce isolation (i.e., the persistent belief that the youth is alone in his or her experience), and transform identity (i.e., by creating and practicing a new identity/role).

Integrated

Treatment should address the multiple ways trauma affects a youth's life. For example, trauma treatment should address a youth's substance use and mental health needs. Likewise, substance abuse treatment also should address trauma and mental health issues. The most effective models are those that integrate trauma, mental health, and substance abuse treatment within one program (group or individual). In the absence of this possibility, all treatment providers should be trained and prepared to discuss issues outside their primary expertise.

Embedded in Trauma-Sensitive Environment

Treatment effectiveness is enhanced when treatment is provided in a trauma-sensitive environment. What is learned in sessions is reaffirmed in the larger environment. This means that the correctional environment also must be trauma-informed, as previously noted.

Fidelity

If a manualized group curriculum is used, fidelity to model is important. Inclusion of all topics, the order of the topics, and recommended training and supervision of the group leader(s) should be followed.

Evidence-Based Treatment Models

Cognitive-behavioral therapies appear to show the most promise for treating youth and adults with histories of repeated abuse. Two evidence-based models are designed for at-risk youth with multiple problems: multisystemic therapy (MST) and functional family therapy (FFT). (These are described by Guerra and colleagues in Chapter 4 and are not discussed here.) Two models are designed specifically to address the cognitive and behavioral consequences of trauma. These are Seeking Safety (Najavits, 2002) and the trauma recovery and empowerment model (TREM; Harris, 1998). An additional model, dialectical behavior therapy (DBT; Linehan, 1993), initially designed to address problems common to persons diagnosed with borderline personality disorder, has also been applied to trauma survivors. Other promising models include the addiction and trauma recovery integration model (ATRIUM; Miller & Guidry, 2001) and Beyond Trauma (Covington, 2003).

The juvenile justice-based models (i.e., FFT and MST) do not provide mental health, substance abuse, or trauma service directly, but support the youth in the context of his or her family to improve family strengths and resiliencies. With other professional services coordinated, these programs are highly effective in achieving justice agency goals of reduced violence, drug use, and re-offending.

The initial design of DBT arose to meet the therapeutic needs of persons who repeatedly attempted suicide. The model has been evaluated and found to reduce various psychiatric symptoms and self-injury (see, e.g., Bohus et al., 2000). The modality has been broadened for use with other diagnostic groups. It also has been applied and tested with juvenile offenders with mental health problems and demonstrated a small reduction in recidivism (Drake & Barnoski, 2006).

The integrated trauma models share several characteristics. First, they focus heavily on teaching concrete strategies for coping with trauma symptoms. They also do not place an emphasis on, or even necessarily attend to, traumatic memories. Second, they are designed based on groups of people who typically have long histories of abuse, often beginning in childhood. Therefore, they tend to be more responsive to complex PTSD. They also are designed for multiproblem individuals (i.e., persons with substance use or mental disorders) and address issues in a holistic and integrated fashion. Because of this previous point, the interventions have been used on many different types of populations whose characteristics are more likely to reflect those of juvenile offenders. They are all manualized. In general, these therapies have been shown to be effective in comparison to no treatment or treatment-as-usual conditions.

Seeking Safety has been the most researched model and has been found to be effective in a wide variety of settings. It has been used successfully with many different types of individuals, including female outpatients (Najavits, Weiss, Shaw, & Muenz, 1998), low-income women (Hien, Cohen, Litt, Miele, & Capstick, 2004), adolescent girls (Najavits, Gallop, & Weiss, 2006), women in a community mental health center (Holdcraft & Comtois, 2002), male and female veterans (Cook, Walser, Kane, Ruzek, & Woody, 2006), male outpatients (Najavits, Schmitz, Gotthardt, & Weiss, 2005), and women in prison (Zlotnick, Najavits, & Rosenow, 2003).

TREM has been shown to be effective in increasing overall functioning, decreasing psychiatric symptoms, decreasing hospitalization and emergency room use, and decreasing HIV-risk behavior in several pilot studies of women trauma survivors with serious mental disorders (Fallot & Harris, 2002). TREM was initially designed for use by women with mental health diagnoses who also had histories of physical and/or sexual abuse. It also has been adapted for use by two different age groups of girls, one for adult men and one for adolescent boys.

Summary and Conclusion

The relationship of childhood abuse and neglect to adolescent mental health and substance use problems, delinquency and violence, and, indeed, to adult health, behavioral health, and early death demands that all agencies providing services to at-risk and justice-involved youth be trauma-informed. Primary care and behavioral health providers are only now becoming aware of the wide-ranging impact of early childhood events. No system has yet to devise a comprehensive plan to respond to these interlocking issues.

It is not surprising, then, that juvenile justice agencies are struggling to find ways to manage and treat these same difficult youth. Every day practitioners and corrections staff members express their frustration. They see complex problems and inexplicable behavior and have no training to solve them or help the youth who have these problems. More importantly, they struggle to find empathy for the youth who are violent and sexually abusive and at the same time victims of violence and sexual abuse.

This chapter was designed to help juvenile justice personnel understand the experiences of many of the youth in their care, the connections among presenting problems, and what may be anticipated from these youth. In addition, practical guidance is presented in how to approach these problems, and suggestions for the use of one or more cognitive-behavioral interventions are offered in the hope that this will not be a lost generation of missed opportunities.

Notes

1. Trauma is defined as the physiological consequences of extreme negative events. Repeated childhood abuse commonly, but not always, results in "trauma." When abuse occurs in childhood, the developing personality is affected by the events, which always leaves a mark, even when the child does not present with the full spectrum of trauma reactions.
2. Of the available studies, variation existed in sample size, location of the study, point in the justice system, mean age and range, prevalence estimates, and measures used.

References

Anda, R. F., Felitti, V. J., Walker, J., Whitfield, C. L., Bremner, J. D., Perry, B. D., et al. (2006). The enduring effects of abuse and related adverse experiences in childhood. A convergence of evidence from neurobiology and epidemiology. *European Archives of Psychiatry and Clinical Neuroscience, 256*(3), 174–86.

Bickel, R., & Campbell, A. (2002). Mental health of adolescents in custody: The use of the "Adolescent Psychopathology Scale" in a Tasmanian context. *Australian and New Zealand Journal of Psychiatry, 36,* 603–609.

Bohus, M., Haaf, B., Stiglmayr, C., Pohl, U., Bohme, R., & Linehan, M. (2000). Evaluation of inpatient dialectical behavioral therapy for borderline personality disorder: A prospective study. *Behavior Research and Therapy, 38,* 875–887.

Brannon, J. M., Larson, B., & Doggett, M. (1989). The extent and origins of sexual molestation and abuse among incarcerated adolescent males. *International Journal of Offender Therapy and Comparative Criminology, 33*(2), 161–171.

Brosky, B. A., & Lally, S. J. (2004). Prevalence of trauma, PTSD, and dissociation in court-referred adolescents. *Journal of Interpersonal Violence, 19*(7), 1–14.

Cauffman, E., Feldman, S., Alterman, J., & Steiner, H. (1998). Posttraumatic stress disorder among female juvenile offenders. *Journal of the American Academy of Child and Adolescent Psychiatry, 37*(11) 1209–1216.

Chapman, D. P., Whitfield, C. L., Felitti, V. J., Dube, S. R., Edwards, V. J., & Anda, R. F. (2004). Adverse childhood experiences and the risk of depressive disorders in adulthood. *Journal of Affective Disorders, 82*(2), 217–225.

Cook, J. M., Walser, R. D., Kane, V., Ruzek, J. I., & Woody, G. (2006). Dissemination and feasibility of a cognitive-behavioral treatment for substance use disorders and posttraumatic stress disorder in the Veterans Administration. *Journal of Psychoactive Drugs, 38,* 89–92.

Covington, S. S. (2003). *Beyond trauma: A Healing Journey for Women.* Center City, MN: Hazelden.

Dong, M., Anda, R. F., Felitti, V. J., Dube, S. R., & Giles, W. H. (2003). The relationship of exposure to childhood sexual abuse to other forms of abuse, neglect and household dysfunction during childhood. *Child Abuse and Neglect, 27*(6), 625–639.

Drake, E., & Barnoski, R. (2006). *Recidivism findings for the juvenile rehabilitation administration's dialectical behavior therapy program: Final report.* Olympia, WA: Washington State Institute for Public Policy.

Dube, S. R., Anda, R. F., Felitti, V. J., Chapman, D., Williamson, D. F., & Giles, W. H. (2001). Childhood abuse, household dysfunction and the risk of attempted suicide throughout the life span: Findings from adverse childhood experiences study. *Journal of the American Medical Association, 286,* 3089–3096.

Dube, S. R., Anda, R. F., Whitfield, C. L., Brown, D. W., Felitti, V. J., Dong, M., et al. (2005). Long-term consequences of childhood sexual abuse by gender of victim. *Journal of Preventive Medicine, 28,* 430–438.

Dube, S. R., Felitti, V. J., Dong, M., Chapman, D. P., Giles, W. H., & Anda, R. F. (2003). Childhood abuse, neglect and household dysfunction and the risk of illicit drug use: The adverse childhood experiences study. *Pediatrics, 111*(3), 564–572.

Dube, S. R., Miller, J. W., Brown, D. W., Giles, W. H., Felitti, V. J., Dong, M., et al. (2006). Adverse childhood experiences and the association with ever using alcohol and initiating alcohol use during adolescence. *Journal of Adolescent Health, 38*(4) 444.e, 1–10.

Duclos, C. W., Beals, J., Novins, D. K., Martin, C., Jewett, C. S., & Manson, S. M.

(1998). Prevalence of common psychiatric disorders among American Indian adolescent detainees. *Journal of the American Academy of Child and Adolescent Psychiatry, 37,* 866–873.

Edwards, V. J., Holden, G. W., Anda, R. F., & Felitti, V. J. (2003). Relationship between multiple forms of childhood maltreatment and adult mental health: Results from the adverse childhood experiences study. *American Journal of Psychiatry, 160*(8), 1453–1460.

Eppright, T. D., Kashani, J. H., Robison, B. D., & Reid , J. C. (1993). Comorbidity of conduct disorder and personality disorders in an incarcerated juvenile population. [author, complete this ref]

Fallot, R. D., & Harris, M. (2002). The trauma recovery and empowerment model (TREM): Conceptual and practical issues in a group intervention for women. *Community Mental Health Journal, 38*(6), 475–485.

Famularo, R., Kinscherff, R., Fenton, T., & Bolduc, S. M. (1990). Child maltreatment histories among runaway and delinquent children. *Clinical Pediatrics, 29*(12), 713–718.

Flannery, D. J. (1998). Adolescent violence exposure and victimization at home: Coping and psychological trauma symptoms. *International Review of Victimology, 6*(1), 29–48.

Harris, M. (1998). *Trauma recovery and empowerment: A clinician's guide for working with women in groups.* New York: Free Press.

Henggeler, S. W., Melton, G.B., Smith, L. A., Schoenwald, S. K., & Hanley, J. H. (1993). Family preservation using multisystemic treatment: Long-term follow-up to a clinical trial with serious juvenile offenders. *Journal of Child and Family Studies, 2,* 283–293.

Herrera, V. M., & McCloskey, L. A. (2003). Sexual abuse, family violence, and female delinquency: Findings from a longitudinal study. *Violence and Victims, 18*(3), 319–334.

Hien, D. A., Cohen, L. R., Litt, L. C., Miele, G. M., & Capstick, C. (2004). Promising empirically supported treatments for women with comorbid PTSD and substance use disorders. *American Journal of Psychiatry, 161,* 1426–1432.

Higgins, G. O. (1994). *Resilient adults: Overcoming a cruel past.* San Francisco: Jossey-Bass.

Hillis, S. D., Anda, R. F., Felitti, V. J., & Marchbanks, P. A. (2001). Adverse childhood experiences and sexual risk behaviors in women: A retrospective cohort study. *Family Planning Perspectives, 33,* 206–211.

Hillis, S. D., Anda, R. F., Dube, S. R., Felitti, V. J., Marchbanks, P. A., & Marks, J. S. (2004). The association between adolescent pregnancy, long-term psychosocial outcomes, and fetal death. *Pediatrics, 113*(2), 320–327.

Holdcraft, L. C., & Comtois, K. A. (2002). Description of and preliminary data from a women's dual diagnosis community mental health program. *Canadian Journal of Community Mental Health, 21,* 91–109.

Horwitz, A. V., Widom, C. S., McLaughlin, J., & White, H. R. (2001). The impact of childhood abuse and neglect on adult mental health: A prospective study. *Journal of Health and Social Behavior, 42*(2), 184–201.

Johnson, R. J., Ross, M. W., & Taylor, W. C. (2006). Prevalence of childhood sexual abuse among incarcerated males in county jails. *Child Abuse and Neglect, 30*(1), 75–86.

Kankar, S., Friedmann, M. L., & Peck, L. (2002). Girls in detention: The results of focus group discussion interviews and official records review. *Journal of Contemporary Criminal Justice, 18*(1), 57–73.

Kaufman, J. G., & Widom, C. S. (1999). Childhood victimization, running away, and delinquency. *Journal of Research in Crime and Delinquency, 36*(4), 347–370.

Linehan, M. M. (1993). *Cognitive behavioral treatment of borderline personality disorder.* New York: Guilford Press.

Miller, D. (1994). Exploring gender differences in suicidal behavior among adolescent offenders: Findings and implications. *Journal of Correctional Education, 45*(3), 134–138.

Miller, D., & Guidry, L. (2001). *Addictions and trauma recovery: Healing the mind, body and spirit.* New York: Norton.

Najavits, L. M. (2002). *Seeking safety: A treatment manual for PTSD and substance abuse.* New York: Guilford Press.

Najavits, L. M., Gallop, R. J., & Weiss, R.D. (2006). Seeking Safety therapy for adolescent girls with PTSD and substance abuse: A randomized controlled trial. *Journal of Behavioral Health Services and Research, 33,* 453–463.

Najavits, L. M., Schmitz, M., Gotthardt, S., & Weiss, R. D. (2005). Seeking safety plus exposure therapy: An outcome study on dual diagnosis men. *Journal of Psychoactive Drugs, 37*(4), 425–435.

Najavits, L. M., Weiss, R. D., Shaw, S. R., & Muenz, L. (1998). "Seeking safety": Outcome of a new cognitive-behavioral psychotherapy for women with posttraumatic stress disorder and substance dependence. *Journal of Traumatic Stress, 11,* 437–456.

Perez, D. M. (2000). The relationship between physical abuse, sexual victimization, and adolescent illicit drug use. *Journal of Drug Issues, 30*(3), 641–662.

Perry, B. D. (2002). Childhood experience and the expression of genetic potential: What childhood neglect tells us about nature and nurture. *Brain and Mind, 3,* 79–100.

Randall, J., Henggeler, S. W., Pickrel, S. G., & Brondino, M. J. (1999). Psychiatric comorbidity and the 16-month trajectory of substance-abusing and substance-dependent juvenile offenders. *Journal of the American Academy of Child and Adolescent Psychiatry, 38*(9), 1118–1124.

Read, J., Perry, B. D., Moskowitz, A., & Connelly, J. (2001). The contribution of early traumatic events to schizophrenia in some patients: A traumagenic neurodevelopmental model. *Psychiatry, 64*(4), 319–345.

Rohde, P., Mace, D., & Seeley, J. (1997). The association of psychiatric disorders with suicide attempts in a juvenile delinquent sample. *Criminal Behavior and Mental Health, 7,* 187–200.

Rohde, P., Seeley, J. R., & Mace, D. E. (1997). Correlates of suicidal behavior in a juvenile detention population. *Suicide and Life-Threatening Behavior, 27*(2), 164–175.

Ryan, J. P. (2006). Dependent youth in juvenile justice: Do positive peer culture programs work for victims of childhood maltreatment? *Research on Social Work Practice, 16*(5), 511–519.

Ryan, J. P., & Testa, M. F. (2005). Child maltreatment and juvenile delinquency: Investigating the role of placement and placement instability. *Children and Youth Services Review, 27*(3), 227–249.

Sandberg, D. N. (1986). The child abuse–delinquency connection: Evolution of a therapeutic community. *Journal of Psychoactive Drugs, 18*(3), 215–220.

Siegel, J. A., & Williams, L. M. (2003). The relationship between child sexual abuse and female delinquency and crime: A prospective study. *Journal of Research in Crime and Delinquency, 40*(1), 71–94.

Stouthamer-Loeber, M., Loeber, R., & Hornish, D. L. (2001). Maltreatment of boys and the development of disruptive and delinquent behavior. *Development and Psychopathology, 13*, 941–955.

Teicher, M. H., Samson, J. A., Polcari, A., & McGreenery, C. E. (2006). Sticks, stones and hurtful words: Relative effects of various forms of childhood maltreatment. *American Journal of Psychiatry, 163*, 993–1000.

Teplin, L. A., Abram, K. M., McClelland, G. M., Dulcan, M. K., & Mericle, A. A. (2002). Psychiatric disorders in youth in juvenile detention. *Archives of General Psychiatry, 59*(12), 1133–1143.

Timmons-Mitchell, J., Brown, C., Schulz, S. C., Webster, S. E., Underwood, L. A., & Semple, W. E. (1997). Comparing the mental health needs of female and male incarcerated juvenile delinquents. *Behavioral Sciences and the Law, 15*, 195–202.

Ulzen, T. P. M., & Hamilton, H. (1998). The nature and characteristics of psychiatric comorbidity in incarcerated adolescents. *Canadian Journal of Psychiatry, 43*(1), 57–63.

Van Dorn, R. A., & Williams, J. H. (2003). Correlates associated with escalation of delinquent behavior in incarcerated youths. *Social Work, 48*(4), 523–531.

Wasserman, G., Ko, S., & Jensen, P. (2001, Winter). Columbia guidelines for child and adolescent mental health referral. *Emotional and Behavioral Disorders in Youth*, 9–14, 23.

Weeks, R., & Widom, C. S. (1998). Self-reports of early childhood victimization among incarcerated adult male felons. *Journal of Interpersonal Violence, 13*(3), 346–361.

White, H. R., & Widom, C. S. (2003). Intimate partner violence among abused and neglected children in young adulthood: The mediating effects of early aggression, antisocial personality, hostility and alcohol problems. *Aggressive Behavior, 29*(4), 332–345.

Whitfield, C. L., Dube, S. R., Felitti, V. J., & Anda, R. F. (2005). Adverse childhood experiences and hallucinations. *Child Abuse and Neglect, 29*(7), 797–810.

Widom, C. S. (1989). Child abuse, neglect, and violent behavior. *Criminology, 27*(2), 251–271.

Widom, C. S., & Ames, M. A. (1994). Criminal consequences of childhood sexual victimization. *Child Abuse and Neglect, 18,*(4), 303–318.

Widom, C. S., Schuck, A. M., & White, H. R. (2006). An examination of path-
    ways from childhood victimization to violence: The role of early aggres-
    sion and problematic alcohol use. *Violence and Victims, 21*(6), 675–690.
Widom, C. S., & White, H. R. (1997). Problem behaviours in abused and
    neglected children grown up: Prevalence and co-occurrence of substance
    abuse, crime and violence. *Criminal Behaviour and Mental Health, 7*(4), 287–
    310.
Wright, J., Friedrich, W., & Cinq-Mars, C. (2004). Self-destructive and delin-
    quent behaviors of adolescent female victims of child sexual abuse: Rates
    and covariates in clinical and non-clinical samples. *Violence and Victims,
    19*(6), 627–643.
Zlotnick, C., Najavits, L. M., & Rohsenow, D. J. (2003) A cognitive-behavioral
    treatment for incarcerated women with substance use disorder and post-
    traumatic stress disorder: Findings from a pilot study. *Journal of Substance
    Abuse Treatment, 25* 99–105.

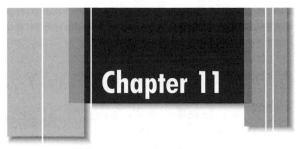

Chapter 11

Juvenile Offenders
with Special Education Needs

Carolyn Eggleston

> Surely, then, if the present system has totally failed, there
> must be something radically wrong in it, and it ought to be
> changed.
> —CARPENTER (1864/1969)

Although these words were spoken in the 19th century, they remain relevant today. Mary Carpenter was an English reformer who, appalled by the conditions of prisons for juveniles and women, set about to provide inmates with the most basic of care as well to develop programs for reading and writing—which were nonexistent at the time. Nor is the awareness of prisoners with disabling conditions new— there were references to learning-disabled prisoners in the United States as early as 1888. Elmira Reformatory, in New York State, operated a showcase facility for young adult offenders and experimented with specialized programs for disabled prisoners (Brockway, 1912/ 1968).

In the annual reports of the managers of the reformatory, there was a reference to a program designed for the first recognized learning-disabled prisoner. This specialized program was started in 1896, and was one among a series of experiments with disabled prisoners. Superintendent Brockway discussed an educational program designed for students who were "exceptionally stupid or deficient in a single faculty such as the arithmatical" [sic] (Brockway, 1912/

1968, p. 360). This is an early reference to students who seemed able to function in most areas, but who found a particular area difficult. Such a difficulty is consistent with what is known today about learning disabilities. In summary, the current emphasis on programs for incarcerated juvenile offenders with educational disabilities is not new, although solutions continue to evade us.

Juvenile offenders often bring to the institutional school experiences that are negative at best and horrendous at worst. They may have been the "bad actors" in public school, either to hide a learning problem, dangerous home experience, or the effects of poverty. They may have been, as Tyack (1974) suggests, "push outs" instead of "drop-outs" from the public school. A poor school experience contributes to the wariness with which students approach institutional schools. It also speaks to the necessary changes in instruction that must take place in the correctional classroom; unsuccessful methods and instruction should not be repeated.

Many dropouts had learning and behavior problems that went undiagnosed in the public classroom. Students may have been "bad actors" to avoid discovery of such a problem. The troublemakers would have been easier to expel had they not been identified by special education procedures. This identification may be one factor to consider in view of the high percentage of special education students in juvenile facilities. The number of public school children with disabilities may be depressed, not actually representative of the total. Research has shown that special education students in the juvenile system have significantly lower academic skills than nondelinquent students at equivalent age levels, and that male juvenile offenders have lower academic skills than female juvenile offenders (Zabel & Nigro, 2001).

The question has to be asked if return to a regular public school is appropriate for offenders. The returning student is not only famous for being a bad actor, but now is also a felon. Public schools have demonstrated an unwillingness to accept returning adjudicated delinquents at all, and when they do, are anxious to find excuses for expulsion as soon as possible. Policymakers should consider the best alternatives for returning students, rather than concentrating on the use of existing resources to manage them.

Prevalence of Students with Disabilities in Corrections

A number of studies have been undertaken to determine the numbers of special education students identified in correctional facilities, beginning not long after the passage of Public Law 94-142, the Education of All Handicapped Children Act (EHA), in 1975. These studies have continued through the 2004 reauthorization of Individuals with Disabilities Education Act (IDEA) (Morgan, 1979; Rutherford, Nelson, & Wolford, 1985; Murphy, 1986; Robinson & Rapport, 1999; Zenz & Langelett, 2004). The findings of these studies and the experience of professionals in the field suggest that the number of students in the juvenile justice field with identifiable disabilities is much higher than in the population at large. The public schools report that between 11 and 13% of the school population possesses educational disabilities, whereas the range reported in the literature for incarcerated populations is from 30 to 70% (Rutherford et al.,1985; Robinson, & Rapport, 1999; Zenz & Langelett, 2004). Most systems report that approximately 45% of the incarcerated population possesses educational disabilities, according to special education definitions. Yet even with these high numbers, incarcerated students remain unserved or underserved in juvenile institutions.

It is important to note, however, that despite the overrepresentation of students with disabilities in juvenile corrections, the majority may be normal or even gifted learners, and the needs of these populations should not be overlooked. There have been cases in which corrections systems have treated the school population as if it were totally educationally disabled (which does a disservice to those without disabilities) or funneled existing resources into education for special education students only, because these students are protected by increased legal mandates. Programs for nonidentified students have been substantially decreased or eliminated altogether. These two responses are inappropriate and unsuccessful. When a correctional system identifies all students as educationally disabled, specialized services become extremely expensive and are quickly eliminated. Furthermore, in addition to being unethical, such a policy typically elicits lawsuits by normal learners.

Braithwaite (1980) discussed whether prisoners deserve fewer or increased educational services. The principle of lesser eligibility suggests that juvenile and adult prisoners are guilty of terrible crimes and therefore do not deserve anything but the most basic of services. The contrasting perspective, the principle of greater eligibility, proposes that prisoners are generally disadvantaged, and incarceration is even more of a disadvantage, so they deserve as much assistance as possible to help them develop skills that will increase their employability outside prison. These principles should be discussed by correctional systems to clarify their orientation toward levels of services. The political reality is that most systems provide the most basic of programming to juvenile and adult prisoners—a reaction to the long-standing negative perspective of the public (described in the introduction to the current volume and throughout the chapters in this book).

The requirements of the new Title I Act, "No Child Left Behind" (NCLB) have caused particular problems for correctional settings. Both public school and correctional systems are having difficulty certifying that teachers have appropriate subject matter competencies. There is another area in the legislation that will never be able to be met by correctional systems: that of school choice. The law allows for some school choice related to annual yearly performance (AYP) scores reported by schools (Leone & Cutting, 2004). Even though the neglected and delinquent (N&D) portion of NCLB is specific to corrections, most provisions cannot fully be implemented in corrections. Provisions such as teacher licensure in specific subjects and collaboration with home community schools are very difficult to implement.

Because placement in a correctional institution, detention facility, or adult prison is not based on education but conviction, choice of school is not an option. In fact, some institutions are not only non-educational facilities, they are actively anti-education. There may even be disincentives to education in juvenile facilities where students almost always fall under compulsory attendance requirements because of their ages. School can be disrupted for a variety of reasons and individual students removed from class for appointments, discipline, or any number of other reasons.

Disability Categories in Juvenile Justice Facilities

All 13 disability categories can be found in facilities for juvenile delinquents, although the most frequent are sometimes called "the big three": specific learning disabilities, mental retardation, and emotional disturbance. In addition, there are offenders with oppositional defiant disorder, autism, and those who are deaf and hard of hearing and visually impaired. Juveniles with these less common disabilities are often not served to any degree, unless they present a management problem to the institution.

Students with specific learning disabilities are more highly represented in corrections than in public schools. A body of research regarding the link between learning disabilities and juvenile delinquency has developed since the early 1970s (U.S. Department of Justice, 1976; Ramos, 1978). There are three distinct explanations for this supposed link. The first theory, the school failure theory, suggests that as a result of doing so poorly in school, learning-disabled students act out and engage in illegal acts to prove that they can be successful at something. In the susceptibility theory, in contrast, students with learning disabilities are considered to be more susceptible to juvenile offending behavior because they are easily influenced by others, and may do illegal acts in attempts to fit in with a peer group. The third theory, the differential treatment theory, suggests that students with learning disabilities tend to get into trouble more easily than their nondisabled peers, and when they do, they then further penetrate the juvenile justice system because they do not know how to talk their way out of trouble (Eggleston, 1995; Leone, Meisel, & Drakeford, 2002).

It is possible that all three theories point to valid reasons that explain the overrepresentation of learning-disabled juvenile delinquents, although each is insufficient on its own. There may be additional factors not identified in the literature on learning-disabled students in trouble with the law. Certainly one characteristic is not considered carefully enough regarding students in correctional facilities. Students with learning disabilities often have problems with social perceptions—that is, misreading, or not reading, interaction with others. This characteristic supports the differential treatment theory in part. Meadan and Halle (2004) suggest that the way a learning-disabled student with social perception problems interprets a social situation can be related to his or her social status. Learning-disabled prisoners should not be expected to hold high status in the institution. Even if their crime is so dramatic that they get some attention, inappropriate behaviors can quickly diminish any benefit.

The more significant issue is that misreading social cues in a correctional facility may lead to problems with security staff, or, at its worst, dangerous consequences with others (Eggleston, 1995). It can be a matter of life or death to misinterpret an interaction with other youth or personnel in the institution. For this reason, if no other, students with learning disabilities should be given special consideration when they are housed in a general population.

Another overrepresented group in the institutional population consists of students with emotional disturbances. This group is one that likely experienced behavior problems during their public school experience, and may or may not have been properly identified. Because special education law requires that the behavior be serious, occur over a long time, and affect educational performance, students may be misidentified or not identified at all. Those with serious mental illnesses are often not properly served in public schools or in correctional facilities. This population of students with disabilities remains the largest in corrections (Quinn, Rutherford, & Leone, 2001). Many of them have had contact with the child welfare system prior to incarceration, even though they may not have been identified (Jonson-Reid, Williams & Webster, 2001). Incarcerated students with behavior disorders often had problems in public schools, including suspensions and expulsions (Rutherford, Quinn, & Mathur, 2004). Jonson-Reid et al. (2001) cite studies that suggest that mental health disorders occur in the correctional population at "two to four times" the prevalence of their peers in the public sector. In a study of delinquent girls, there was little difference noted in the characteristics of girls housed in mental health facilities over those in correctional facilities (Ruffolo, Sarri, & Goodkind, 2004). There was a high level of depression noted in both settings, with the only real difference being the level of violence exhibited. A study in England supported this finding, indicating that students in "welfare" or "penal" institutions were distinct only in the articulated level of violent behavior (Nicol et al., 2000). Treatment for students in both groups was not being addressed fully; for example, therapy for sexual and physical abuse, psychosis, and other mental health problems was inadequate.

The problems exhibited by students who have emotional disturbance or mental illness can range from disruption in the classroom to true mental breakdown. Ironically, the class behavior that was so disruptive in the public school setting is often not exhibited in the correctional classroom—a result of the increased structure of the correctional system. This should not imply that intervention is not necessary, but therapy may be the most significant immediate need for these students.

Limitations in cognitive functioning present a third area of disability that large numbers of juveniles in corrections exhibit (Robinson & Rapport, 1999; Steelman, 1987). These youth are often overrepresented in corrections not because of the supposed link between mental retardation and crime, but because there are few placement alternatives for older adolescent students with mental retardation once they exhibit criminal behavior (Santamour, 1987). Most systems have few specialized programs or units for this population (Leone, 2001). In California the adult corrections system reported that between 2 and 4% of the population in their state prisons has developmental disabilities (Petersilia, 1997, 2000). Most of the programs that do exist consist of focus on segregation in specialized housing units. These units may not have adequate programs. Juveniles in this population of the disabled, who may have spent most of their childhoods in institutions or residential community settings, require a great deal of service in order to experience success upon release.

The range and nature of the different disabilities create significant problems for corrections systems. The focus on most programs in the institution is a "one-size-fits-all" model. This model is less expensive to administer and requires less consistent effort. But prisoners with disabilities do not fit nicely into standard programs. Even when systems make attempts to address prisoners with disabilities, there is often little understanding of distinctions between the disabilities.

Requirements of Special Education Implementation

The basic tenets of special education law have addressed problems with special education students in public schools. Before the passage of these laws, some states provided relatively sound programs, but there was no clear requirement to do so, and when states ran short of money, programs suffered. One major area addressed by legislation and litigation included parental involvement. Prior to 1975, parents were often not even notified if their child was placed in special education, and they had very little access to student records. On the other hand, because of few confidentiality requirements, others (such as insurance companies) could access student records without the consent or knowledge of parents. In addition, because programs were so limited, not all children with special needs were served. The EHA and IDEA require that special education services be provided and cannot be limited because of financial constraints. School districts must actively attempt to locate and serve eligible special needs students through a process called Child Find. Also, the resultant educational placement must be determined by the needs of the student, not the availability of a particular program. The requirement of least restrictive environment (LRE) means that a student must be placed in a setting that is the least restrictive for meeting individual educational goals. This does not always mean a regular education classroom, but it does mean that the setting must meet the student's needs.

Once a child entered a special education program, the lack of evaluation ensured that he or she would stay in special education, no matter how large the academic gains made. Now, procedures for evaluation, using multiple measures by more than one person, help to determine who truly needs special services and how to measure gains. Definitions of the disability categories are provided in the regulations, so that the multidisciplinary team has criteria for eligibility decisions. Once a student is identified for special services, the development of an educational plan specific to that child's individual student needs must be developed. This individualized education plan (IEP) has strict guidelines and timelines for service delivery, with a built-in process of reevaluation.

An area of particular importance to this population is that of transition services. This problem was not addressed in the first wave of special education law (EHA), but it was handled in IDEA. Awareness that students with special needs require extra help in transitioning from the school to community led to requirements for transition programming before leaving the school environment.

Providing Appropriate Services to Students in Juvenile Justice Facilities

Implementation of special education programs has presented challenges for correctional systems across the country. Although there are some variations in level or degree, generally speaking, the same areas of special education implementation present challenges to most states.

Free Appropriate Public Education

The first area is the underlying concept in special education law—the provision of a Free, Appropriate Public Education (FAPE). This concept requires that proper education and related services be provided to each student identified as eligible for special education services. Although great strides in services have been made in juvenile corrections in providing FAPE, a number of problems continue to persist. For example, students in special or restrictive housing are often not provided with appropriate education; students may receive reduced or no educational services. The movement of students within corrections makes continuity of service very difficult. The length of stay in many facilities is limited, and transfers occur for reasons that relate to discipline or custody, not education. In addition, actual hours of service provision are often inadequate due to employee absences or competition for student time. This lack of service provision is one of the most disturbing aspects of institutional services, because it occurs with such frequency. State departments of education find the problem of services not being provided regularly in many correctional systems, and it is often the area that is likely to be cited.

Child Find

A second area that presents major problems for special education implementation in corrections is the requirement of Child Find. School systems actively search for students who need special education; they do not simply wait until a student or parent comes forward to request special help. An important distinction in special education legislation requires that students are to be identified in all kinds of schools. The original legislation includes the statement that children, "wherever they are found, including corrections," must be served (20 USC 1412 sec 612 2 c 30). Child Find requirements state that students in any setting are eligible for special education, including custodial facilities. The lack of Child Find efforts in juvenile facilities has been cited as a deficiency by most departments of education. The recent changes in IDEA diminished the requirement for adult corrections, in that they obligate adult systems to merely provide services to students who previously were identified for special education. Although eliminated for adult corrections, the Child Find requirement is still needed in juvenile systems. The practice of recording transfers from juvenile to adult prisons has long been deficient and needs to be improved for those juvenile offenders who are either transferred or recommitted to the adult system upon reaching majority.

Least Restrictive Environment

Another problem in implementing special education in juvenile facilities is that of providing services in the LRE. This was initially a much broader problem than it is currently, as questions were asked about whether special education students were *ever* appropriately educated in prison, which is the most restrictive environment. The intent of the law is that students with special education needs not be educated in environments that are more restrictive than those for their nondisabled peers—which may mean nondisabled juveniles in the institution. It has been determined that as long as students with disabilities are not housed within the institution in more restrictive environments than other correctional students *because* of their disability, then the obligation of LRE has been met. Where the LRE continues to be a problem is with students who have a mental illness or severe emotional disturbance. The behaviors exhibited by these individuals often result in more restrictive housing placements, where education opportunities can be seriously curtailed. Determining whether an emotional disturbance creates problems for educational success is a challenging requirement of special education law. Also, students with severe mental illness may be so seriously disturbed that the need for formal educational experiences should be limited for a brief period while concentrating on therapeutic efforts.

Parental Involvement

The parental involvement portions of the federal and state statutes present particular problems in corrections. Although it is clear that the corrections agency must have parental consent to evaluate a student for special education, for IEP development, and for any changes in program, some systems make limited effort to find and involve the natural parent or legal guardian. If is often difficult for a corrections system to find parents; sometimes they are incarcerated themselves or have not been in the student's life for years. However, unless parental rights have been removed legally, attempts must be made to find and coordinate services with parents. When efforts to find a natural parent or legal guardian have been exhausted, a surrogate parent must be appointed.

There are clear requirements for using and training surrogate parents to serve as advocates for students eligible for special education services. The surrogate may not be an employee of the agency housing the student, and must be allowed access to the student and his or her records. This open exchange is often difficult for correctional systems. The provision that a student may serve as his or her own parent after age 18 has been used in many correctional systems, sometimes to students' detriment. Correctional systems have implemented programs for students to serve as their own guardian, but do not always provide the required support and training. Many times students are encouraged to sign themselves out of special education altogether, which makes life easier for the system but may be a disservice to the student. The effect can be seen not only during incarceration but after release as well. Students may lack access to programs they may need in the community setting.

Confidentiality of Records

Confidentiality of records remains a significant issue in many correctional systems. Because there had been problems in lack of confidentiality in public schools regarding special education information, a system for the use and transfer of confidential records was established. When this was implemented on top of correctional confidentiality policies, there were a number of resultant problems, not all of which have yet been resolved.

The transfer of records from public school systems continues to be a nightmare for many correctional systems. Students may have been out of school for a long time before they attend correctional schools, and simply identifying the proper school district can be problematic. A student's sporadic school history may require that a correctional school attempt to get records from several schools or even several states. Public schools have established restrictive confidentiality structures that can inhibit access by legitimate systems, such as corrections.

There is often a significant wait for records, and in some cases, public schools do not recognize correctional schools as real schools, so they are unwilling to submit records. The unfortunate truth is that at times the restrictive confidentiality structures established by the corrections agency may conflict with special education confidentiality measures. It is not uncommon to encounter a state system in which personnel in the same agency are not allowed access to student records, even educational records.

Timelines

Overrestrictive confidentiality procedures affect another requirement of special education in which corrections systems continue to fail—that of meeting timelines for special education implementation. Special education requirements, by both federal and state statutes, have clear timelines for when evaluation, identification, IEP program development, and services must be accomplished. These timelines were developed to solve the situation in public schools whereby the schools "dragged their feet" in developing a special education program for a child because of expense, lack of services, or other factors. But the timelines do not account for the physical movement that many correctional students make—from detention, to an evaluation center, to a facility, and then perhaps another facility. Due to security concerns, custodial level, gang separation, or bed space availability, a juvenile offender may be moved several times before settling at one facility. The emphasis is rarely, if ever, on educational considerations. If a student is found eligible for special education at a diagnostic center, services must be provided within a very short time, and the student may not have a permanent placement for several weeks. To make matters more difficult, the length of stay at an institution may vary a great deal.

Many states have elected to provide the required comprehensive evaluation procedures at central receiving units, a procedure that concentrates staffing for psychologists, educational evaluators, or social work evaluation. The problem of meeting timelines becomes critical when the identification is made, but school services are not available at the unit. An alternative that some states have explored is to have all evaluation services—eligibility, reevaluation, IEP development for special education—occur at the actual placement site. This approach requires that the full range of diagnostic services be available at each site, which is more expensive, even though it better meets student needs. Some states have been hesitant to implement such a system.

Assessment and Evaluation

The question of educational assessment and type/scope of evaluation is often problematic in a corrections system. The full range of screening and testing services and the opportunity to use an appropriate multi-disciplinary team for special education are not always available. The evaluation may be completed by one or two people, at best, and the requirement of observing a student in several educational settings may not occur. The use of up-to-date and appropriate assessment materials is not always evident. When a student is identified and the educational program is developed, the services identified as needed may be influenced by the knowledge of which services are available at the sites, rather than actual need.

Continuum of Educational Placement

The full continuum of educational placements may not be available in correctional environments. This fact relates to the LRE issue, wherein the student is required to be served in an environment that is least restrictive to meet his or her specific educational needs. For example, a student who requires only a few hours of support services should be placed in a regular classroom, with a special education teacher who provides resource help in the regular classroom. The educational needs of this student would not be best met if he or she were placed in a special day class or an all-day special education program, just because that is the only option available at that particular school.

Many students who require increased special education services may receive only part-time resource help from a special education teacher because there are not enough special education teachers to serve all students. This system leads to the problem often cited by state departments of education and, through litigation, to the correctional system, wherein the appropriate level of compensatory education has not been provided for all students with disabilities. "Appropriate level" can mean both placement options and number of hours served by special education.

Qualified Personnel

The next significant problem has remained one of the central issues in special education implementation: the provision of qualified personnel. This problem occurs at every level of the process, from the provision of school psychologists rather than clinical psychologists, to insufficient educational evaluators, to limited numbers of special education endorsed teachers. There is a shortage of special education qualified personnel in the public schools, particularly in low-incidence areas such as visual impairment or autism. The categorical certification in some states, where a teacher must be licensed in many different areas of special education, is also challenging. The problem is even more severe in correctional systems and further exacerbated by hiring issues. Salaries may not be equivalent to public school salaries, the correctional schools may be located in remote areas with a general absence of professional services, and public attitudes toward the field of corrections and criminality make this career path uninviting to many. Many state correctional systems worsen the problem by maintaining an outdated hiring system that takes so long and is so complex that interested professionals find other employment well before state processes are completed.

When considering low-incidence disabilities, such as services for the deaf or visually impaired, the provision of appropriate staff becomes even more difficult. In addition, the correctional educators who are licensed in regular education areas such as elementary or secondary education usually consider the special education student to be the sole obligation of the special education teacher (Moody, 2003). Opposed to inclusion and already overworked, they are often reluctant to take on the responsibility of students with disabilities.

Related Services

Provision of related services is a particular problem within the general area of staffing concerns. Special education law is clear about the spectrum of services required for students with disabilities. These may include speech, occupational, or physical therapy, or counseling. Correctional schools often do a very poor job of providing the appropriate level of services because they are unable to hire and keep qualified specialists; many identified services remain undermet or unmet. Indeed there is a tendency to overlook certain services a student needs when the school knows such services are unavailable. Some correctional systems have attempted innovative ways to overcome these constraints, for example, by creating a traveling team of professionals who work at several school sites, hiring public school professionals to provide services after their regular workday, or contracting with local agencies to provide services. These strategies work best in areas where several institutional schools are located in close proximity to one another or are in urban environments. Such efforts have improved the situation to some degree, but it can be said that many, if not most, correctional systems continue to have problems in this area.

Preparation of Teachers

Even when an agency can hire qualified special education personnel, many are underprepared for work in an institutional environment. Teacher preparation programs prepare educators to work in public school settings, but it is very rare for someone to get instruction in working with institutional populations. Teaching strategies, curriculum, and instruction are designed for children and for teaching in traditional settings. Without specialized preparation, correctional educators learn on the job—which is sufficient if the teacher next door is enthusiastic and dedicated (i.e., not burned out and counting the days until retirement). Specialized pre- and inservice programs are needed to help correctional educators succeed and flourish.

There is a significant problem with collaboration, or the lack thereof, between agencies and disciplines. This problem occurs within the institution as well as with outside agencies. Specialized services that are not fully available in all settings should be provided through interagency agreements. Within the institution there is often a problem with turf issues and professionals not cooperating as well as they should. Each discipline is dedicated to the provision of that particular service but may not consider others as important. The outside agencies are often reluctant to work with an institutional population or to provide quality services after release. These agencies are often overburdened and understaffed, and released students typically have multiple issues and need extensive services.

Transition

Transition services, despite being arguably the single most important effort for the correctional student, remain poorly implemented in many systems. The school in the institution is usually not funded to provide any kind of transition service beyond a short prerelease program required for all students. Transition is considered a function of the custodial staff. Sometimes there is a state prohibition against institutional employees having any contact with students once they leave the institution, which makes follow-up impossible. There is often a lack of collaboration between educational personnel and treatment staff regarding transition, making the efforts of both ineffective. The central issue seems to be a general lack of understanding about what transition should be, even though it is very important. Instead, a "one-size-fits-all" approach is often used. The transition efforts for purposes of special education should be a significant part of the overall treatment plan for transition from the institution. Educational transition efforts may include transition from the institutional school to the general population of the institution, or to educational services on the outside.

In a review of 12 years of research studies on special education student transition from institutions, Baltodano, Mathur, and Rutherford (2005) found that there were several factors common to success after release. These included planning prior to release, an emphasis on community member support, follow-up educational services, and recognition of differences in gender needs. Significant work needs to be done in this area.

Training for Educators in Juvenile Institutions

As noted above, there continues to be a substantial need for teacher preparation specific to correctional facilities. Educators come to corrections with licensure in elementary education, secondary education, special education, or with vocational certificates. They rarely, if ever, have been trained to work in the environment in which they find themselves. A system of pre- and inservice training must be developed to teach skills specific to working in a correctional environment.

For most public school settings, the emphasis for instruction is on knowledge, skills, and attitudes. This is an appropriate trajectory for a developing child, as it follows a natural developmental path. However, students in corrections are older and have demonstrated that they have not been good community members. Instead, they need a curriculum that emphasizes *attitudes,* skills, and knowledge (Gehring, Eggleston, & Ashcroft, 1992). The fact that they cannot perform two-digit multiplication is not the reason they became incarcerated.

On the other hand, professionals in an institutional setting cannot avoid recognizing that these students have had life experiences that they bring to the classroom or clinical setting and that need to be acknowledged and appreciated. This does not mean that the educational content should be substantially different from that in the public school. Every effort should be made to facilitate high school completion, and students in the correctional setting deserve the same level of content as their public school counterparts. But correctional educators need to adapt the curriculum to the student and the environment, and not simply repeat instructional strategies that were not successful the first time around in their K–12 school experience.

The issue of teacher preparation for educators in correctional settings is one that must be addressed by every system. Current inservice activities in institutional schools often have little to do with this necessary training—they tend to focus on maintaining clean classrooms, filling out forms properly, or repeated trainings on how dangerous the students are.

Correctional educators need to learn not only how to adapt curricula but how to maintain their own educational excellence in the environment. Institutions can damage workers as well as clients. There has been a body of research dating from the early 1980s on determining the skills and characteristics of correctional educators (Gehring et al., 1992). Experienced correctional educators—academic and vocational instructors, educational administrators, in varied juvenile and adult correctional settings—have been asked what they consider the most important things correctional educators need to know to be successful. These include the things educators need to do to make sure they stay knowledgeable and focused, such as professional development and pursuing interests outside the job.

Specific personal characteristics are important as well. For example, it is particularly important for a correctional teacher to have a sense of humor, not take him- or herself too seriously, have interests outside work, and continue to learn and study, so that the difficult environment does not result in jaded disinterest.

Treatment versus Education in Institutions

The roles of various professionals working with institutionalized juveniles, including those with special education needs, have often conflicted. Competing interests of the various groups, each of which considers his or her discipline the most important, may mean that the interests of the student are not best met. Educational staff believe the time in school to be the most important rehabilitative effort available to students, and there are legal requirements for certain hours and types of services. On the other hand, mental health, medical, and psychological service providers consider their own efforts to be most important, and since there is so little staffed evening time available, they consider it appropriate to remove a student from school, if necessary. Each discipline lacks tolerance for the efforts of other disciplines, focusing instead on its piece of the treatment process. It is critically important that ineffective "turf" squabbles be reexamined and eliminated. Treatment team models that have been most effective in the past should be reconsidered, with each discipline holding equal status on the team. Unless professionals are willing to abolish the disjointed, often-contradictory approaches of their various disciplines, students will be poorly served.

A Recommendation: Establishing a Collaborative Model

It is critically important that professionals from every discipline work together to provide services for incarcerated juveniles. Service providers should not compete for time with students, consider their own piece of the treatment the most important, and devalue other disciplines. This approach has never worked.

Leone and Cutting (2004) suggest that a lack of collaboration has increased the problem of implementing IDEA in corrections systems. It certainly makes rehabilitation more difficult. A symptom can be seen in the professional publications. There is a tendency for each discipline to discuss research for its portion of the rehabilitative effort, often ignoring, or just briefly acknowledging, other groups.

A recommendation would be to establish a treatment team approach that works with a student before placement and continues beyond release. Transition efforts should start at this beginning point. Each discipline (custody, medical, psychological, educational, social work) must have an equal part in the effort. Although this is potentially an expensive process to develop, and statutory or regulatory changes might be necessary, it is much less expensive than repeated incarcerations. Rutherford et al. (2004) recommend a "network" of effective community services—which is critically important once a student is released, but a network should also be established *within* the institution. The various networks should focus together on the needs of the student.

References

Baltodano, H., Mathur, S., & Rutherford, R. (2005). Transition of incarcerated youth with disabilities across systems into adulthood. *Exceptionality, 13,* 103–124.

Braithwaite, J. (1980). *Prisons, education, and work: Towards a national employment strategy for prisoners.* Queensland, Australia: University of Queensland Press.

Brockway, Z. (1968). *Fifty years of prison service: An autobiography.* Montclair, NJ: Patterson Smith. (Original work published 1912)

Carpenter, M. (1969). *Our convicts.* Montclair, NJ: Patterson Smith. (Original work published 1864)

Eggleston, C. (1995). *Learning disability and the justice system.* Washington, DC: Their World.

Gehring, T., Eggleston, C., & Ashcroft, R. (1992). *Correctional teacher skills, characteristics, and performance indicators.* Riverside, CA: Robert Presley Institute of Corrections Research and Training.

Jonson-Reid, M., Williams, J., & Webster, D. (2001). Severe emotional disturbance and violent offending among incarcerated adolescents. *Social Work Research, 25* 213–222.

Leone, P. (2001, November). *Accommodating the needs of inmates with developmental disabilities in the California Department of Corrections.* Proceedings from the American Association of Criminology annual meeting, Atlanta, GA.

Leone, P., & Cutting, C. (2004). Appropriate education, juvenile corrections, and No Child Left Behind. *Behavioral Disorders, 29,* 260–265.

Leone, P., Meisel, S., & Drakeford, W. (2002). Special education programs for youth with disabilities in juvenile corrections. *Journal of Correctional Education, 53,* 46–50.

Meadan, H., & Halle, J. (2004). Social perceptions of students with learning disabilities who differ in social status. *Learning Disabilities Research and Practice, 19,* 71–82.

Moody, B. (2003). Juvenile corrections educators: Their knowledge and understanding of special education. *Journal of Correctional Education, 54,* 105–107.

Morgan, D. (1979). Prevalence and types of handicapping conditions found in juvenile correctional institutions: A national survey. *Journal of Special Education, 13,* 283–295.

Murphy, D. (1986). The prevalence of handicapping conditions among juvenile delinquents. *Remedial and Special Education,7,* 7–17.

Nicol, R., Stretch, D., Whitney, I., Jones, K., Garfield, P., Turner, K., et al. (2000). Mental health needs and services for severely troubled and troubling young people including young offenders in an N. H. S. region. *Journal of Adolescence, 23,* 243–261.

Petersilia, J. (1997). Justice for all? Offenders with mental retardation and the California corrections system. *Prison Journal, 77,* 358–380.

Petersilia, J. (2000). *Doing justice? Criminal offenders with developmental disabilities.* Berkeley, CA: University of California, California Policy Research Center.

Quinn, M., Rutherford, R., & Leone, P. (2001). *Students with disabilities in correctional facilities.* [ERIC EC Digest #E621]. ERIC Clearinghouse on Disabilities and Gifted Education, December.

Ramos, N. (Ed.) (1978). *Delinquent youth and learning disabilities.* San Rafael, CA: Academic Therapy Publications.

Robinson, T., & Rapport, M. (1999). Providing special education in the justice system. Remedial and Special Education, 20, 19–26.

Ruffolo, M., Sarri, R., & Goodkind, S. (2004). Study of delinquent, diverted, and high-risk adolescent girls: Implications for mental health intervention. *Social Work Research, 28* 237–245.

Rutherford, R., Nelson, M., & Wolford, B. (1985). Special education in the most restrictive environment: Correctional special education. *Journal of Special Education, 19* 59–71.

Rutherford, R., Quinn, M. M., & Mathur, S. (Eds.). (2004). *Handbook of research in emotional and behavioral disorders.* New York: Guilford Press.

Santamour, M. (1987). The mentally retarded offender. In M. Nelson, R. Rutherford, & B. Wolford (Eds.), *Special education in the criminal justice system* (pp. 105–119). Columbus, OH: Merrill.

Steelman, D. (1987). *The mentally impaired in New York's prisons: Problems and solutions.* New York: Correctional Association of New York.

Tyack, D. (1974). *The one best system: A history of American urban education.* Cambridge, MA: Harvard University Press.

U.S. Department of Justice. (1976). *The link between learning disabilities and juvenile delinquency: Current theory and knowledge.* Washington, DC: National Institute for Juvenile Justice and Delinquency Prevention, Law Enforcement Assistance Administration.

Zabel, R., & Nigro, F. (2001). The influence of special education experience and gender of juvenile offenders on academic achievement scores in reading, language, and mathematics. *Behavioral Disorders, 26,* 164–172.

Zenz, T., & Langelett, G. (2004). Special education in Wisconsin's juvenile detention. *Journal of Correctional Education, 55,* 60–68.

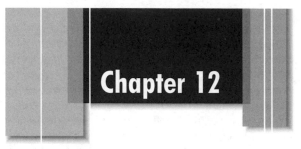

Chapter 12

The Female Juvenile Offender

Robert D. Hoge
Lynda Robertson

Official statistics and self-report data indicate that girls are less likely than boys to commit serious delinquent acts. These gender differences are consistent across time and cultures (Elliott, 1994; Gottfredson & Hirschi, 1990; Office of Juvenile Justice and Delinquency Prevention, 2006). This disparity between girls and boys in the incidence of antisocial behaviors may help to explain why most attempts to explore the correlates, causes, and treatment of youth crime have focused on males. However, girls do engage in criminal behavior, particularly less serious forms, suggesting that understanding the unique and shared (with boys) causes of this behavior is an important concern for justice professionals and service providers. It is for this reason that criminologists and psychologists have increasingly turned their attention to the criminal activity of females.

This chapter focuses specifically on what we know about the causes and treatment of juvenile offending among girls. We begin with a brief review of the nature and incidence of female antisocial behavior, followed by an overview of the major theoretical issues regarding the correlates and causes of girls' offending. We then turn to a discussion of treatment, highlighting programs designed specifically for female offenders.

The Nature and Incidence of Female Juvenile Crime

The criminal code makes no reference to gender differences. Mischief, theft, assault, and prostitution are considered crimes whether committed by boys or girls. Nevertheless, there are two issues to keep in mind when evaluating information about the incidence of criminal activity in girls and boys.

First, boys and girls display consistent differences in the expression of conduct disorders and aggressive behaviors (Moffitt, Caspi, Rutter, & Silva, 2001; Zoccolillo, 1993). Girls are more likely than boys to express conduct disorder and aggression through covert (e.g., lying, gossiping, shunning) rather than overt (e.g., physical aggression, property destruction) actions. To the extent that the justice system focuses on overt antisocial acts, boys are more likely to be involved than girls. In this regard, indices of criminal activity based on official records would tend to underestimate the extent of antisocial activity in girls (although such covert action typically is not criminal in nature).

Second, under some circumstances girls are treated differently by juvenile justice systems (Chesney-Lind & Shelden, 1992). Data indicate that girls tend to be dealt with more harshly for status offenses (e.g., running away, curfew violations, truancy) and sex offenses such as prostitution. This tendency would tend to inflate crime statistics for girls for these low-level offenses.

These considerations should be kept in mind in evaluating the following observations regarding gender differences in offending:

- Rates of conduct disorder, neurological impairment, and other developmental disabilities assessed during preschool years are relatively low for girls, particularly when compared with the rates for boys. These are important early predictors of later antisocial and delinquent behaviors.
- Gender differences in levels of externalizing problems, including physical aggression, are similar for girls and boys until around 3 and 4 years of age, following which the rates for boys begin to exceed that of girls and remain higher throughout the lifespan.
- There is some evidence that rates of covert or relational aggression (expressed, e.g., in lying, rejection of peers, gossiping) are higher for girls than boys, although the research on this is still limited.
- Girls are more likely than boys to be diagnosed with depression, anxiety, and general psychopathology, although gender biases in the diagnosing of these conditions complicate the matter.

- Rates of criminal activity are lower for girls across the lifespan, particularly rates for criminal activities involving violence. The latter remain relatively rare for girls.
- Some have suggested that criminal activities, including acts of violence, committed by girls have increased over the past 10 or so years, but the evidence for this contention is limited and difficult to interpret.
- Girls are more likely than boys to be charged with status offenses.
- Girls generally begin criminal activities during early adolescence and desist by the end of adolescence; life-course persistent criminal activity is much rarer in girls than in boys.
- Although girls who engage in criminal activity during adolescence are at low risk for involvement in criminal activities as adults, they are high risk for other problematic conditions (e.g., alcohol/drug problems, depression, eating disorders, personality disorders).

Although levels of serious antisocial behavior, including violent actions, are lower for girls than for boys, the fact remains that significant numbers of girls are involved with the juvenile justice system, with critical costs to those girls and society.

Major Theoretical and Research Issues

We have two sources of information concerning the causes of antisocial behavior in young girls. The first includes a growing body of correlational (and some longitudinal) research on risk factors associated with female antisocial behavior; and the second, a considerable body of speculative theoretical literature attempting to identify causal factors and how they may differ between boys and girls.

Prior to reviewing research and theory, it is important to consider how and why gender differences in delinquency may arise. We suggest three possibilities: (1) the same risk and protective factors and processes that predict delinquency in boys may also be operating for girls, but girls may simply display lower levels of risk and higher levels of protective factors; (2) risk and protective factors may portend different outcomes for girls and boys and may lead to different types of maladjustment (e.g., depression) in girls but not boys; (3) unique risk factors may be present for girls but not boys related to biological, psychological, or social determinants linked to gender. Although less research has focused on the correlates of delinquency in girls compared with boys, a growing body of data suggests that all three of these mechanisms are implicated in our understanding of gender differences.

First, let us consider the shared risk and protective factors and whether girls simply display lower levels of risk and higher levels of protection. Looking at individual-level predictors that emerge early in development, several empirical studies have demonstrated that many risk factors for girls are essentially the same as for boys, but are less likely among girls (Moffitt et al., 2001; Rowe, Vazonyi, & Flannery, 1995; Silverthorn, Frick, & Reynolds, 2001; Simourd & Andrews, 1994). For example, symptoms of conduct disorder, neurological impairments, hyperactivity, and learning disabilities appearing during the preschool years, although rarer in girls than boys, predict later criminal activity for both girls and boys. Others have implicated genetically based gender differences in aggressive impulses as primary determinants of differences in the rates of antisocial behavior (Quinsey, Skilling, Lalumiere, & Craig, 2004).

From this perspective, gender differences in antisocial behavior can be attributed, in part, to differences in levels of a subset of risk factors, although the process of influence on risk is the same. Many of the risk factors that differentially affect boys, described above, cluster around early neurological and biological risk factors that have also been implicated in the early-starter, life-course persistent group of offenders (Moffitt et al., 2001). Gender differences in these early predictors can also shed light on why girls are much less likely to display life-course persistent patterns of offending than boys.

Beyond individual risk and protective factors, it is also likely that contextual risk factors vary between boys and girls, in part, as a function of differential socialization. Contextual predictors of risk that begin in childhood and continue through adolescence include inadequate parenting/poor parent–child relations, educational failure, exposure to community violence, and associations with antisocial peers (one of the most robust predictors of delinquency during adolescence). Consider, for example, parent–child relations. The socialization literature suggests that parents respond to and treat boys differently than girls from infancy through adolescence. To the extent that parents respond more gently to girls, reserving harsh and aggressive actions for boys, the risk factor of harsh parenting is simply less likely for girls than for boys.

A second plausible explanation for gender differences is that similar levels of a risk factor may predict different outcomes for boys and girls. As noted previously, although girls are less likely to engage in antisocial and delinquent behavior, they are more likely to experience a different set of adjustment problems, such as depression and eating disorders. It may be that certain risk factors predict externalizing behaviors for boys but predict internalizing behaviors for girls. This is certainly the case with exposure to violence: Empirical studies have found that community violence exposure predicts aggression in school-age boys but predicts depression in girls (Attar, Guerra, & Tolan, 1994; Guerra, Huesmann, & Spindler, 2003). Thus identified risk factors in boys may have weaker effects in girls, although there is some evidence to suggest that other risk factors (e.g., such as family conflict) may portend more difficulties for girls than boys (Lee, Burkam, Zimiles, & Ladewski, 1994). Still, these stressors tend to predict psychological dysfunction rather than delinquency in girls.

A third possibility is that there may simply be different risk and protective factors and associated mechanisms of influence that uniquely affect girls. Because so much of the research on causes and correlates of delinquency has been designed to understand boys' delinquency, even when girls are included as participants, the risk and protective factors measured tend to be linked to previous findings for boys. Even developmental life-course (DLC) models emphasizing mechanisms of desistance from offending, discussed by Guerra et al. in Chapter 2 of this volume, identify particular events and "turning points" that predict desistance for males. Yet, there may be other factors related to girls' unique place in society, including considerations of patriarchal oppression, that predict risk only for girls (Regoli & Hewitt, 1994). Similarly, boys who do not adopt conventional pathways during adolescence may be easily drawn into the tough, streetwise criminal and gang culture, whereas girls may be more likely to become pregnant and drop out of school. This pattern suggests that not only may some risk factors be different for girls and boys, but the available nonconventional pathways may also differ by gender.

Interventions with the Female Young Offender

Our responsibility is to deal with the young person before us, to ensure that services are available to address his or her specific needs. In that sense race, ethnicity, or gender are really irrelevant. However, because many girls do present with special needs and because they have often been neglected relative to boys, it is also our responsibility to be sensitive to them as an identifiable group.

Research on Best Practices

Earlier chapters in this volume provide conclusions from research on best practices for use with juvenile offenders, with most of the research based on studies of male offenders. However, the limited research that has evaluated programming for female offenders (Dowden & Andrews, 1999) and clinical experience suggests that the basic principles of best practice are similar for girls and boys. Risk–need and responsivity are key concepts in the best-practice model; these are discussed next with specific reference to female offenders.

Risk–Need Factors

We have seen that empirically based information is now available about the risk–need factors associated with female juvenile offending (Moffitt et al., 2001; Rowe et al., 1995; Simourd & Andrews, 1994). The identification of these factors is important because the targets of intervention should match the specific risk and need factors of the youth. Although we have noted potentially different explanations for the lower rates of serious offending among girls, most of the research from which we draw has concentrated on risk and protective factors that affect both boys and girls. We now provide a more detailed discussion of these risk factors and their implications for interventions with girls.

- *Early risk factors* evident during preschool years serve as major predictors of antisocial behavior. These include neurological impairments, attention disorders, hyperactivity, learning disabilities, and early conduct disorders. Although these are worthy targets for early prevention and early intervention programs, they are less relevant to the treatment of older juvenile offenders—the major subject matter of this volume.
- *Family dynamics and parenting practices* consistently emerge as significant correlates of female juvenile offending. Family discord and conflict comprise one dimension of this issue. There is evidence that girls are particularly sensitive to conflict within the family (Lee, Burkam, Zimiles, & Ladewski, 1994). Although stressors associated with the conflict are likely not direct causes of criminal activity, they can impact on parenting behavior and the emotional well-being of the youth, serving as indirect contributors to antisocial actions. Counselors are often called on to deal with the stressors associated with that discord.

Parenting practices and parent–child relations often have direct and indirect impacts on antisocial behaviors. Unfortunately, many girls are subject to sexual, physical, or emotional abuse. Although the evidence linking abuse and neglect to criminal activity in girls is contradictory (Langhinrichsen-Rohling & Neidig, 1995; Wekerle & Wolfe, 1998), there may be consequences of the youth's emotional state (e.g., anxiety, a mood disorder, low self-esteem) that have implications for treatment. These are discussed in the following section on responsivity considerations.

Parent supervision, communication, and disciplinary practices are directly linked with antisocial behaviors. Highly punitive (or highly permissive) disciplinary practices, a failure to supervise behavior, and inconsistent parenting are all associated with increased risk for criminal activities (Dodge, Bates, & Pettit, 1990; Loeber & Stouthamer-Loeber, 1986; Maughan, Pickles, & Quinton, 1995; Pepler & Craig, 2004). We should also recognize that the impact of parenting practices and parent–child relations is often heightened during adolescence. The onset of puberty may be associated with personality and emotional changes in the youth. A desire for increased independence from the parent is often the catalyst for significant conflicts between parent and youth and the onset of antisocial behaviors in the youth. The finding that criminal activity in girls often begins around the period of puberty onset suggests that parental influences might be particularly salient.

Effecting improvements in parenting and parent–child relations presents a serious challenge. We are sometimes dealing with uncooperative parents, parents with very limited competencies, and situations that have developed to a point where they appear nearly hopeless. Nevertheless, and as we will see, there are treatment methods available to help us address this important area.

• *Educational achievement and experiences* have frequently emerged as areas of significant risk for juvenile offending. Academic failure, conflicts with teachers and peers, truancy, and learning disabilities are often associated with antisocial activities (Pepler & Craig, 2004; Robins, 1986). Although the direction of effect is not always clear in these cases (what is the real causal factor?), many of the girls we encounter present problems in these areas, and clinical experience shows that improvements can have a positive impact on antisocial behaviors and the general well-being of the youth.

The school is the logical place for dealing with these issues for youth in the community, but we are often handicapped by limited resources in that setting for assessing and treating academic and behavioral problems. There are also significant challenges for dealing with educational issues for youth in custody, particularly arising from the disconnection from their home school. In Chapter 11 of this volume, Eggleston provides useful discussions of addressing educational problems in the community school and institutional settings.

• *Antisocial peer group associations* consistently emerge as risk factors. There are suggestions that the dynamics of the peer group experience–criminality behavior link is different for male and female youth, with boys more adversely affected by these associations than girls (Rutter, Giller, & Hagell, 1998). However, there is evidence that delinquent girls are more likely to report antisocial peer associations than nondelinquent girls Dishion, 2000; Giordano, Cernkovich, & Pugh, 1986). Further, some empirical support is emerging for the suggestion that an absence of positive peer associations is directly associated with antisocial behaviors (Woodward & Fergusson, 1999).

In any case, it is clear from both research and clinical experience that antisocial behavior of girls is sometimes directly linked to their associations with antisocial peers (Caspi, Lynman, Moffitt, & Silva, 1993; Dishion, 2000; Leve & Chamberlain, 2005). This association may occur in the context of individual pairings (boyfriend–girlfriend), loose friendship associations (either mixed [boys and girls] or all girls), or membership in an organized gang. The forces operating within these associations can be very strong: They often provide important emotional support for the girl (in many cases substituting for its absence in the family) and are, at the same time, models of antisocial behavior. For this reason, targeting this area of need can be very difficult. Some specific guidance is presented below.

• *Substance abuse* is identified as a risk factor in many cases (Ellickson, Saner, & McGuigan, 1997). This may involve abuse of prescription drugs, illicit drugs, or other substances (e.g., gasoline, glue). The causes of substance abuse are complex, as is the link between substance abuse and criminal activity. Under some circumstances, for example, both substance abuse and antisocial behavior may be products of emotional disorders (mood disorders, anxiety, posttraumatic stress) linked with earlier physical, sexual, or emotional abuse. Under other circumstances both the substance abuse and the criminal activity may be the result of associations with antisocial peers.

The issue of the dynamics of the substance abuse is important because the choice of interventions will depend very directly on the causes of the condition. It is usually a mistake in substance abuse treatment to focus exclusively on the pattern of substance use. Responsivity factors are important here as well. Because of physical factors, girls are often highly susceptible to developing a substance abuse problem and to suffering the physical consequences of that abuse.

• *Use of leisure time,* although not extensively researched with females, does emerge as a risk–need factor for boys, and clinical experience would suggest that it affects girls as well. In many cases the youth gets into trouble simply because of boredom and having so much free time. Clinical experience suggests that this may be less of a problem for girls than boys, but in many cases intervention plans must include some means for ensuring that the girl is involved in positive activities.

• *Personality/behavior traits* encompass a broad range of individual characteristics associated with antisocial behaviors (Cottle, Lee, & Heilbrun, 2001; Loeber & Keenan, 1994; Sroufe, 1997). The list for boys includes patterns of physical and verbal aggression, hyperactivity, attention disorders, and impulsivity. Although levels of risk factors, including physical aggression and attention disorders, may be lower for girls, there is no reason to think that they are lesser predictors for girls. As well, there are suggestions that levels of covert relational aggression are frequent in girls and may also serve as risk–need factors.

Dysfunctional personality and behavioral patterns constitute important targets of service. For example, impulsivity and sensation seeking are often associated with engagement in antisocial acts. Similarly, a proneness to respond to frustration with aggressive actions place the youth at high risk for violent criminal activity. Unfortunately, these personality and behavior traits may be well established by the time we deal with the offender, and this entrenchment presents significant challenges in addressing the problems. Some therapeutic tools are discussed below.

• *Antisocial attitudes, values, and cognitions* form an important group of predictors of antisocial behavior for girls (see Simourd & Andrews, 1994). Many of the youth we treat hold negative attitudes toward parents, teachers, police, the courts, and the law in general, and those attitudes are often directly linked with their criminal activity. Also, there is often an absence of positive values about academic achievement or responsible behavior. An absence of empathy or the ability to adopt the perspective of another is implicated as well.

The current literature often analyzes these modes of thought in terms of social cognitions (Dodge, 2003). The antisocial behavior of the young person is seen as a product of distorted cognitions regarding the actions of others and the available alternative courses of action. The girl may have a tendency to perceive social cues in a negative light, and her behavior may be guided by an implicit belief that all perceived slights merit a hostile response.

One of the key tasks in working with antisocial youth is to address these dysfunctional and damaging attitudes and cognitions and replace them with more positive modes of thinking and behaving. Some approaches are discussed below.

Responsivity Considerations

The need principle of case classification directs that interventions should target the specific risks and needs exhibited by the youth. However, there may be other characteristics of the youth or her circumstances that, although not directly related to criminal activity, should be considered in planning an intervention. For example, substance abuse treatment may constitute a major need for two girls, but in one case the abuse may be primarily associated with depression and anxiety and in the other case with newly formed associations with antisocial peers. The interventions would have to be somewhat different in the two cases. Consider another example. Intelligence is normally not directly linked to criminal activity; however, it may be a relevant consideration in selecting an intervention program. A cognitive modification program that involves reading complicated material and understanding abstract thought would probably be inappropriate for a youth with limited reading skills and more concrete in her thinking.

Table 12.1 identifies some important responsivity and protective considerations. All of these are potentially important, but some of the personality factors bear special consideration. It is well established that many girls who come into contact with the juvenile justice system have serious emotional disorders (Abram, Teplin, & McClelland, 2003; Abrantes, Hoffmann, & Anton, 2005; Grisso, Barnum, Fletcher, Cauffman, & Peuschold, 2001; Pepler & Sedighdeilami, 1998). These include mood disorders, anxiety, posttraumatic stress, and suicidal ideation. Other issues may include poor self-esteem, low assertiveness, and body-image problems. Although these considerations may not be directly associated with criminal activity, they are characteristics that require careful attention in case planning. Similarly, and as is elaborated below, girls seem to be more affected by social relationships than boys (Acoca, 1995; Artz, 1997, 1998). This factor should be an important consideration in any treatment decisions.

Protective Factors

Strength or protective factors can also be regarded as responsivity considerations. That is, consider the situational factors and characteristics of the youth that serve to buffer or moderate the effects of risk. Table 12.1 provides a partial list of potential protective factors. Some of those

TABLE 12.1. Examples of Responsivity and Protective Factors

Situational characteristics	Characteristics of the youth
Stable and cohesive family unit	Emotionally mature
Supportive parent, teacher, or other adult	Highly intelligent
Accessible and effective school services	Positive, prosocial attitudes
Accessible and effective mental health services	Good prosocial skills
Positive/prosocial neighborhood environment	Good problem-solving skills
	Positive academic attitudes
	Positive leisure/sport activities
	Motivated to address problems

are situational, such as the availability of a supportive parent or quality school services, and others relate to characteristics of the youth, such as emotional maturity and good problem-solving skills. It is amazing how some girls exposed to extraordinarily stressful circumstances continue to show resilience, and it is important to recognize that fact.

Although theoretical debates about the way in which strength or protective factors operate remain (see Rutter et al., 1998), there are two reasons to consider them in case planning. First, establishing a relationship with the client is easier and more effective when discussions involve positive topics rather than solely focusing on negative aspects of the young person. Second, case plans are more effective when they integrate strengths of the young person. For example, an effort to address a girl's poor use of leisure time might utilize her interest in basketball or photography. Similarly, physical aggression associated with anger over an abusive father might be ameliorated by time spent with a supportive and cooperative father figure.

A Holistic View

Although the identification of individual need and responsivity factors is important, we should not lose sight of the youth before us. Two aspects of this point bear special mention. First, the various risk–need and responsivity factors do not operate independently of one another; rather, very complex interactions may exist. For example, there is often a close link among substance abuse, antisocial peer associations, and depression. Focusing narrowly on substance abuse in a case like this will likely not be very effective. This interactiveness is one reason why multimodal interventions are usually recommended. Second, the girl before us is more than the sum of her needs and other characteristics and circumstances. She must always be valued as an important human being.

Intervention Guidelines

As we saw in Chapter 3, the first step in developing an intervention program involves conducting a careful evaluation of risk and need considerations. Girls come to us with a broad range of needs, and it is important to ensure that any plan of action is based on the situation of the individual client.

The second step is careful case planning based on the risk–need assessment. This plan is constrained, of course, by the resources available, but to the extent possible, it should target the specific needs of the young person and take account of responsivity considerations.

Guidelines regarding the specifics of treatment have been presented in earlier chapters, and most of those apply equally well to boys and girls. However, here we outline some special considerations that may apply specifically to girls.

The Office of Juvenile Justice and Delinquency Prevention (1998) recommends that all efforts begin with the development of policies regarding the treatment of female juvenile offenders in a system. The following steps should be considered:

- Form a task force or other body to systematically explore needs and options.
- Define a mission and set of goals for the interventions.
- Collect information on the needs of female juvenile offenders in the jurisdiction.
- Develop a community action plan in cooperation with related agencies.
- Confront barriers to implementing needed changes.
- Lobby for necessary legislative changes.
- Engage in community education and advocacy.

An example of such an effort can be found in the Cook County (Illinois) Juvenile Justice System, where committees composed of representatives of all agencies providing services to female juvenile offenders were formed. The four committees focused on advocacy, education, policy development, and programming. The committees ultimately created a set of gender-specific initiatives impacting assessment and programming for female offenders and the training of case workers.

Leschied, Cummings, Van Brunschot, Cunningham, and Saunders (2001), the Office of Juvenile Justice and Delinquency Prevention (1998), and the Valentine Foundation (1990) have also articulated a set of general guidelines to be followed in developing gender-specific programming for girls. The following is a summary of those guidelines.

- *Provide a physical space that is physically and emotionally safe.* Many of the girls have been neglected or abused by family members or others, and it is important that that threat be removed. A period of freedom from dealing with relations with male peers may be advised under some circumstances.
- *Provide girls with an opportunity to develop relationships of trust with other females.* This concern with developing normal relationships with females extends to peers, female staff members, and, when possible, female adults in their lives (e.g., mother, aunt, teacher). Female mentors may also be an important resource, particularly those who had experiences similar to those of the offender at an earlier age. This is not to say that the girl's relationships with men are unimportant, but many of the girls with whom we work have never had an opportunity to develop meaningful relationships with other females.
- *Provide meaningful education of sexual issues.* Some of the girls with whom we work are uneducated or misinformed about sexual issues, including safe sex practices, contraception, and dealing with peer pressure regarding sex. They may also need counseling in dealing with their own sexuality, no matter what their orientation. This is an issue that must be addressed in any programming involving adolescent females.
- *Provide education and treatment relating to substance abuse.* Significant numbers of girls have more or less disabling problems with alcohol and/or drugs. This is typically a difficult intervention target because the substance abuse is often complicated by mental health and peer association issues. Nevertheless, reduction in the girl's risk for future offending and other negative outcomes depends on confronting the issue.
- *Provide opportunities to enhance competencies.* This is perhaps the key recommendation. Many of our clients have experienced nothing but failure in the past. Their relationships in their home may have been negative, they may have experienced school failure, been the subject of rejection by peers, or other types of stress. Assertiveness and problem-solving skills, anger management, academic competencies, and healthy physical development are some of the areas often requiring attention. Enhancing self-esteem is typically mentioned as a goal of programming. Although improved self-esteem is important, it must be

grounded in the development of competencies—the true foundation for a healthy self-image.

- *Other considerations.* Several other considerations may be raised in case planning with girls. First, as elaborated above, any case plan should recognize the strengths that girls bring to the therapeutic setting. This recognition helps to establish a therapeutic relationship with the client and develop an effective intervention. Second, particularly in the case of higher risk–need cases, coordinated services from the juvenile justice, education, mental health, and social service systems may be required. Too often fragmented systems produce fragmented and ineffective interventions.

The selection and training of staff working with these girls is extremely important. Because of the emotional and personality problems presented by some of the girls, many people find it difficult and unrewarding to work with them. Only individuals prepared to deal with the special challenges of these clients, and with the required training and support, will succeed at this task.

A number of points should be observed when a residential placement is required. These placements should represent the least restrictive environment consistent with the needs of the girl and the community, and should be located as close to her home as possible. These facilities should also have a full range of services available to meet the academic, cognitive, social, and emotional needs of the young person. Too often custody settings for girls offer no provisions that meet their needs.

Finally, a growing body of research evidence shows that behavioral and cognitive-behavioral modification strategies are most effective in addressing many of the behavioral and attitudinal deficits exhibited by female juvenile offenders. Much of that research is based on exclusively or predominantly male samples (Andrews et al., 1990; Lipsey, 1995; Lipsey & Wilson, 1998; Losel, 1996). Nevertheless, a meta-analysis by Dowden and Andrews (1999) concludes that this principle applies to girls as well.

Examples of Intervention Programs

Several specialized programs for female juvenile offenders have been developed (see Office of Juvenile Justice and Delinquency Prevention, 1998). Although none has been subjected to an impact evaluation (with one exception noted below), features of the programs can serve as useful models. A few of the programs are described here for illustrative purposes.

Harriet Tubman Residential Center

The Harriet Tubman Residential Center residential facility in Auburn, New York, is designed for first-time or status offenders, or girls convicted of minor assaults. Many of the girls come from unstable home environments and have been exposed, directly or indirectly, to abuse or neglect. Unfortunately, girls are often removed some distance from their homes, but the confinement is kept as brief as possible, depending on the progress of the client.

Emphasis is placed on forming an ethnically diverse staff of males and females and on training staff in gender-specific programming. The latter is based on 10 hours of training prior to delivery of services, 120 additional hours during the first year of employment, and 40 hours each subsequent year.

A treatment plan is developed for each client that focuses on the development of self-control competencies and relationship building. The program is highly structured initially, with the girls permitted increased freedom as they acquire better self-control and decision-making skills. Deficiencies in education and independent living skills are also addressed.

This program is typical of many programs that specifically addresses the needs of high-risk girls. An additional strength is the emphasis on training staff in delivering gender-sensitive services.

Boys Town USA, Staff-Secure Detention Program for Female Offenders

The Detention Program for Female Offenders that is part of Boys Town USA is a somewhat unusual program in that it was designed for high-risk girls detained prior to trial. Although girls remain in the program for relatively short periods, an intensive assessment is conducted at intake, and the plan developed on the basis of that assessment is designed to follow the client through subsequent placements. The plan encompasses both short- and long-term goals. Most of the girls accepted for the program are members of minority groups, come from high-risk family environments, and exhibit a range of academic, social, behavioral, and emotional needs.

The staff of the program is predominantly female, and all are given intensive training in gender-specific programming. Individual and group treatment is focused on mental health and behavioral issues as well as developing life skills. Treatment involves families whenever possible. The ultimate goal is to address deficits in the young woman and assist her reintegration into society.

Although the intervention process in this program is brief, two positive features bear mention. First, in too many cases no effort is made in detention settings to address the needs of the young person. It is simply regarded as a holding action. Second, the comprehensive assessment accomplished at intake and the development of long-term actions and goals can serve a very useful and far-reaching purpose.

Moving On

Moving On, developed by Marilyn Van Dieten and Patricia MacKenna in association with Dodge–Olmsted–Filmore County (Minnesota) Community Corrections, is designed for adult females but easily adapted for older female juvenile offenders. This 26-session curriculum-based program can be delivered over 9–13 weeks in group or individual formats.

The goal of the program is to "provide women with alternatives free from criminal activity by assisting them to identify and mobilize both personal and community resources" (Van Dieten & MacKenna, 2002, p. 1). The programming is based on behavioral and cognitive-behavioral therapeutic principles. Considerable emphasis is placed on developing motivation for change, encouraging personal responsibility, and fostering skill enhancement. Careful selection and training of program facilitators are emphasized. The developers acknowledge that the program is not designed to address needs relating to psychiatric or substance abuse issues, but it can be an important supplement to those treatments by developing general competencies in the client.

Although this program was developed for adult female offenders, many features are relevant to the treatment of female juvenile offenders. A major strength of the program is the highly structured curriculum for training individuals in program delivery.

Multidimensional Treatment Foster Care

Multidimensional Treatment Foster Care was developed by Patricia Chamberlain and her associates at the Oregon Learning Center. It is a multidimensional treatment program for high-risk youth and families and designed for delivery in foster homes. It is an alternative to more restrictive residential environments.

The careful selection, training, and supervision of the foster parents are important features of this program and are recognized as a key to the successful management of difficult youth. Provision is made to address social, emotional, behavioral, and educational problems of the youth and to counsel primary caregivers. A case manager and clinical consultant maintain close relations with the foster parents, meeting weekly to coordinate treatment and supervision activities.

Preliminary evaluation studies have indicated that the program is as effective for girls as boys in reducing offending behavior (Leve & Chamberlain, 2005). However, early research also suggests that foster parents found the girls more difficult to deal with than boys, and that behavioral problems tended to escalate over time rather than decline, as is usually the case for boys. Some modifications have been made in the program to tailor it more for the needs of females, including helping girls cope with the experience of abuse.

This is a well-developed program that continues to be the subject of evaluation. A major strength of the program is the effort to tailor it to the needs of the high-risk female adolescent and to make adjustments to the program as a result of evaluation research.

A Final Word

This chapter has stressed the importance of focusing carefully on the specific needs of the female adolescent client. We should not enter the therapeutic process with preconceived ideas about the young girl, but rather be sensitive to all behavioral and emotional issues displayed by the girl: the kinds of stressors she is experiencing in the home, school, and community; her expectations and dreams; and, of particular importance, the strengths that she brings to her situation.

References

Abram, K. M., Teplin, L., & McClelland, G. M. (2003). Co-morbid psychiatric disorders in youth in juvenile detention. Archives of General Psychiatry, 60, 1097–1108.

Abrantes, A. M., Hoffmann, N. G., & Anton, R. (2005). Prevalence of co-occurring disorders among juveniles committed to detention centers. International Journal of Offender Therapy and Comparative Criminology, 49, 179–193.

Acoca, L. (1995). Breaking the cycle: A developmental model for the assessment and treatment of adolescents with alcohol and other drug problems. Juvenile and Family Court Journal, 46, 1–45.

Andrews, D. A., Zinger, I., Hoge, R. D., Bonta, J., Gendreau, P., & Cullen, F. T. (1990). Does correctional treatment work? A psychologically informed meta-analysis. Criminology, 28, 369–404.

Artz, S. (1997). On becoming an object. Journal of Child and Youth Care, 11, 17–37.

Artz, S. (1998). Where have all the school girls gone? Violent girls in the school yard. *Child and Youth Care Forum, 27* 77–107.

Attar, B., Guerra, N. G., & Tolan, P. (1994). Neighborhood disadvantage, stressful life events, and adjustment in elementary school children. *Journal of Clinical Child Psychology, 23*, 394–400.

Caspi, A., Lynam, D., Moffitt, T. E., & Silva, P. A. (1993). Unraveling girls' delinquency: Biological, dispositional, and contextual contributions to adolescent misbehavior. *Developmental Psychology, 29*, 19–30.

Chesney-Lind, M., & Sheldon, R. (1992). *Girls delinquency and juvenile justice.* Pacific Grove, CA: Brooks/Cole.

Cottle, C. C., Lee, R. J., & Heilbrun, K. (2001). The prediction of criminal recidivism in juveniles. *Criminal Justice and Behavior, 28*, 367–394.

Dishion, T. J. (2000). Cross-setting consistency in early adolescent psychopathology: Deviant friendships and problem behavior sequelae. *Journal of Personality, 68*, 1109–1126.

Dodge, K. A. (2003). Do social information-processing patterns mediate aggressive behavior? In B. B. Lahey, T. E. Moffitt, & A. Caspi (Eds.), *Causes of conduct disorder and juvenile delinquency* (pp. 254–274). New York: Guilford Press.

Dodge, K. A., Bates, J. E., & Pettit, G. S. (1990). Mechanisms in the cycle of violence. *Science, 250*, 1678–1683.

Dowden, C., & Andrews, D. A. (1999). What works for female offenders: A meta-analytic review. *Crime and Delinquency, 45*, 438–452.

Ellickson, P., Saner, H., & McGuigan, K. A. (1997). Profiles of violent youth: Substance use and other concurrent problems. *American Journal of Public Health, 87*, 985–991.

Elliott, D. S. (1994). Serious violent offenders: Onset, developmental course, and termination: The American Society of Criminology 1993 presidential address. *Criminology, 32*, 1–21.

Giordano, P. C., Cernkovich, S. A., & Pugh, M. D. (1986). Friendship and delinquency. *American Journal of Sociology, 91*, 1170–1201.

Gottfredson, M., & Hirschi, T. (1990). *A general theory of crime.* Palo Alto, CA: Stanford University Press.

Grisso, T., Barnum, R., Fletcher, K., Cauffman, E., & Peuschold, D. (2001). Massachusetts Youth Screening Instrument for mental health needs of juvenile justice youth. *Journal of the American Academy of Child and Adolescent Psychiatry, 40*, 541–548.

Guerra, N. G., Huesmann, L. R., & Spindler, A. (2003). Community violence exposure, social cognition, and aggression among urban elementary-school children. *Child Development, 74*, 1507–1522.

Langhinrichsen-Rohling, J., & Neidig, P. (1995). Violent backgrounds of economically disadvantaged youth: Risk factors for perpetrating violence? *Journal of Family Violence, 10*, 379–397.

Lee, V. E., Burkam, D. T., Zimiles, H., & Ladewski, B. (1994). Family structure and its effect on behavioral and emotional problems in young adolescents. *Journal of Research on Adolescents, 4*, 405–437.

Leschied, A. W., Cummings, A. L., Van Brunschot, M., Cunningham, A., & Saunders, A. (2001). Aggression in adolescent girls: Implications for policy, prevention, and treatment. *Canadian Psychology, 42,* 200–215.

Leve, L. D., & Chamberlain, P. (2005). Girls in the juvenile justice system: Risk factors and clinical implications. In D. J. Pepler, K. C. Madsen, C. Webster, & K. S. Levene (Eds.), *The development and treatment of girlhood aggression* (pp. 191–215). Mahwah, NJ: Erlbaum.

Lipsey, M. W. (1995). What do we learn from 400 research studies on the effectiveness of treatment with juvenile delinquents? In J. McGuire (Ed.), *What works: Reducing reoffending* (pp. 63–78). Chichester, UK: Wiley.

Lipsey, M. W., & Wilson, D. B. (1998). Effective intervention for serious juvenile offenders: A synthesis of research. In R. Loeber & D. P. Farrington (Eds.), *Serious and violent juvenile offenders: Risk factors and successful interventions* (pp. 313–345). Thousand Oaks, CA: Sage.

Loeber, R., & Keenan, K. (1994). The interaction between conduct disorder and its co-morbid conditions: Effects of age and gender. *Clinical Psychology Review, 14* 497–523.

Loeber, R., & Stouthamer-Loeber, M. (1986). Prediction. In H. C. Quay (Ed.), *Handbook of juvenile delinquency* (pp. 325–382). New York: Wiley.

Losel, F. (1996). Working with young offenders: The impact of meta-analysis. In C. R. Holling & K. Howells (Eds.), *Clinical approaches to working with young offenders* (pp. 57–82). New York: Wiley.

Maughan, B., Pickles, A., & Quinton, D. (1995). Parental hostility, childhood behavior, and adult social functioning. In J. McCord (Ed.), *Coercion and punishment in long-term perspectives* (pp. 34–58). New York: Cambridge University Press.

Moffitt, T. E., Caspi, A., Rutter, M., & Silva, P. A. (2001). *Sex differences in antisocial behavior: Conduct disorder, delinquency, and violence in the Dunedin Longitudinal Study.* Cambridge, UK: Cambridge University Press.

Office of Juvenile Justice and Delinquency Prevention. (1998). *Guiding principles for promising female programming: An inventory of best practices.* Washington, DC: U.S. Department of Justice.

Office of Juvenile Justice and Delinquency Prevention. (2006). *Juvenile offenders and victims: 2006 national report.* Washington, DC: Department of Justice.

Pepler, D. J., & Craig, W. (2004). Aggressive girls on troubled trajectories: A developmental perspective. In D. J. Pepler, K. C. Madsen, C. Webster, & K. S. Levene (Eds.), *The development and treatment of girlhood aggression* (pp. 3–28). Mahwah, NJ: Erlbaum.

Pepler, D. J., & Sedighdeilami, F. (1998). *Aggressive girls in Canada.* Manuscript #W-98–30E, Applied Research Branch, Human Resources, Ottawa, Canada.

Quinsey, V. L., Skilling, T. A., Lalumiere, M. L., & Craig, W. M. (2004). *Juvenile delinquency: Understanding the origins of individual differences.* Washington, DC: American Psychological Association.

Regoli, R., & Hewitt, J. (1994). *Delinquency in society: A child-centered approach.* New York: McGraw-Hill.

Robins, L. N. (1986). The consequences of conduct disorders in girls. In D. Olweus, J. Block, & M. Radke-Yarrow (Eds.), *Development of antisocial and prosocial behavior: Research, theories, and issues* (pp. 385–414). Orlando, FL: Academic Press.

Rowe, D. C., Vazonyi, A. T., & Flannery, D. J. (1995). Sex differences in crime: Do means and within-sex variation have similar causes? *Journal of Research in Crime and Delinquency, 32,* 84–100.

Rutter, M., Giller, H., & Hagell, A. (1998). *Antisocial behavior by young people.* Cambridge, UK: Cambridge University Press.

Silverthorn, P., Frick, P. J., & Reynolds, R. (2001). Timing of onset and correlates of conduct problems in adjudicated girls and boys. *Journal of Psychopathology and Behavioral Assessment, 23,* 171–181.

Simourd, L., & Andrews, D. A. (1994). Correlates of delinquency: A look at gender differences. In R. A. Silverman, J. J. Teevan, & V. F. Sacco (Eds.), *Crime in Canadian society* (6th ed., pp. 44–76). Toronto, ON: Harcourt Brace.

Sroufe, L. A. (1997). Psychopathology as an outcome of development. *Development and Psychopathology, 9,* 251–268.

Valentine Foundation. (1990). *A conversation about girls.* Bryn Mawr, PA: Author.

Van Dieten, M., & MacKenna, P. (2002). *Moving On manual.* Ottawa, ON: Orbis Partners.

Wekerle, C., & Wolfe, D. A. (1998). The role of child maltreatment and attachment style in adolescent relationship violence. *Development and Psychopathology, 10,* 571–586.

Woodward, L. J., & Fergusson, D. M. (1999). Early conduct problems and later risk of teenage pregnancy in girls. *Development and Psychopathology, 11,* 127–141.

Zoccolillo, M. (1993). Gender and the development of conduct disorder. *Development and Psychopathology, 5,* 65–78.

Epilogue

Robert D. Hoge
Nancy G. Guerra
Paul Boxer

This book has provided an introduction to recent theoretical and practical developments relating to the treatment of the juvenile offender. Our chapters show that the combined efforts of researchers in a number of social science disciplines have yielded a comprehensive and nuanced understanding of youth crime, from development through treatment. We have endeavored to use that knowledge to provide concrete guidance regarding the treatment of youth in juvenile justice and correctional systems, believing that contemporary research on best practices offers clear, portable, and verifiable guidelines in this respect.

Considerable space also has been devoted to a review of relevant theory and research. This reflects our belief that practitioners in the field will benefit from a solid foundation in basic models and observations regarding the origins and development of antisocial behaviors in youth. We turn now to some directions for research and policy emerging from our reviews.

Future Research Directions

The chapters in this book highlight the considerable progress made in developing our understanding of the causes and treatment of antisocial behavior in youth. This understanding has emerged from a number of social science disciplines, but especially noteworthy is research and theory from the fields of developmental psychology and the psychology of youthful criminal conduct. This work has been facilitated by methodological advances, particularly those relating to meta-analysis and multivariate statistics. However, despite these significant advances, research gaps remain.

Research and theory have advanced our understanding of the individual and situational factors placing the youth at risk for criminal activity. However, knowledge of the dynamics of those risk factors is limited. For example, while we know that antisocial peer associations constitute a risk factor, the way in which they actually have an impact on the youth's behavior—particularly in the context of treatments for antisocial behavior—is not always clear. Only recently have investigators begun to specify and fully test hypotheses regarding peer contagion effects in group-based interventions for delinquency. Another illustration involves a callous and unemotional interpersonal style. This is clearly a risk factor, but our understanding of how this style emerges and influences behavior remains somewhat limited. Despite a wealth of evidence linking callous–unemotional traits to general antisocial and violent behavior, it has yet to be shown whether these traits are driven by variations over time in emotional processing or moral reasoning, or how these traits are influenced by parents, peers, and communities.

Another gap in our knowledge concerns desistance from continued criminal activity. We have an understanding of what leads youth to antisocial behavior, but only limited understanding of why some youth persist in the criminal behavior and some do not. On a related note, our understanding of personal and contextual factors that promote or inhibit amenability to treatment is present only in broad strokes. These are issues that clearly have implications for treatment strategies.

Our understanding of the developmental processes involved in the emergence and maintenance of antisocial behaviors is also lacking. The distinction between life-course persistent and adolescent-onset delinquency is useful, but we require a more detailed picture of the factors influencing the appearance of antisocial behaviors at each stage of development, as well as of the factors that contribute to antisocial behavior sustained over time within individuals. A related area requiring more attention concerns the nature of the antisocial behavior. Researchers have identified a variety of useful distinctions, such as proactive versus reactive aggression and covert versus overt antisocial behavior, but much more work needs to be done. Studies of treatments for youth offenders still largely treats criminal activity as a uniform composite variable and fail to account for variability in the nature, severity, and chronicity of the activity.

Much research on antisocial behavior of youth has focused on Caucasian and African American males. Although the literature base is growing, information about the emergence and treatment of antisocial behaviors in females and other minority groups is still quite limited. Future research should recognize that the situation of youth can vary considerably according to individual and situational factors. For example, the needs of an African American adolescent female in a rural Southern U.S. community may differ in many respects from her counterpart in a large Northern city.

Various chapters in this book have shown considerable advances in our understanding of best practices. Sophisticated evaluation research combined with meta-analytic strategies has yielded important information about the features of effective programming. However, much of that research has been based on limited samples of youth and programming has been applied primarily under ideal experimental conditions high only in internal validity. We need more information about the features of programming that have an impact on outcomes, especially with regard to outcomes observed under more naturalistic experimental designs high in external or ecological validity—that is, those that mirror practices in the "real world."

The failure of some of our intervention efforts does not necessarily correspond to an unwillingness to apply best practices or implement high-quality research designs; rather, it points to practical, economic, and political constraints that impede our efforts. We turn now to some of the policy implications of our reviews.

Policy Implications

Four general principles have guided the recommendations provided in this book: closer-to-home; rehabilitation; evidence-based; and risk-focused, strengths-based. Implementing programming based on these principles requires considerable efforts to influence public policy at national, local, and agency levels.

Perhaps the key policy initiative involves educating policy makers and the public about the efficacy of those principles. The major barriers to accomplishing that goal are the public's fear of crime and the tendency of some politicians and policy makers to play on those fears and advocate the use of punitive crime-control strategies. However, public support for a system reflecting the four principles is essential for their implementation.

A second policy initiative should focus on creating the conditions for strong and viable families in which youth have an opportunity to develop their cognitive, emotional, and social competencies. This may involve effective early childhood and family support programs as well as family-friendly employment policies and more comprehensive and consistent strategies to reduce crime and other indicators of social and physical disorder in communities prone to those problems.

A third policy initiative involves ensuring that quality educational, mental health, and family support/protection services are available for all youth and all families. It is now clear that early prevention efforts represent the most effective means of discouraging the development of antisocial behaviors.

A fourth initiative should focus on providing coordinated services for all special-needs youth. This means that schools, mental health agencies, child protection services, and juvenile offender services must work together cooperatively to meet the needs of youth in a timely and effective manner. Confidentiality and other legal issues impeding this coordination must be resolved to ensure that effective services are provided.

A fifth initiative would focus on creating conditions within juvenile justice and correctional systems to ensure that the principles outlined above can be observed. This means obtaining adequate funds for creating these conditions, often a challenging barrier requiring considerable educational and political efforts. Efforts within agencies are also required. The careful selection and training of personnel is required for insuring that agency professionals are capable and motivated to deliver effective services. The mental health practitioner working in the system—whether psychologist, psychiatrist, or social worker—has an important role to play in encouraging the development of rehabilitative attitudes and practices among all workers in the system.

All of these policy initiatives involve challenging educational and political efforts. However, we have seen growing empirical support for the efficacy of interventions reflecting the closer-to-home, rehabilitation, evidence-based, and risk-focused, strengths-based principles. Also, as we have observed, growing evidence demonstrates that programs reflecting these principles are cost effective. In other words, they are important investments that can pay for themselves many times over in future reductions in criminal activity, school drop-out rates, and rates of mental health problems.

Index

Page numbers followed by an *f, t,* or *n* indicate figures, tables, or notes.